P9-CCB-856

Microsoft®
Outlook 2000
Step by Step

Microsoft Outlook ☒

⚠ You cannot assign a task from a public folder. To assign the task, open the task, and then click Copy To Personal Task List on the Actions menu. Then assign the task from your private Tasks folder.

[OK]

Catapult **Microsoft** Press

PUBLISHED BY
Microsoft Press
A Division of Microsoft Corporation
One Microsoft Way
Redmond, Washington 98052-6399

Copyright © 1999 by Catapult, Inc.

Library of Congress Cataloging-in-Publication Data
Microsoft Outlook 2000 Step by Step / Catapult, Inc.
    Includes index.
    ISBN 1-57231-982-8
    1. Microsoft Outlook. 2. Time management--Computer programs. 3. Personal information management--Computer programs. I. Catapult, Inc.
    HD69.T54M537   1999
    005.369--dc21   98-48190

Printed and bound in the United States of America.

7 8 9   QWT   7 6 5 4 3 2

Distributed in Canada by Penguin Books Canada Limited.

A CIP catalogue record for this book is available from the British Library.

Microsoft Press books are available through booksellers and distributors worldwide. For further information about international editions, contact your local Microsoft Corporation office or contact Microsoft Press International directly at fax (425) 936-7329. Visit our Web site at www.microsoft.com/mspress. Send comments to *mspinput@microsoft.com*.

Expedia, Microsoft, Microsoft Press, NetMeeting, Outlook, PowerPoint, Windows, and Windows NT are either registered trademarks or trademarks of Microsoft Corporation in the United States and/or other countries. Other product and company names mentioned herein may be the trademarks of their respective owners.

The example companies, organizations, products, domain names, e-mail addresses, logos, people, places, and events depicted herein are fictitious. No association with any real company, organization, product, domain name, e-mail address, logo, person, place, or event is intended or should be inferred.

For Catapult, Inc.
Directorof Publications: Bryn Cope
Project Editor: Margery Spears
Production Manager: Carolyn Thornley
Production/Layout: Sue Prettyman, Editor;
        Marie Hammer; Kim McGhee
Manuscript Editor: Jennifer Angier
Writers: Christine Di Terlizzi, Aidan Kelly
Technical Editors: Jesse Braswell, Jim Simonson
Copy Editor: Sam Ferriss

For Microsoft Press
Acquisitions Editor: Susanne Forderer
Project Editor: Jenny Moss Benson

Body Part No. 097-0008414

Contents

*Quick*Look Guide

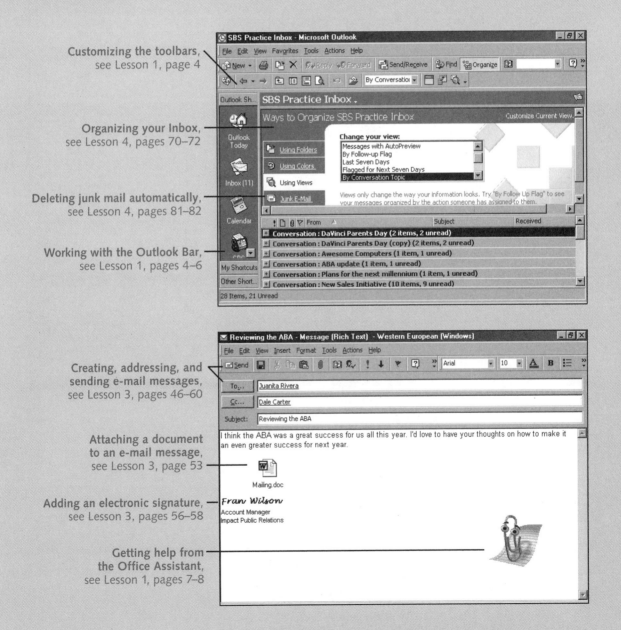

Customizing the toolbars,
see Lesson 1, page 4

Organizing your Inbox,
see Lesson 4, pages 70–72

Deleting junk mail automatically,
see Lesson 4, pages 81–82

Working with the Outlook Bar,
see Lesson 1, pages 4–6

Creating, addressing, and sending e-mail messages,
see Lesson 3, pages 46–60

Attaching a document to an e-mail message,
see Lesson 3, page 53

Adding an electronic signature,
see Lesson 3, pages 56–58

Getting help from the Office Assistant,
see Lesson 1, pages 7–8

Navigating in Calendar,
see Lesson 2, pages 28–33

Setting reminder notices,
see Lesson 7, pages 145–147

Scheduling a
recurring appointment,
see Lesson 7, pages 140–141

Starting a Task list,
see Lesson 9, page 186–190

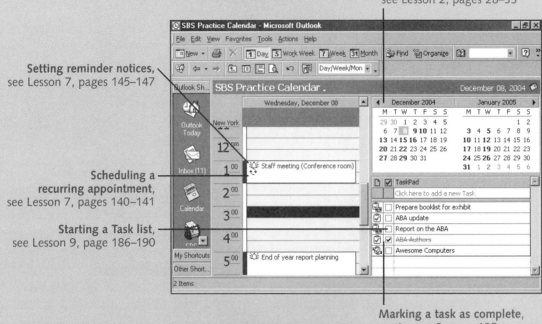

Marking a task as complete,
see Lesson 9, page 195

Adding contacts
to your Contact list,
see Lesson 5, pages 92–94

Creating a customized
view of your Contact list,
see Lesson 5, pages 100–101

Flagging a contact for follow-up
see Lesson 5, pages 95–96

Organizing Your
contacts by categories
see Lesson 5, page 104

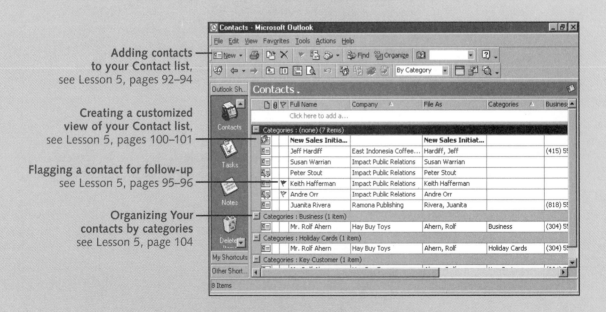

Redesigning an existing form,
see Lesson 12, pages 270–277

Creating a note,
see Lesson 1, pages 21–22

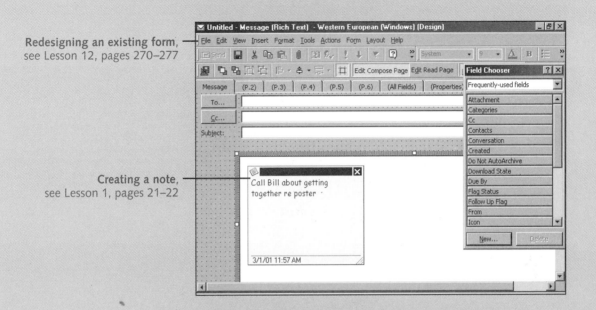

Previewing your e-mail messages
see Lesson 1, pages 13–14

Setting the importance level
see Lesson 3, page 58

**Adding a shared folder
to your Folder List,**
see Lesson 11, pages 256–257

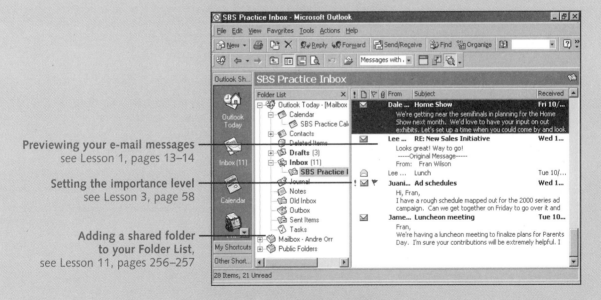

Finding Your Best Starting Point

Microsoft Outlook 2000 is an integrated electronic mail, calendar, and task management program that you can use to efficiently communicate with others, schedule appointments and tasks, record information about your personal and business contacts, and organize your files. In addition, Outlook can be optimized for use in a corporate workgroup or for use in small businesses or homes that have an Internet connection. With *Microsoft Outlook 2000 Step by Step*, you'll quickly and easily learn how to use Outlook 2000 to get your work done.

important

This book is designed for use with Microsoft Outlook 2000 for the Windows operating system. To find out which version of Outlook you're running, you can check the product package or you can start the program, click the Help menu, and then click About Microsoft Outlook. If your software is not compatible with this book, a Step by Step book matching your software is probably available. Please visit our World Wide Web site at *http://mspress.microsoft.com* or call 1-800-MSPRESS (1-800-677-7377) for more information.

Finding the Best Starting Point for You

This book is designed for beginning users of e-mail, scheduling, and contact management programs, as well as for readers who have had experience with these types of programs and are switching to Outlook or upgrading to Outlook 2000. Use the following table to find your best starting point in this book.

If you are	Follow these steps
New	
to computers	➊ Install the practice files as described in "Using the Microsoft Outlook 2000 Step by Step CD-ROM."
to graphical (as opposed to text-only) computer programs	➋ Become acquainted with the Windows operating system and how to use the online Help system by working through Appendix A, "If You're New to Windows or Outlook 2000" on the companion CD-ROM.
to Windows	➌ Learn basic skills for using Microsoft Outlook 2000 by working through Lessons 1 and 2. Then you can work through Lessons 3 through 6. Lessons 7 through 12 can be completed in any order.

If you are	Follow these steps
Switching	
from Lotus Notes or Lotus Organizer	➊ Install the practice files as described in "Using the Microsoft Outlook 2000 Step by Step CD-ROM."
	➋ Learn basic skills for using Microsoft Outlook 2000 by working through Lessons 1 and 2. Then you can work through Lessons 3 through 6. Lessons 7 through 12 can be completed in any order.

If you are	Follow these steps
Upgrading	
from Microsoft Outlook 97 or Outlook 98	➊ Learn about the new features of Outlook 2000 that are covered in this book by reading through the following section, "New Features in Microsoft Outlook 2000."
	➋ Install the practice files as described in "Using the Microsoft Outlook 2000 Step by Step CD-ROM."
	➌ Complete the lessons that cover the topics you need. You can use the table of contents and the *Quick*Look Guide to locate information about general topics. You can use the index to find information about a specific topic or feature.

If you are	Follow these steps
Referencing	
this book after working through the lessons	❶ Use the index to locate information about specific topics, and use the table of contents and the *Quick*Look Guide to locate information about general topics.
	❷ Read the Quick Reference at the end of each lesson for a brief review of the major tasks in the lesson. The Quick Reference topics are listed in the same order as they are presented in the lesson.

New Features in Microsoft Outlook 2000

Workgroup

Internet only

Microsoft Outlook 2000 contains new and enhanced features that make it easier than ever to organize, find, and view electronic mail, personal and group calendars, and task and contact management information. These features are integrated into a powerful communications program that offers collaboration and information-sharing capabilities in a workgroup environment or via the Internet. Outlook 2000 can help you work better and more effectively than ever before.

When you install Outlook 2000, you optimize the computing environment to best suit your individual needs. For example, if you work in a corporate setting or other organization with an internal network and server, you can set up Outlook for a Workgroup environment. If you are a home user or work in a small business that is not part of an internal network, you can set up Outlook for an Internet only environment. You can even set up Outlook with a No E-mail option if you plan to use an e-mail program other than the Outlook Inbox.

Whichever environment you choose, certain features designed only for that environment will be enabled during installation. Exercises specific to only one environment are identified in each lesson by either an Internet only icon or a Workgroup icon. If you selected the No E-mail option, you will be unable to do the exercises requiring the use of the Outlook Inbox.

The following table lists the major new or enhanced features of Microsoft Outlook 2000 that are covered in this book and the lesson in which you can learn how to use each feature. You can also use the index to find specific information about a feature or a task that you want to perform.

To learn how to	See
Find answers to your questions about Microsoft Outlook with the enhanced Office Assistant.	Lesson 1; Appendix A on the CD-ROM
Customize your Outlook menu options.	Lesson 1
Easily create personal distribution lists of contacts from one or more Contacts folders and the Global Address List.	Lesson 3
Run rules on the contents of any folder at any time using the enhanced Rules Wizard.	Lesson 4
Track all e-mail, tasks, appointments, and documents related to each contact.	Lesson 10
Work offsite using enhanced capabilities for remote access.	Appendix C on the CD-ROM

Corrections, Comments, and Help

Every effort has been made to ensure the accuracy of this book and the contents of the Microsoft Outlook 2000 Step by Step CD-ROM. Microsoft Press provides corrections and additional content for its books through the World Wide Web at

http://mspress.microsoft.com/support

If you have comments, questions, or ideas regarding this book or the CD-ROM, please send them to us.

Send e-mail to:

mspinput@microsoft.com

Or send postal mail to:

Microsoft Press
Attn: Step by Step Editor
One Microsoft Way
Redmond, WA 98052-6399

Please note that support for the Outlook 2000 software product itself is not offered through the above addresses. For help using Outlook 2000, you can call Outlook 2000 Technical Support at (425) 635-7070 on weekdays between 6 A.M. and 6 P.M. Pacific Time.

Visit Our World Wide Web Site

We invite you to visit the Microsoft Press World Wide Web site. You can visit us at the following location:

http://mspress.microsoft.com

You'll find descriptions of all of our books, information about ordering titles, notices of special features and events, additional content for Microsoft Press books, and much more.

You can also find out the latest in software developments and news from Microsoft Corporation by visiting the following World Wide Web site:

http://www.microsoft.com/

We look forward to your visit on the Web!

Using the Microsoft Outlook 2000 Step by Step CD-ROM

The CD-ROM inside the back cover of this book contains the practice files that you'll use as you perform the exercises in the book and multimedia files that demonstrate 11 of the exercises. By using the practice files, you won't waste time creating the samples used in the lessons—instead, you can concentrate on learning how to use Outlook 2000. With the files and the step-by-step instructions in the lessons, you'll also learn by doing, which is an easy and effective way to acquire and remember new skills.

important

Before you break the seal on the practice CD-ROM package, be sure that this book matches your version of the software. This book is designed for use with Microsoft Outlook 2000 for the Windows operating system. To find out which version of Outlook you are running, you can check the product package or you can start the software, click the Help menu, and then click About Microsoft Outlook. If your program is not compatible with this book, a Step by Step book matching your software is probably available. Please visit our World Wide Web site at *http://mspress.microsoft.com* or call 1-800-MSPRESS (1-800-677-7377) for more information.

Installing the Practice Files

Follow these steps to install the practice files on your computer's hard disk so that you can use them with the exercises in this book.

Close

1 If your computer isn't on, turn it on now.

2 If you're using Windows NT, press Ctrl+Alt+Del to display a dialog box asking for your user name and password. If you are using Windows 95 or 98, you will see this dialog box if your computer is connected to a network.

3 If necessary, type your username and password in the appropriate boxes, and then click OK. If you see the Welcome dialog box, click the Close button.

4 Remove the CD-ROM from the package inside the back cover of this book and insert it in the CD-ROM drive of your computer.

5 On the Windows taskbar, click Start, and then click Run.

The Run dialog box appears.

6 Click Browse.

The Browse dialog box appears.

7 If necessary, in the Look In drop-down list, select your CD-ROM drive.

The contents of the CD-ROM are displayed.

8 Double-click Setup.exe, and in the Run dialog box, click OK.

The setup program window appears with the recommended options preselected for you. For best results in using the practice files with this book, accept these preselected settings.

9 Follow the instructions on the screen.

10 When the files have been installed, remove the CD-ROM from your CD-ROM drive and replace it in the package inside the back cover of the book.

A folder called Outlook 2000 SBS Practice has been created on your hard disk, and the practice files have been placed in that folder. A shortcut to the Microsoft Press Web site is placed on your desktop.

If your computer is set up to connect to the Internet, you can double-click the Microsoft Press Welcome shortcut to visit the Microsoft Press Web site. You can also connect to this Web site directly at *http://mspress.microsoft.com*

Using the Practice Files

Each lesson in this book explains when and how to use any practice files for that lesson. When a practice file is needed for a lesson, the book will list instructions on how to open the file. The lessons are built around scenarios that simulate a real work environment, so you can easily apply the skills you learn to your own work. For the scenario in this book, imagine that you're an account manager at Impact Public Relations, a small public relations firm. Your company recently installed Office 2000, and you are eager to use Outlook 2000 for a variety of business tasks.

The screen illustrations in this book might look different from what you see on your computer, depending on how your computer is set up. To help make your screen match the illustrations in this book, please follow the instructions in Appendix B, "Matching the Exercises," on the companion CD-ROM.

For those of you who like to know all the details, here's a summary of the practice files used in the lessons.

Folder name	Description
Lesson01	Sample e-mail messages to open, read, and reply to in the SBS Practice Inbox folder.
Lesson02	Sample appointment files to open and view in the SBS Practice Calendar.
Lesson03	Sample e-mail messages to open, customize, and send in the SBS Practice Inbox folder. Three Microsoft Word documents to open, view, and/or use as attachments to e-mail messages. Sample Contacts cards to use in the Address Book.
Lesson04	Sample e-mail messages to open, view, and organize in the SBS Practice Inbox.
Lesson05	Sample Contacts cards to open, view, and organize in SBS Practice Contacts. Includes the Extras subfolder.
Extras	Subfolder in the Lesson05 folder that contains a Microsoft Word document for mail merging and a Microsoft Access file for importing contact information.
Lesson06	Sample Contacts cards to use in the Address Book. A Microsoft Word document for faxing.
RP02	Sample Contacts cards to use in the Address Book. A Microsoft Word document to use as an attachment and to fax. A sample e-mail message to flag for follow-up.
Lesson07	Sample appointment files to open and view in the SBS Practice Calendar. A sample Contacts card to use in the Address Book. A Microsoft Word document to attach to an appointment.
Lesson08	Sample Contacts cards to use in the Address Book. A sample appointment file to open and view in the SBS Practice Calendar. A sample meeting request e-mail message to open and view in the SBS Practice Inbox.
Lesson09	Sample Contacts cards to use in the Address Book. A sample appointment file to use to create a task. Sample task e-mail messages to open and view in the SBS Practice Inbox.

Folder name	Description
Lesson10	Practice e-mail messages to open and view in the SBS Practice Inbox. Sample Notes files for exporting to a folder.
Lesson11	Sample Contacts cards to use in the Address Book.
Lesson12	No practice files.
Multimedia	Video demonstrations of how to perform some of the more complicated tasks in this book.

Using the Multimedia Files

Throughout this book, you will see icons for multimedia files for particular exercises. Use the following steps to run the multimedia files.

1 Insert the Outlook 2000 Step by Step CD-ROM in your CD-ROM drive.

2 On the Windows taskbar, click Start, and then click Run.

The Run dialog box appears.

3 Click Browse.

The Browse dialog box appears.

4 If necessary, in the Look In drop-down list, select your CD-ROM drive.

The contents of the CD-ROM are displayed.

5 Double-click the Multimedia folder.

The Multimedia folder opens.

6 Double-click the multimedia file you need, and in the Run dialog box, click OK.

Microsoft Camcorder runs the video of the exercise.

7 Return to the exercise in the book.

Uninstalling the Practice Files

Use the following steps when you want to delete the practice files added to your hard disk by the Step by Step setup program.

1 On the Windows taskbar, click Start, point to Settings, and then click Control Panel.

2 Double-click the Add/Remove Programs icon.

The Add/Remove Programs Properties dialog box appears.

3 On the Install/Uninstall tab, select Microsoft Outlook 2000 Step by Step from the list, and then click Add/Remove.

A confirmation message appears.

4 Click Yes or OK.

The practice files are uninstalled.

5 Click OK to close the Add/Remove Programs Properties dialog box.

6 Close the Control Panel window.

Need Help with the Practice Files?

Every effort has been made to ensure the accuracy of this book and the contents of the practice files CD-ROM. If you do run into a problem, Microsoft Press provides corrections for its books through the World Wide Web at:

http://mspress.microsoft.com/support/

We invite you to visit our main Web page at:

http://mspress.microsoft.com

You'll find descriptions of all of our books, information about ordering titles, notices of special features and events, additional content for Microsoft Press books, and much more.

Conventions and Features in This Book

You can save time when you use this book by understanding, before you start the lessons, how instructions, keys to press, and so on are shown in the book. Please take a moment to read the following list, which also points out helpful features of the book that you might want to use.

Conventions

▪ Hands-on exercises for you to follow are given in numbered lists of steps (1, 2, and so on). A round bullet (●) indicates an exercise that has only one step.

▪ Text that you are to type appears in **bold**.

▪ A plus sign (+) between two key names means that you must press those keys at the same time. For example, "Press Alt+Tab" means that you hold down the Alt key while you press Tab.

▪ The following icons are used to identify certain types of exercise features:

Icon	Alerts you to
	Skills that are demonstrated in multimedia files available on the Microsoft Outlook 2000 Step by Step CD-ROM.
	New features in Outlook 2000.

Icon	Alerts you to
 Workgroup	Features available only when Outlook is optimized for the Corporate Or Workgroup environment.
 Internet only	Features available only when Outlook is optimized for the Internet only environment.

Other Features of This Book

- You can get a quick reminder of how to perform the tasks you learned by reading the Quick Reference at the end of each lesson.

- You can practice the major skills presented in the lessons by working through the Review & Practice sections at the end of each part.

- You can see a multimedia demonstration of some of the exercises in the book by following the instructions in "Using the Multimedia Files" in the "Using the Microsoft Outlook 2000 Step by Step CD-ROM" section of this book.

PART 1

Getting Started with Outlook 2000

1

Jumping into Your E-mail

ESTIMATED TIME
45 min.

In this lesson you will learn how to:

✔ *Start Microsoft Outlook 2000.*

✔ *Navigate in the Outlook Bar.*

✔ *Review e-mail messages and attachments.*

✔ *Reply to and forward e-mail messages.*

✔ *Save e-mail messages and check sent messages.*

✔ *Format and print a copy of e-mail messages.*

✔ *Use Notes as a reminder.*

✔ *Customize your Inbox.*

Managing personal communications and information is essential for success in today's business world. With Microsoft Outlook 2000, you have complete command over your business communications and schedule. You can:

■ Track your tasks, assignments, and appointments on your calendar.

■ Record and classify information about any business or personal matter.

■ Keep track of detailed information on all your business and personal contacts, including e-mail addresses, Web page addresses, and meeting notes.

■ Send e-mail messages and electronic business cards.

■ Organize your files.

■ Access any other Microsoft files you need—such as Microsoft Word. documents or Microsoft Excel spreadsheets—directly from Outlook.

You can carry out all these tasks without ever leaving Outlook.

You can configure Outlook to work in a Workgroup environment or just over the Internet.

Workgroup

In a Workgroup environment, your computer is connected to a server. Other computers in your organization can also be connected to the same server or to other servers connected together into a network. You communicate with others in your workgroup and access the Internet via this network of servers.

Internet only

In an Internet only environment, which is more typical for home computers, your computer is connected via modem to an Internet service provider (ISP). Your ISP provides access to the Internet.

Either configuration provides you with powerful tools to completely integrate your e-mail with your calendar, contacts, and task management activities.

Starting Outlook 2000, the Gateway to Your E-mail

The screen you see when you start Outlook has several parts.

- The large area beneath the folder banner is called the Information viewer. Your e-mail, calendar, contacts, tasks, and other information are displayed in this window.

- Above the Information viewer are the Standard and Advanced toolbars. These contain buttons for the commands that you will use most frequently. You can customize the toolbars to make them more useful by adding your own favorite buttons or removing ones you don't use. You can hide one or both of the toolbars, or compress then onto a single row, by using the Toolbar commands in the View menu.

- The vertical column of shortcuts to the left of the Information viewer is the Outlook Bar. Each shortcut on the Outlook Bar will take you directly to the contents of an Outlook folder. Shortcuts eliminate the need to type complicated path names to reach the files you want. Each Outlook folder contains the programs and files for a particular Outlook feature, such as Inbox or Contacts. Outlook folders that do not have an associated shortcut can be opened directly from the Folder List.

- The shortcuts on your Outlook Bar are organized in groups. When you install Outlook, the Outlook Shortcuts, My Shortcuts, and Other Shortcuts groups of shortcuts are automatically created. You can create new groups and place new shortcuts within those groups. You can also add shortcuts to groups that already exist.

Appointment area   Date Navigator

*If your screen
looks different
from this illus-
tration, see
Appendix B,
"Matching the
Exercises," on
the CD-ROM
in the back of
this book.*

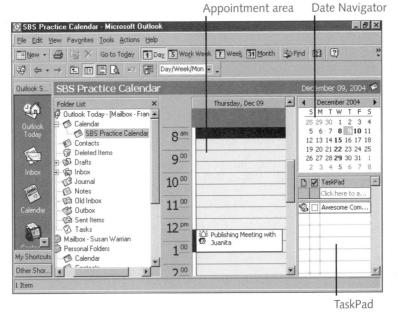

TaskPad

Internet only

This table shows the different groups and shortcuts included in the standard installation of Outlook 2000. Other configurations may display different shortcuts, depending on how you set up your program.

Group	Shortcut	Description
Outlook Shortcuts	Outlook Today	Opens the "day-at-a-glance" view with an overview of your Calendar, e-mail messages, and tasks.
	Inbox	Opens the Inbox folder, which contains your e-mail messages.
	Calendar	Opens the Calendar folder, which displays your appointments.
	Contacts	Opens the Contacts folder, which stores the names, phone numbers, and addresses of the important people in your life.
	Tasks	Opens your Task list, which displays a to-do list.
	Notes	Opens the Notes folder, which stores general information, such as ideas, reminders, lists, and directions, in the form of notes.

(continued)

continued

Group	Shortcut	Description
Outlook Shortcuts	Deleted Items	Opens the Deleted Items folder, which temporarily stores the items you delete until you permanently delete them.
My Shortcuts	Drafts	Opens the Drafts folder, which stores e-mail messages that you have created but have not sent.
	Outbox	Opens the Outbox folder, which holds e-mail messages that you are sending until you are connected to your mail server.
	Sent Items	Opens the Sent Items folder, which stores copies of e-mail messages you have sent.
	Journal	Opens the Journal folder, which displays a history of your recorded activities in a timeline format.
Other Shortcuts	My Computer	Provides access to the drives, folders, and files on your computer.
	My Documents	Provides access to the My Documents folder on your hard disk.
	Favorites	Opens the Favorites folder, which stores shortcuts to your favorite Internet addresses or to other items on your computer.

E-mail is now the preferred method of communication for business and many other purposes. It combines the immediacy and informality of a phone call with the benefits of written correspondence.

As a new account manager at Impact Public Relations, your daily tasks include reading and responding to e-mail messages, some of which have important documents attached. Because you are busy with several clients at once, you also need an effective way to record and organize miscellaneous ideas and information as you think of them. In this lesson, you begin using Outlook 2000 to manage your e-mail and create electronic notes.

You begin by starting Microsoft Outlook 2000, and then you open Outlook Today for an overview of your day. The Outlook Today pane displays your calendar for up to seven days, your list of tasks, and whether you have any e-mail messages—all on one screen. In order to have a more realistic experience accessing e-mail messages, you then create a practice Inbox and copy messages into it from the Outlook 2000 SBS Practice folder on your hard drive that is created during Setup. Using this practice Inbox ensures that these exercises will not interfere with your actual Inbox and e-mail messages.

Start Outlook 2000 for the first time

Outlook

For more information about installing and configuring Outlook 2000, see Appendices B and D on the CD-ROM in the back of this book.

Maximize

❶ On the desktop, double-click the Microsoft Outlook 2000 icon.

The Microsoft Outlook 2000 startup screen appears.

❷ Click Next.

❸ In the E-Mail Service Options area, select either the Internet Only or the Corporate Or Workgroup option, depending on your setup.

❹ Click Next.

Outlook's configuration will be tailored to your work needs.

❺ Click Yes to make Outlook your default manager for Mail, News, and Contacts.

❻ The first time you open Outlook, Clippit, the default Office Assistant, and the Welcome to Microsoft Outlook Help balloon appear. Click Start Using Microsoft Outlook.

❼ Maximize the Outlook window.

Meet the Office Assistant

If you have started Microsoft Outlook 2000 before, some of the opening screens described here might not appear.

The Office Assistant probably just popped up on your screen. So, now is a great time to introduce it. If it did not appear, you can easily reach it—on the Help menu, click Show The Office Assistant.

The default Office Assistant for Office 2000 is Clippit the paper clip, an animated character that automatically appears on your screen to offer help.

(continued)

continued

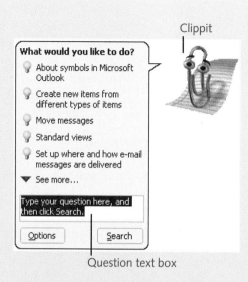

Clippit

Question text box

To get help from the Office Assistant, simply click in the Type Your Question Here, And Then Click Search box, and then type your question. Then click the Search button or press Enter. After a few moments of pondering, the Office Assistant displays a list of possible topics relating to your question. You can check out these topics by clicking your choice.

From time to time as you work, the Office Assistant automatically appears with a light bulb overhead. When this happens, the Office Assistant has a tip about the action that you are performing. Simply click the light bulb to display the helpful information.

If you receive the message "The selected Assistant character is not available... Would you like to install it now?" click No, and then click Cancel.

You can specify the type of assistance that you want from the Office Assistant for both help and tips. To do so, right-click the Office Assistant, and then on the shortcut menu, click Options. This opens the Office Assistant dialog box. On the Options tab, customize the Office Assistant by clearing the check boxes for those options that you want turned off (by default, all check boxes should already be selected). You can also turn off the Office Assistant entirely by simply clearing the Use The Office Assistant check box.

You can even select a different animated character as your Office Assistant—for example, Rocky, the Dot, the Genius, or Mother Nature. To do so, on the bottom of the Office Assistant box, click the Options button. Then, on the Gallery tab, scroll through the characters using the Back and Next buttons. When you see the one you'd like, click OK.

Jumping into Your E-mail

Open Outlook Today for an overview of your day

Outlook Today provides a quick overview of the day's appointments, tasks, and the number of e-mail messages you have. In this exercise, you open Outlook Today and make it your *default* page, the first page you see when you start Outlook.

Outlook Today

1 On the Outlook Bar, click the Outlook Today shortcut.

The Outlook Today screen appears. Your screen should look similar to the illustration below.

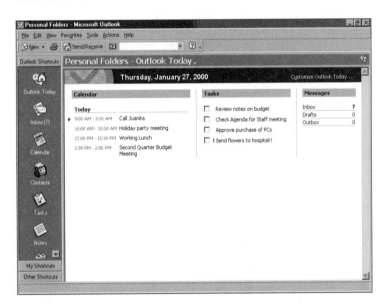

2 Scroll right, if necessary, and then click the Customize Outlook Today link.

The Outlook Today options for Startup, Messages, Calendar, Tasks, and Styles appear in the Information viewer.

3 In the Startup area, be sure that the When Starting, Go Directly To Outlook Today check box is selected.

Clicking a folder in the Folder List displays the files or sub-folders that it contains.

4 Click the Save Changes button.

The Outlook Today screen reappears.

5 If the Folder List is not displayed, on the View menu, click Folder List.

The Folder List appears.

More Buttons

important

If you don't see a button on your toolbar, click the More Buttons drop-down arrow for that toolbar. Point to the Add Or Remove Buttons drop-down arrow to display a list of additional toolbar buttons. In this list, click the button that you want to use. This executes the command and adds the button to the toolbar, replacing one that has not been used for a while.

Create an SBS Practice Inbox

In order to keep your practice e-mail messages separate from your real messages, in this exercise you'll set up a practice Inbox and create a shortcut to it.

Inbox

1. On the Outlook Bar, click the Inbox shortcut.

2. Be sure that the Folder List is displayed.

New Mail Message

3. On the Standard toolbar, click the New Mail Message button drop-down arrow, and then click Folder.

   The Create New Folder dialog box appears.

4. Be sure that the Folder Contains box displays Mail Items.

5. In the Name box, type **SBS Practice Inbox** and click OK. You'll create the shortcut to it in step 8.

6. If you are prompted to Add Shortcut to Outlook Bar? click No.

   The SBS Practice Inbox folder appears in the Folder List as a subfolder of your Inbox.

7. On the Standard toolbar, click the New Mail Message button drop-down arrow, and then click Outlook Bar Shortcut.

   The Add To Outlook Bar dialog box appears.

To quickly add a shortcut to the Outlook Bar, right-click the folder in the Folder List and click Add To Outlook Bar.

8. In the Folder List, click the plus sign (+) next to the Inbox folder to display the subfolders, click the SBS Practice Inbox folder, and click OK.

   The new SBS Practice Inbox shortcut appears at the bottom of the Outlook Bar.

Set up practice e-mail

In real life, e-mail messages arrive over the Internet or your office network and pop up automatically in your Inbox. In these lessons, you won't be working with real e-mail messages. Instead, you will drag e-mail messages from the Outlook 2000 SBS Practice folder to your SBS Practice Inbox folder.

1. Click the Start button, point to Programs, and then click either Windows Explorer or Windows NT Explorer, whichever is on your computer.

The Windows Explorer or Windows NT Explorer window opens on top of your Outlook window.

important

If you have not yet installed the Outlook 2000 SBS Practice folder, you need to do so now in order to continue with these lessons. See "Installing the Practice Files" in "Using the Microsoft Outlook 2000 Step by Step CD-ROM" in the front of this book.

2 Browse through the folders on your hard disk until you locate the Outlook 2000 SBS Practice folder.

3 Double-click the Outlook 2000 SBS Practice folder.

The contents of the folder are displayed.

4 Open the Lesson01 folder.

The contents of the folder are displayed.

5 Right-click a blank area on the taskbar (the horizontal bar across the bottom of the screen), and then click Tile Vertically if you have Windows 95, or Tile Windows Vertically if you have Windows 98 or Windows NT.

The Explorer and SBS Practice Inbox windows are now arranged side by side. Your screen should look similar to the following illustration.

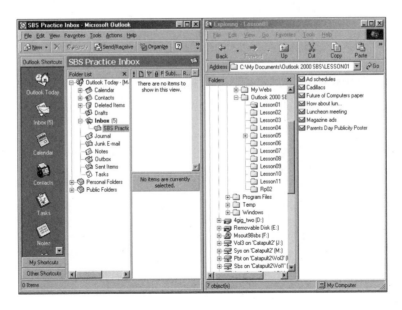

To select all three messages at once, click the first message, and then hold down the Shift key while clicking the last message.

6   Drag the practice e-mail message files, indicated by envelope icons, from the Lesson01 folder in the Outlook 2000 SBS Practice folder to your SBS Practice Inbox folder in the Folder List.

7   In the Explorer window, click the Close button.

8   Maximize the SBS Practice Inbox window.

The e-mail messages are displayed in the Information viewer.

Reviewing Your E-mail Messages and Attachments

You have arrived early for work one Tuesday morning at Impact Public Relations. Looking at your Inbox, you discover several e-mail messages, including some from Five Lakes Publishing, Awesome Computers, and the DaVinci School of Arts and Crafts, three of your client accounts.

With Outlook 2000, you can quickly preview e-mail messages without actually opening them so that you can identify and deal with the urgent ones immediately and save the rest for later. One especially useful feature of e-mail is that documents can be attached to and sent with messages. An attached document remains in the format in which it was created, such as Microsoft Word. If you have the application that was used to create the attachment, you can open and edit the attachment directly. Even without that particular application, if the attachment is in almost any standard format, it can be converted into text that can be read and edited.

In the following exercises, you open, read, reply to, and forward messages, and save an e-mail attachment to use later.

Open and read a message

1   If the SBS Practice Inbox is not open, on the Outlook Bar, click the SBS Practice Inbox shortcut.

2   In the Information viewer, double-click the Magazine Ads message from Juanita Rivera.

The text of the message appears in the Message form. In the header, the names of the sender and the recipients, and the date and time of the message appear.

Your screen should look similar to the following illustration.

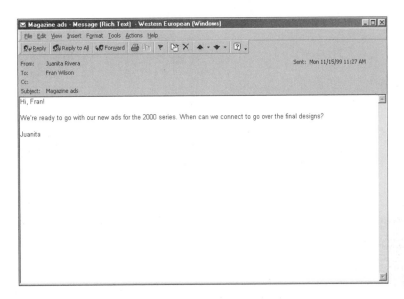

Close

❸   After reading the e-mail message, on the Message form title bar, click the Close button.

The message closes and the envelope icon in the SBS Practice Inbox changes from closed to open to indicate that the message has been read.

Save time by previewing messages

You have an important company meeting this morning and no time to read all of your e-mail messages. You know that at least some of them require immediate attention. You need to preview them to find out which ones are urgent.

In this exercise, you practice two ways to preview your messages. First, with AutoPreview, you can see the first few lines of all of your unread messages. Second, using the Preview Pane, you can see the complete text of a selected message without opening it.

AutoPreview

❶   On the View menu, click AutoPreview.

The first few lines of all messages are displayed. Your screen should look similar to the following illustration.

AutoPreviewed messages are still flagged as unread—the envelope icon is still sealed—which is useful for sorting them later.

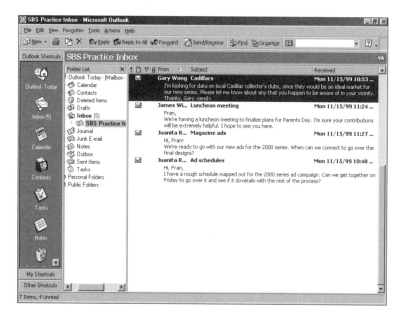

2 Click a message in order to select it.

3 On the View menu, click Preview Pane.

The Preview pane opens in a separate window at the bottom of the Information viewer, and you can read the complete text of the message.

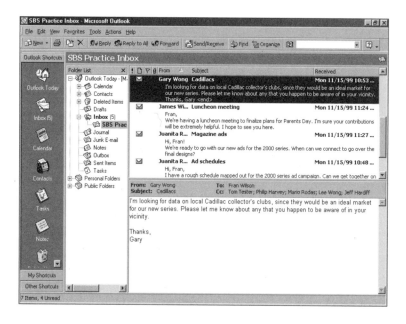

tip

You can choose to be notified as soon as new e-mail messages arrive. On the Tools menu, click Options. On the Preferences tab, click the E-Mail Options button, and then select the Display A Notification Message When New Mail Arrives check box. Click OK twice to close all open dialog boxes. Now, when a new e-mail message arrives, a message appears on your screen to let you know.

Open and save an attachment

Your colleague at the DaVinci School, Bill Carter, has created a publicity poster for the upcoming Parents Day at the school, and he has sent you a copy of it as an attachment to his e-mail message. In this exercise, you open the poster and save it to a folder on your hard disk in case you need to use it later.

1   Double-click the message from Bill Carter entitled Parents Day Publicity Poster.

The message is displayed, and an attachment icon similar to the one shown below appears at the bottom of the message window.

POSTER.doc

To quickly save an attached file without opening it, right-click the attachment icon. On the shortcut menu, click Save As.

2   Double-click the attachment icon.

The Opening Mail Attachment dialog box may appear.

3   In the dialog box, click the Open It option, and click OK.

The attachment opens in Microsoft Word or, if you don't have Word, in WordPad. You can now read, change, and save the document, and print copies of it.

Attachments are deleted only when the e-mail message is deleted or when you manually delete the attachment from the message and save the change.

4   On the File menu, click Save As.

The Save As dialog box appears.

5   In the Save As dialog box, in the Save In drop-down list, select a folder on your hard disk. In the File Name box, select the current filename, type **Parents day poster** and click the Save button.

Bill's poster has been saved in the folder. The original attachment is still attached to the e-mail message and can be opened again later.

6   Close Microsoft Word (or WordPad).

7   Close the message.

🗙

Close

Outlook Menus
Automatically Customize Your Options

Outlook menus logically group commands together, making it easy to access a feature. For example, all formatting commands are grouped on the Format menu. To access a particular menu, simply point to it on the menu bar and click. Initially, the most frequently used features are displayed as menu commands. However, if you hold the mouse pointer still for a moment, the menu expands and the full selection of commands is displayed. You can also expand a menu by double- clicking the arrows at the bottom of the menu. Once one full menu is displayed on the menu bar, all other menus that you click display their expanded menus as well. As shown in the following illustration, when fully expanded, a menu always indicates infrequently used commands by displaying them against a lighter, recessed background.

Short menu

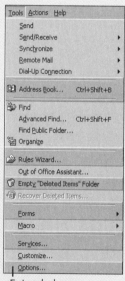

Extended menu

Replying to E-mail Messages

Outlook provides three different methods to respond to messages. You can choose to send your reply to the sender alone or to the sender *and* to everyone else listed in that message's Cc and Bcc boxes. You can also choose to forward the message, along with any attachments, to the sender, to other recipients, or to another person. Knowing how to apply each of these three methods will provide great flexibility in your e-mail communications.

One difference between replying to a message and forwarding a message is this: if the original message included an attachment, the attachment is not sent back if you use Reply or Reply To All. To include the attachment in your reply or to send the e-mail message to someone who was not on the original recipient, Cc, or Bcc lists, you must forward the message.

If you don't see a Bcc box in your Message form, on the View menu, click Bcc Field.

tip

If you need to ensure that other people see a copy of an e-mail message, on the Message form, type their e-mail addresses in the Cc (courtesy copy) box. You can also send a blind courtesy copy by typing their addresses in the Bcc box. When you send a blind copy, the recipients in the To and Cc boxes are unaware of the copy that was sent to the people listed in the Bcc box.

In the following exercises, you practice all three methods of replying to a message. Because e-mail addresses in these exercises are fictitious, all replies will be returned as undeliverable and can be deleted at your leisure.

Reply to a message

Dr. James Wilson has invited you to a luncheon meeting at the DaVinci School. Attending the meeting promises to be both a pleasant social occasion and useful for your role as the school's publicist. You decide to accept his e-mail invitation.

SBS Practice Inbox

To enter the meeting in your Calendar, see Lesson 2, "Learning the Basics of Scheduling."

1   On the Outlook Bar, click the SBS Practice Inbox shortcut.

The SBS Practice Inbox appears.

2   In the SBS Practice Inbox Information viewer, double-click the message from James Wilson.

The message appears.

3   On the Message form Standard toolbar, click the Reply button.

The Reply form appears. James Wilson already appears in the To box as the recipient.

4   In the message area of the Reply form, type the following:

Dr. Wilson: I'd be honored to attend your luncheon. I'll see you there.

5   Click the Send button.

The Reply form disappears, and your message is sent.

Internet only

If you are working in an Internet only environment, after you click the Send button on the Message form Standard toolbar, your message is placed in the Outbox. To send the message, on the Standard toolbar, click Send/Receive. If you are not presently connected to the Internet, you may be prompted to connect. Complete the instructions from your Internet service provider to access the Internet.

Close

6 On the Message form, click the Close button.

James Wilson's message to you closes.

Reply to everyone who received a message

Gary Wong is the sales manager for Five Lakes Publishing, which publishes a series of books about classic American cars. He has sent a request to various colleagues for information about clubs for Cadillac collectors. You happened across a new club at the county fair last weekend, and you suspect that he and the others might be interested. In this exercise, you send your reply to everyone who received Gary's message.

1 In the SBS Practice Inbox Information viewer, open the message from Gary Wong entitled Cadillacs.

The message appears.

2 On the Message form Standard toolbar, click the Reply To All button.

The Reply form appears.

3 Type the following response:

Check out the King County Classic Cadillac Collector's Club.

4 Click the Send button.

The Reply form disappears, and your message is sent to Gary Wong and to everyone listed in the Cc box in his message.

Internet only

If you are working in an Internet only environment, after you click the Send button on the Message form Standard toolbar, your message is placed in the Outbox. To send the message, on the Standard toolbar, click Send/Receive. If you are not presently connected to the Internet, you may be prompted to connect. Complete the instructions from your Internet service provider to access the Internet.

5 On the Message form, click the Close button.

Forward a message

Let's suppose that Bill Carter at the DaVinci School wants to have your advice before he shows his poster to Dr. Wilson. You think that the poster is not only professional, but also attractive, and you decide to forward it to Dr. Wilson.

1 In the SBS Practice Inbox Information viewer, open the message from Bill Carter entitled Parents Day Publicity Poster.

2 On the Message form Standard toolbar, click the Forward button.

3 In the To box, type Dr. Wilson's e-mail address: **Jamesw@davinci.davinci**

4 In the message window, type your praise of Carter's poster:

Dr. Wilson: I am very impressed with Mr. Carter's efforts here. I think this will provide excellent exposure for the school.

5 Click the Send button.

The message window closes. In addition to your message, the attachment containing a copy of Bill's poster is now sent to Dr. Wilson.

Internet only

If you are working in an Internet only environment, after you click the Send button on the Message form Standard toolbar, your message is placed in the Outbox. To send the message, on the Standard toolbar, click Send/Receive. If you are not presently connected to the Internet, you may be prompted to connect. Complete the instructions from your Internet service provider to access the Internet.

6 On the Message form, click the Close button.

The message from Bill Carter closes.

Saving and Checking Your Sent Messages

When you send an e-mail message, you do not necessarily lose the information contained in the message. You can store a copy of any e-mail message that you send in the Sent Items folder, where you can later review it. If you decide that you no longer need a message, you can delete it from the Sent Items folder. Even then, you still retain a copy of the item in the Deleted Items folder; these items remain until you permanently remove them. This system of backup copies helps you avoid losing important information.

Keep copies of your sent e-mail messages

You can choose whether or not to have copies of all your e-mail messages stored in the Sent Items folder. In this exercise, you retain the option of keeping your e-mail messages stored in Sent Items so that later exercises proceed correctly.

1 On the Tools menu, click Options.

The Options dialog box appears.

2 In the Options dialog box, on the Preferences tab, click the E-mail Options button.

The E-mail Options dialog box appears.

❸ Be sure the Save Copies Of Messages In Sent Items Folder check box is selected.

❹ In the E-mail Options dialog box, click OK.

❺ In the Options dialog box, click OK.

Formatting and Printing Copies of E-mail Messages

Sometimes you need hard copies of an e-mail message, for example, to distribute at a meeting. You can format and print copies of the e-mail messages you receive and the ones you send, just as you can with any other document.

Format and print an e-mail message

To make the message easier to read, you can click the Actual Size button on the Print Preview toolbar.

In this exercise, you make changes in the formatting of an e-mail message and then print a copy of the result.

❶ If the SBS Practice Inbox is not open, on the Outlook Bar, click the SBS Practice Inbox shortcut.

❷ In the Information viewer, click the message from James Wilson.

tip
If no changes are needed in the format or layout of the e-mail message, you can print the message immediately by clicking the Print button on the Standard toolbar.

Print

Print Preview

❸ On the File menu, click Print Preview.

In the Print Preview window, you now see an image of the message as it will appear when printed.

❹ On the Print Preview toolbar, click the Page Setup button.

The Page Setup dialog box appears.

❺ On the Format tab, in the Fonts area, click the Font button next to the Fields box.

The Font dialog box appears. The current font size and style choices are displayed in the Sample box.

❻ In the Font list, select Times New Roman.

7 In the Size list, type or select 12.

The text has now been reformatted to be displayed in 12-point Times New Roman font.

8 In the Font dialog box, click OK, and then in the Page Setup dialog box, click OK.

9 In the Print Preview dialog box, click the Print button.

The Print dialog box appears.

10 In the Print dialog box, click OK.

The message is printed.

Using Notes to Store Information

Many people jot down notes—ideas, messages, chores, and reminders—on notepads or sticky notes as they think of them during the course of a day. In Outlook, you can capture these spontaneous thoughts in electronic form. Outlook's Notes takes the place of sticky notes. The note will stay on your screen when Outlook is minimized, and when you click the note on the taskbar, it will reappear on your screen no matter what Microsoft Office 2000 program you are running.

In the following exercise, you write yourself a reminder to get together with Bill Carter to discuss printing and distributing his poster, and then you save the reminder for later use.

Create a note

Notes

New Note

1 On the Outlook Bar, scroll if necessary to bring the Notes shortcut into view. Click the Notes shortcut.

2 On the Standard toolbar, click the New Note button.

A new blank note form that looks like a yellow sticky note appears.

3 Type **Call Bill about getting together re poster**

The note should look similar to the following illustration.

4 On the note, click the Close Note button.

Your note closes, and a shortcut appears in the Information viewer with the first few words of the content listed underneath.

5 Double-click the note.

The complete note reappears on the screen.

Close Note

6 On the note, click the Close Note button.

Views in Notes

As you accumulate notes, you will want to organize them. This is easily done in Outlook. To use any of the views below, on the Outlook Bar, click the Notes shortcut. On the View menu, point to Current View, and then click the view you want.

Click this view	To see notes
Icons	Represented by icons arranged from left to right by creation date.
Notes List	In a list sorted by creation date.
Last Seven Days	In a list created during the last seven days.
By Category	In a list grouped by categories and sorted by creation date within each category.
By Color	In a list grouped by color and sorted by creation date for each color.

One Step Further

Customizing Your Inbox

You can rearrange the way your Inbox is set up and how it handles your e-mail to better suit your personal work style. You can change how your incoming e-mail is displayed, in which font it appears, and where it is automatically filed when you are finished with it, all of which can contribute to your efficiency at Impact Public Relations. In this exercise, you set Outlook to automatically open the next item in your Inbox after you delete the previous one, thus saving you a step in reading your mail.

Jumping into Your E-mail

Automatically open the next item after a message is deleted

1 On the Tools menu, click Options.

The Options dialog box appears.

2 On the Preferences tab, click the E-mail Options button.

The E-mail Options dialog box appears.

The Advanced E-mail Options button gives you even more ways to customize your Inbox.

3 In the After Moving Or Deleting An Open Item box, click the drop-down arrow, and then select Open The Next Item.

Your screen should look similar to the following illustration.

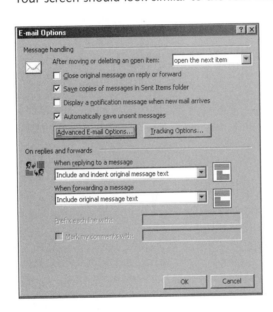

4 In the E-Mail Options dialog box, click OK, and then in the Options dialog box, click OK.

Finish the lesson

Calendar

1 If you want to continue to the next lesson, on the Outlook Bar, click the Calendar shortcut.

2 If you have finished using Outlook for now and are working in a Workgroup environment, click File, and then click Exit And Log Off. If you are working in an Internet only environment, click File, and then click Exit.

Lesson 1 Quick Reference

To	Do this	Button
Start Outlook 2000	On the desktop, double-click the Outlook 2000 shortcut.	
Open Outlook Today	On the Outlook Bar, click the Outlook Today shortcut.	
Make Outlook Today your default page	On the Outlook Bar, click the Outlook Today shortcut. Click the Customize Outlook Today link, select the When Starting, Go Directly To Outlook Today check box, and then click the Save Changes button.	
Read an e-mail message	In the Inbox Information viewer, double-click the message.	
Partially preview all e-mail messages	On the View menu, click AutoPreview.	
Preview a complete message	On the View menu, click Preview Pane.	
Open an attachment	Open the e-mail message, and then double-click the attachment icon.	
Save an attachment	Double-click the attachment icon, and on the File menu, click Save As. Find the folder that you want to use, type a name for the file in the File Name box, and then click the Save button.	
Reply to the sender of an e-mail message	Open the message, click the Reply button, type your response, and then click the Send button. In an Internet only environment, on the Standard toolbar, click the Send/Receive button.	
Reply to the sender of an e-mail message and all who received it	Open the message, click the Reply To All button, type your response, and then click the Send button. In an Internet only environment, on the Standard toolbar, click the Send/Receive button.	

Lesson 1 Quick Reference

To	Do this	Button
Forward a message	Open the message and click the Forward button. Type e-mail addresses in the To and Cc boxes, and then click Send. In an Internet only environment, on the Standard toolbar, click the Send/Receive button.	
Keep copies of all your sent e-mail messages	On the Tools menu, click Options. In the Options dialog box, on the Preferences tab, click the E-mail Options button. Select the Save Copies Of Messages In Sent Items Folder check box. In the E-mail Options dialog box, click OK. In the Options dialog box, click OK.	
Format and print an e-mail message	Open the message and then click the Print button; or on the File menu, click Print Preview, and then click the Page Setup button. In the Page Setup dialog box, select or clear the options you want, and click OK. In the Print Preview, click the Print button, and click OK.	
Create a note	On the Outlook Bar, click the Notes shortcut. On the Standard toolbar, click the New Note button. Type the note.	
Customize your Inbox	On the Tools menu, click Options, and then click the E-mail Options button. Select or clear your preferred settings. Click the Advanced E-mail Options button for additional choices. Click OK twice to close the dialog boxes.	

2

Learning the Basics of Scheduling

ESTIMATED TIME

25 min.

In this lesson you will learn how to:

✔ *Navigate in your Calendar.*

✔ *Open and view Calendar items.*

✔ *Add appointments to your Calendar.*

✔ *Delete Calendar items.*

✔ *Format and print a copy of your schedule.*

✔ *Create an appointment from an e-mail message.*

Microsoft Outlook 2000 helps you manage all your time commitments. You can view your schedule one day at a time, one week at a time, or for an entire month. You can search for or sort appointments, and you can customize your Calendar to display the information in a way that's convenient for you.

As the Impact Public Relations account manager, you have appointments with many different clients, and many meetings and events to attend. In this lesson, you begin to gain control of your schedule by practicing how to add and delete Calendar items, how to format your Calendar to match your own preferences, and how to print a copy of your schedule in several different formats.

Getting Ready for the Lesson

In this exercise, you start Outlook 2000 and prepare the practice folders and files that you need. You create a practice Calendar folder, add a shortcut to the Outlook Bar, and then copy the files to the folder.

Start Outlook and copy the practice files

In this exercise, you start Outlook and set up the special files and folders needed for this lesson. This keeps the lesson materials separate from your own daily work.

Microsoft Outlook

1   On the desktop, double-click the Microsoft Outlook icon.

Outlook 2000 opens.

2   If necessary, maximize the Outlook window.

3   On the Outlook Bar, click the Calendar shortcut.

Your Calendar appears with today's date displayed in the Appointment area.

Calendar

4   On the Standard toolbar, click the New Appointment button drop-down arrow, and then click Folder.

The Create New Folder dialog box appears.

New Appoint-ment

5   Be sure that the Folder Contains box displays Appointment Items.

6   In the Name box, type **SBS Practice Calendar** and click OK.

A Calendar folder called SBS Practice Calendar is created.

For a detailed example of how to copy practice files to a practice folder, see the exercise "Set Up Practice E-mail" in Lesson 1.

7   If you get the message Add Shortcut to Outlook Bar? click No. You'll create the shortcut to it in step 9.

8   On the Standard toolbar, click the New Appointment button drop-down arrow, and then click Outlook Bar Shortcut.

The Add To Outlook Bar dialog box appears.

9   Click the plus sign (+) next to the Calendar folder, click SBS Practice Calendar, and click OK.

An SBS Practice Calendar shortcut is added to the bottom of the Outlook Bar.

SBS Practice Calendar

10 Drag the practice Calendar files, indicated by calendar icons, from the Lesson02 folder in the Outlook 2000 SBS Practice folder on your hard disk to your SBS Practice Calendar folder in the Folder List.

11 Drag the practice e-mail message files, indicated by envelope icons, from the Lesson02 folder in the Outlook 2000 SBS Practice folder to your SBS Practice Inbox folder in the Folder List.

12 On the Outlook Bar, click the SBS Practice Calendar shortcut.

The SBS Practice Calendar appears in the Information viewer.

Navigating in Calendar

When you open Calendar, the Information viewer displays the Appointment area, the TaskPad, and the Date Navigator.

Appointment area   Date Navigator

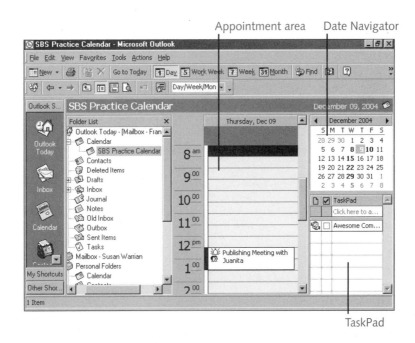

TaskPad

The Appointment area is divided into half-hour time slots. The schedule is highlighted from 8:00 A.M. to 5:00 P.M., but you can enter appointments for other times as well. You can also customize the schedule to display a week at a time or a month at a time. By using the Right and Left arrow keys on the keyboard, you can scroll forward and backward through your daily schedule one day at a time.

The small monthly calendar in the upper-right corner of the Information viewer is the *Date Navigator*. Instead of scrolling through your Calendar day by day to get to a specific date, you can use the Date Navigator to go directly there. By dragging the Date Navigator's left border to the left or right, you can choose to display either one or two monthly calendars at once. By clicking the right and left arrows next to the name of the month, you can scroll month by month. By clicking a specific date in the Date Navigator, the schedule jumps directly to that date, which then is displayed in your Appointment area. You can also tell instantly whether you have anything scheduled for a specific day by scrolling through the Date Navigator to the appropriate month. Dates displayed in boldface type have at least one scheduled event.

For more information about using the TaskPad, see Lesson 9, "Taking Charge of Tasks."

Below the Date Navigator is the TaskPad, which shows a quick overview of the tasks that are currently on your Task list.

Go directly to a date

As a busy account manager, you sometimes need to schedule appointments far in advance.

❶ On the Date Navigator, click the right scroll arrow twice to move forward two months.

❷ Click any date.

The page for that date appears in your Appointment area.

Go to a date far in the future

Let's say that you want to schedule a trade show for the year 2004. You can go quickly to that date without scrolling month by month through the Date Navigator.

❶ On the View menu, point to Go To, and then click Go To Date.

The Go To Date dialog box appears.

You can type the date as 09-17-05 or as Sept 17, 2005, or in any other form; AutoDate converts the information into the correct form.

❷ In the Date box, type or select the date **09-17-04** and click OK.

The Appointment area and the Date Navigator now display the date: Saturday, September 17, 2004.

Using Ordinary Phrases to Set the Date and Time

Calendar's AutoDate feature allows you to type ordinary phrases and abbreviations for a specific date or time and converts them to a numerical date format. Examples of phrases that you can type in the Go To Date dialog box (and in other date boxes in Outlook) include: *first of October; from Friday to Wednesday; in three weeks; July twenty-third; last Saturday; next Friday noon; one week from today; six weeks ago; ten days from now; the week ending next Saturday; this Friday; tomorrow; until June sixth;* and *yesterday*. Examples of phrases that you can type in time boxes include: *eight am; midnight; noon; and six-fifteen*.

Outlook interprets ordinary phrases based on today's date. For example, if the current date is Monday, October 1, and you type *this Thursday*, Outlook's Calendar jumps to Thursday, October 4; but if you type *next Thursday*, the Calendar jumps to Thursday, October 11. You can also type names of holidays and then jump to those dates. To find out how to add holidays, see Lesson 7, "Managing Your Calendar."

Open a Calendar item

In this exercise, you've been asked to speak to a group of prospective clients on December 10, 2004. You check to see if you are available on that date.

1 On the Date Navigator, click the right arrow until you locate the month of December 2004.

The calendar for December 2004 is displayed on the Date Navigator with the date for December 10 in boldface type.

2 Click December 10.

Holiday Shopping appears in the schedule. You decide that your clients are more important than the shopping.

3 Double-click the Holiday Shopping entry.

The Holiday Shopping appointment form appears.

4 Select the text in the Subject field, and type the following:

Meet with colleagues from publishing companies

5 Click Save And Close.

A warning dialog box appears.

6 Click Yes to accept the changes.

The new appointment appears in your schedule. Your screen should look similar to the following illustration.

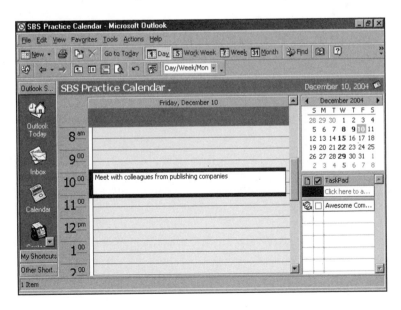

View your future appointments

As an account manager, you must always stay on top of your schedule; being aware of your existing commitments helps you realistically manage your workload. In this exercise, you take a look at your future appointments.

1   On the Date Navigator, scroll to the second week in December 2004, and then click a date that appears in boldface type. The daily schedule for that date appears in the Appointment area.

2   On the Date Navigator, click the following day.

The schedule for the following day appears in the Appointment area.

3   On the Standard toolbar, click the Week button to view your schedule for the week.

A one-week calendar showing all of your appointments appears in the Appointment area.

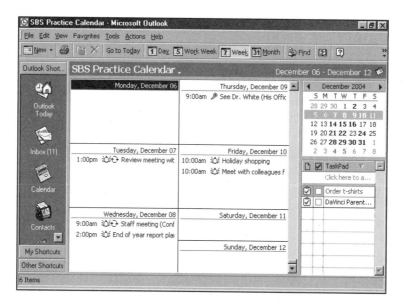

4   On the Standard toolbar, click the Month button to see your schedule for the month.

A one-month calendar showing all of your appointments appears in the Appointment area.

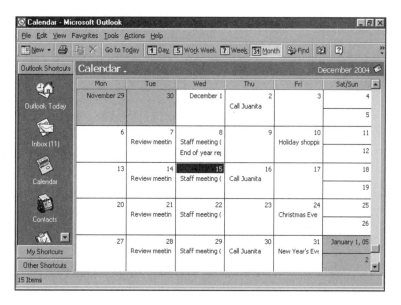

⑤   On the Standard toolbar, click the Day button to return to the daily view.

Adjusting Your Schedule

Keeping on top of your time commitments may mean making frequent adjustments to your schedule. The electronic schedule is as easy to use as a desktop calendar. In this exercise, you add an appointment to the Calendar and then delete an appointment that has been canceled.

Add an appointment directly to your Calendar

In this exercise, you schedule an appointment to meet with your colleague Jim for lunch.

❶   On the Standard toolbar, click the Go To Today button.

Today's schedule appears in the Appointment area.

❷   On the keyboard, press the Right arrow key to scroll forward to tomorrow's schedule, and then click the 12 P.M. time slot.

The 12 P.M. time-slot area is highlighted.

❸   Type **Meet Jim for lunch** in the time slot, and press Enter.

As your entry appears, the time slot becomes white with a blue border.

tip

You can type appointment information, such as duration and location, directly into your appointment record. To do this, double-click the new appointment when you have completed the entry in your schedule. (You can also right-click the appointment, and then click Open.) When the Appointment form appears, enter your data, and then click the Save And Close button.

Delete an appointment

The Delete key on the keyboard deletes only the displayed text, and not the appointment itself.

Sometimes your colleagues cancel appointments, which must then be deleted from your schedule.

1 Be sure that Calendar is open, and then go to tomorrow's schedule showing the noon appointment with Jim for lunch.

2 Click the 12 P.M. appointment to select it.

3 On the Standard toolbar, click the Delete button.

The appointment is deleted from your Calendar.

Delete

Making a Printed Copy of Your Schedule

Because you have many meetings and events to attend with your clients or on their behalf, you are not always at your computer. Nevertheless, you must keep careful track of your schedule in order not to miss important appointments and commitments. One way to accomplish this is to bring your schedule with you. Outlook 2000 can produce a printed schedule in many different formats. The options available in the Print dialog box allow you to choose:

For additional printing options, on the File menu, click Print, and then scroll through the list in the Print Styles box.

- Whether your daily schedule is printed on one page or on two.
- Whether entries from your Task list and an area for notes are included.
- How many hours of the day are shown.
- What fonts are used for printing.
- Whether to add headers and footers.
- Whether to show a day, a week, or a month on each page.
- Whether to print only those days that have entries and eliminate days that are blank.
- Whether to start a new page every day, every week, or every month.

Choose how your printed schedule looks

Press Ctrl+G to go directly to the Go To Date dialog box.

1 On the Outlook Bar, click the SBS Practice Calendar shortcut.

2 On the View menu, point to Go To, and then click Go To Date. In the Date box, click the drop-down arrow and select January 4, 2005, and click OK.

The daily schedule for that date appears in the Appointment area.

Print

3 On the Standard toolbar, click the Print button.

The Print dialog box appears, with Daily Style selected in the Print Style box.

4 In the Print Style area, click Page Setup.

The Page Setup: Daily Style dialog box appears.

You must have a printer connected to your computer for this exercise to work.

5 On the Format tab, in the Options area, click the Layout drop-down list and select 2 Pages/Day. Click OK.

The Page Setup: Daily Style dialog box closes.

6 In the Print dialog box, click OK.

A two-page daily schedule is printed.

Creating New Calendar Items from Other Types of Outlook Items

When you receive an e-mail message asking for an appointment or meeting, you do not need to retype that information into your Calendar. Outlook can do that for you.

You have received an e-mail message from your colleague Bill Carter. He wants to get together for another working lunch on The DaVinci School of Arts and Crafts Parents Day campaign. In this exercise, you use Mr. Carter's e-mail message as the basis for automatically creating an appointment.

Create an appointment from an e-mail message

SBS Practice Inbox

1 On the Outlook Bar, click the SBS Practice Inbox shortcut.

The SBS Practice Inbox appears in the Information viewer.

2 If the Folder List is not displayed on your screen, on the View menu, click Folder List.

The Folder List appears.

The Subject box of the Appointment form is automatically derived from the subject of the e-mail message. You can edit it as necessary.

3 In the Information viewer, select Bill Carter's How About Lunch? e-mail message, and then drag it onto the SBS Practice Calendar folder in the Folder List.

An Appointment form appears, with some information from the e-mail message filled in.

4 On the Appointment form, in Subject box, select the text and type **Lunch with Bill**. In the Start Time box, click the drop-down arrow and select December 9, 2004. In the next box, change the time to 12:00 P.M., and then click Save And Close.

The e-mail message is saved as an appointment.

SBS Practice
Calendar

5 To view the new appointment in your schedule, click the SBS Practice Calendar shortcut. On the View menu, point to Go To, and then click Go To Date. In the Date box, select the current date and type **December 9, 2004**

The new appointment appears in the Appointment area of your schedule.

tip

Most Outlook items can be turned into other kinds of Outlook items by dragging them onto the Outlook Bar shortcut representing the type of item that you'd like to create. An e-mail message can be turned into an appointment, or a contact, or even a task. Contact information can be turned into an e-mail, and so on.

Finish the lesson

SBS Practice
Inbox

1 If you want to continue to the next lesson, on the Outlook Bar, click the SBS Practice Inbox shortcut.

2 If you have finished using Outlook for now and are working in a Workgroup environment, on the File menu, click Exit And Log Off. If you are working in an Internet only environment, on the File menu, click Exit.

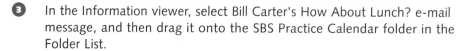

Lesson 2 Quick Reference

To	Do this
Go directly to a date in Calendar	On the Date Navigator, scroll to the month you want, and then click the date you want.
Go to a date in Calendar without scrolling	On the View menu, point to Go To, click Go To Date, type or select a new date in the Date box, and click OK.

Lesson 2 Quick Reference

To	Do this	Button
Open a Calendar item	Double-click the item.	
View appointments for a different date	On the Date Navigator, click the date.	
View appointments for a week or for a month	On the Date Navigator, click a date in the week that you want to view, and then on the Standard toolbar, click the Week or Month button.	
Add an appointment directly to your Calendar	On the Date Navigator, click the day you want, and then in the Appointment area, click the time you want. Type the appointment data in the time slot.	
Delete an appointment	In the Appointment area, click the time slot for the item, and then on the Standard toolbar, click the Delete button.	✕
Print your schedule	On the Date Navigator, click a date, and then on the Standard toolbar, click the Print button, and click OK.	🖨
Create an appointment from an e-mail message	On the Outlook Bar, click the Inbox shortcut. On the View menu, click Folder List. In the Information viewer, select an e-mail message, and drag it onto the Calendar folder in the Folder List. On the Appointment form, edit and complete the information as necessary, and then click the Save And Close button.	

Review & Practice

**ESTIMATED TIME
15 min.**

Before you move on to Part 2, which covers more advanced aspects of e-mail and managing business contact information, you can practice the skills you learned in Part 1 by working through this Review & Practice section. You will review the basic steps involved in sending and replying to e-mail messages and in managing your schedule.

Scenario

As an account manager for Impact Public Relations, you face a demanding schedule and receive many e-mail messages over the course of a day. You want to quickly manage your messages and appointments so that you can devote as much time as possible to preparations for the national sales meeting.

Step 1:   Preview, Open, Reply to, and Print an E-mail Message

An e-mail message has arrived from one of your clients. After you read it and reply, you decide that you need a hard copy.

1 In the SBS Practice Inbox Information viewer, open the message from Juanita Rivera titled Ad Schedules, and preview the complete contents.

2 Click Reply, and type the reply **I think that will work out just right.** Send the message.

3 Print a hard copy of the original, and then close the message.

For more information about	See
Previewing	Lesson 1
Opening an e-mail message	Lesson 1
Replying to an e-mail message	Lesson 1
Printing an e-mail message	Lesson 1

Step 2:   Open and Save an Attachment

You have received a message with an attachment from Gary Wong. You open the attachment, briefly review its contents, and then save it in a folder to read later.

1 Open the message from Gary Wong titled The Future of Computers, and then open the attachment.

2 Save the attachment in your My Documents folder.

For more information about	See
Opening an attachment	Lesson 1
Saving an attachment	Lesson 1

Step 3:   Go Directly to a Date in Calendar, Add an Appointment, and Then Delete It

After entering an appointment into your schedule for a meeting of your professional society, you receive a call canceling the event. You delete the appointment from your Calendar.

1 On the Date Navigator, go to January 15, 2001, and select the time slot for 2:00 P.M. to 4:00 P.M.

2 In the time slot, type **Association of Publicists Steering Committee meeting**

3 After the call canceling the meeting, delete the appointment.

For more information about	See
Viewing future appointments	Lesson 2
Adding an appointment to Calendar	Lesson 2
Deleting an appointment	Lesson 2

Step 4:   View and Print Appointments for January 2005

You find it useful to occasionally survey and print a hard copy of your entire schedule for a month at a time.

1   Find the daily schedule for January 15, 2005.

2   Change the Calendar Information viewer to display a full month of appointments.

3   Print your schedule for the month.

For more information about	See
Viewing future appointments	Lesson 2
Printing your schedule	Lesson 2

Step 5:   Finish the Review & Practice

Follow these steps to delete the practice messages you created in this Review & Practice, and then quit Outlook 2000.

1   Open the Folder List, and then delete the practice messages in the SBS Practice Inbox.

2   Open the Outbox folder and delete any practice messages in it.

3   Locate the attachment file The Future of Computers that you saved, and delete it.

4   If you have finished using Outlook for now and are working in a Workgroup environment, click File, and then click Exit And Log Off. If you are working in an Internet only environment, click File, and then click Exit.

PART 2

Mastering Your Communication with Outlook 2000

3

Creating and Sending E-mail Messages

ESTIMATED TIME
40 min.

In this lesson you will learn how to:

✔ *Compose and send messages.*

✔ *Use the Address Book.*

✔ *Add attachments to messages.*

✔ *Mark messages confidential or urgent.*

✔ *Retrieve messages sent in error.*

✔ *Route files for feedback.*

E-mail is a quick, convenient way to communicate with people both at your workplace and at other locations. Your messages are received almost instantly, and you can attach files and embed Internet links. You can also duplicate many of the formatting features of other written correspondence.

Suppose that you are the account manager at Impact Public Relations. You are responsible for dozens of clients, and you also need to communicate internally with your management and staff. In this lesson, you practice creating and sending e-mail messages and attachments to your clients. After you draft a message, you address it using the Address Book, and then you format the message, mark it confidential and urgent, enclose attachments, and send it. You also learn how to retrieve a message that you've sent by mistake.

Getting Ready for the Lesson

In this exercise, you start Outlook 2000 and prepare the practice files and folders that you need. This keeps the lesson materials separate from your own daily work. If you haven't already done so, you create a practice Inbox, add a shortcut to the Outlook Bar for your practice files folder, and then copy the files to the folder.

Start Outlook and copy the practice files

① On the desktop, double-click the Microsoft Outlook 2000 icon.

Outlook 2000 opens.

② If necessary, maximize the Outlook window.

Maximize

> # important
>
> Before proceeding to the next step, you must have installed this book's practice folder on your hard disk and created an SBS Practice Inbox folder and shortcut.

For a detailed example of how to copy practice files to a practice folder, see the exercise "Set Up Practice E-mail" in Lesson 1.

③ Click the SBS Practice Inbox shortcut.

④ Drag the practice e-mail message files, indicated by envelope icons, from the Lesson03 folder in the Outlook 2000 SBS Practice folder to your SBS Practice Inbox folder in the Folder List.

⑤ Drag the practice Contacts files, indicated by address card icons, from the Lesson03 folder in the Outlook 2000 SBS Practice folder to your Contacts folder in the Folder List.

The three Microsoft Word practice documents should not be copied.

Creating New E-mail Messages

You have just received details about a new sales initiative that must be communicated immediately to your client base. Your support staff must be kept in the loop without your clients' being aware of their behind-the-scenes involvement. Because your client base is geographically diverse and your support staff is organized into geographic units, you need to be especially careful that the internal copies are routed accurately.

In this exercise, you compose and address an e-mail message to one of your clients and then use it as a template for a mass mailing to others in your client base.

Compose a new e-mail message

You begin by drafting the e-mail message to your first client, Dale Carter, with copies to the appropriate internal support staff.

❶ On the Outlook Bar, click the SBS Practice Inbox shortcut.

❷ On the Standard toolbar, click the New Mail Message button.

New Mail Message

A blank Message form appears. Your screen should look similar to the following illustration.

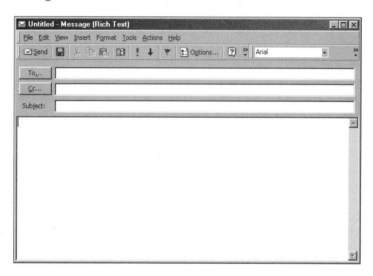

See the following section, "Using the Address Book to Enter E-mail Recipients," to learn how to use the Address Book to address e-mail messages.

important

Throughout this book, you send e-mail to fictitious people. After you send the message, you will receive a screen message telling you that your message is non-deliverable. You can ignore this message and continue with the lesson.

To enter more than one address into the To, Cc, or Bcc box, type an address, insert a semicolon, and then type the next address.

❸ In the Message form, in the To box, type Dale Carter's e-mail address **dalec@millertextiles.millertextiles**, and press Tab.

❹ Type **pstout@ipr.ipr** in the Cc box, and press Tab.

tip

If you want to send a person a copy without others' being aware of it, use the Bcc feature. Click the Cc button, type the address in the Bcc portion of the Select Names dialog box, and click OK. The address then appears in the Bcc box of the message form.

Completing the Subject box is a courtesy that lets readers know what your message is about before they open and read it.

5 In the Subject box, type **New Sales Initiative** and press Tab.

The Message form title bar changes to reflect the subject matter.

6 Type the following in the message area of the form:

Dale—We have a new sales program that I would like to review with you as soon as possible.

Save an unfinished draft of your e-mail message

Already late for a meeting, you decide to finish the message after you return to your desk. Outlook 2000 allows you to save your work in the Drafts folder for later use.

Save

1 On the Standard toolbar, click the Save button, and then close the message.

2 To retrieve the saved draft of your message, in the Folder List, click the Drafts folder.

The Information viewer displays a list of saved drafts. Your screen should look similar to the following illustration.

If your Folder List is not visible on the screen, on the View menu, click Folder List.

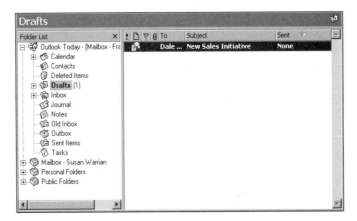

3 Double-click the New Sales Initiative message. Move the insertion point to the end of the text and then type the following:

I will call you tomorrow to discuss this in greater detail.

Check your spelling

To give the message one last quality check before sending it, you run a spelling check.

1 On the Tools menu, click Spelling.

If the Spelling feature detects a potential problem, the Spelling dialog box appears.

2 If a word or group of words are highlighted in boldface type in the dialog box, correct them as appropriate.

3 When the spelling check is complete, click OK, and then click the Minimize button in the upper-right corner of the Message—New Sales Initiative form.

The New Sales Initiative—Message form is reduced to a button on the taskbar. (Later in this lesson, you maximize the New Sales Initiative—Message form again.)

Minimize

If you do not see the Message form on the taskbar, click the Start button, point to Settings, and then click Taskbar. Select the Always On Top check box.

tip

To set Outlook 2000 to check the spelling in your e-mail messages automatically, on the Tools menu, click Options. In the Options dialog box, click the Spelling tab, and then select the Always Check Spelling Before Sending check box.

Using the Address Book to Enter E-mail Recipients

The stack of business cards you brought from a recent trade show provides a good mailing list for prospective clients. Some of the cards represent new contacts; others represent existing contacts already in your database that have relocated to new companies or locations. Because you want to send several of them information on the new sales initiative, you decide to add the new records and change the existing records in your Address Book. Then you use the Address Book to address an e-mail message to one of your new prospects.

Add new contacts to the Address Book

With your stack of business cards in hand, you add information about a new contact, Rob Kahn, to your Address Book.

1 On the Outlook Bar, click the SBS Practice Inbox shortcut.

Address Book

2 On the Standard toolbar, click the Address Book button.

The Address Book dialog box appears.

3 In the Address Book dialog box, click the New Entry button.

The New Entry dialog box appears.

New Entry

4 In the Select The Entry Type area, be sure New Contact is selected, and click OK.

The Untitled—Contact form appears, displaying several tabs.

If you use Outlook 2000 in an Internet only environment, some of these dialog boxes and forms may look different.

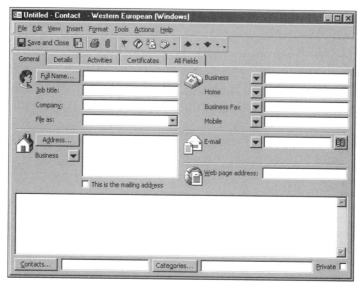

To enter additional information, click the applicable tab and follow the same procedure.

⑤ On the General tab, in the Full Name box, type **Rob Kahn** and then press Tab.

The contact name is automatically recorded as Kahn, Rob in the File As box.

⑥ In the E-mail box, type **robertk@litware.litware**

⑦ Click the Save And Close button.

The Rob Kahn—Contact form closes, and Rob Kahn is added to your Contact list.

Update an Address Book entry

The next card in your stack is for an existing contact, Sue Kennedy, who has changed employers. You update your Address Book to reflect her new e-mail address.

❶ In the Address Book dialog box, in the Show Names From The drop-down list, select Contacts.

❷ In the name list, double-click Sue Kennedy.

The Sue Kennedy—Contact form appears.

tip

You can also select the contact name by typing the first few letters of the person's name in the Type Name Or Select From List box. Outlook 2000 locates the name in the list and selects it for you. Double-click the name, and then type the new information where appropriate.

To change additional information, click the appropriate tab and follow the same procedure.

3 On the General tab, in the E-mail box, update her e-mail address to **skennedy@wcoastsales.wcoastsales**

4 On the Contact Standard toolbar, click the Save And Close button.

Sue Kennedy's updated file is saved and the form closes.

Create distribution lists in the Address Book

You regularly send important e-mail messages about the new sales initiative to certain staff members. To save time and to ensure that no staff member is inadvertently left out, in this exercise you create a *distribution list,* a handy collection of contacts grouped under a single name.

If you use Outlook 2000 in an Internet only environment, some of these dialog boxes and forms may look different.

1 In the Address Book dialog box, click the New Entry button.

The New Entry dialog box appears.

2 In the New Entry dialog box, in the Select The Entry Type area, select New Distribution List, and click OK.

The Distribution List form appears with the Members tab active.

3 On the Distribution List form, in the Name box, type **New Sales Initiative Team**

Your screen should look similar to the following illustration.

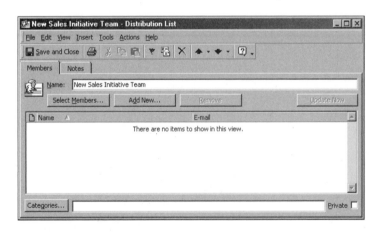

To add a contact not yet in the Address Book to the distribution list, on the Members tab, click the Add New button.

4 Click the Select Members button.

The Select Members dialog box appears.

5 In the Select Members dialog box, in the Show Names From The drop-down list, select Contacts.

6 In the list of contact entries, click Peter Stout, and then click the Add button.

7 Repeat steps 5 and 6 for Susan Warrian.

8 In the Select Members dialog box, click OK.

The Select Members dialog box closes and the New Sales Initiative Team—Distribution List form appears.

9 Click the Save And Close button.

The group appears in the Contact list identified by a group icon and the group name in boldface type.

Close

10 Click the Close button.

> ## tip
> To remove a person from the distribution list, double-click the group name in the Contact list. Click the group member's name in the group member list box, click the Remove button, and then click the Save And Close button.

Enter e-mail addresses from the Address Book

Now that you have correct e-mail addresses for your clients in the Address Book, you can quickly and accurately address your e-mail messages.

1 Click the New Sales Initiative—Message button on the taskbar.

The Message form reappears on your screen.

2 In the New Sales Initiative—Message form, click the To button.

The Select Names dialog box appears.

> ## tip
> To insert a person from the Address Book in the Cc or Bcc box, click the Cc button, select the person's name, and then click the Cc or Bcc button as applicable. Click OK.

3 In the Show Names From The drop-down list, select Contacts.

4 In the name list, select George Ruter and then click the To button.

The name is added after Dale's name in the Message Recipients list.

5 Click OK.

The Select Names dialog box closes and you can now continue working on your message, amending the greeting to read **Dale and George–**

Adding Attachments to Messages

For a demonstration of how to attach files to and address an e-mail message, in the Multimedia folder on the Microsoft Outlook 2000 Step by Step CD-ROM, double-click the Mail icon.

In the next exercise, you forward a variety of supporting information to a prospective client along with your e-mail message. The items include a product data sheet, a testimonial e-mail message from a satisfied client, and a link to your firm's Web site. To assist you in drafting the letter, you use an excerpt from an existing Microsoft Word document in the body of your e-mail message.

Send files with e-mail messages

To send the product data sheet, which is a Microsoft Word document, you attach the file to the e-mail message.

Insert File

1. In the New Sales Initiative—Message form, move the insertion point to the end of the text, and press Enter.

   A blank line is added.

2. On the Message form Standard toolbar, click the Insert File button.

   The Insert File dialog box appears.

3. In the Insert File dialog box, locate the Outlook 2000 SBS Practice folder and double-click it.

   The contents of the folder are displayed.

4. Double-click the Lesson03 folder, and then double-click the Product Data Sheet document.

   An icon representing the attached Word file appears in the message area at the insertion point or at the bottom of the screen.

Workgroup

tip

In a Workgroup environment, coworkers on the same server can access your attachment using a shortcut that you send to them. To send a shortcut, click the Insert File button, select the file you want to attach, click the Insert drop-down arrow, and then select Insert As Shortcut. A shortcut linking your message to the appropriate file on the server appears in the message area.

Attach other e-mail messages

Over time, you have collected a wonderful set of e-mail messages from satisfied clients. In this exercise, you attach a testimonial e-mail message to your original e-mail message.

❶ On the Message form, click the Insert menu, and then click Item.

The Insert Item dialog box appears.

❷ In the Insert Item dialog box, in the Look In list, click the plus sign (+) next to the Inbox folder, and then click the SBS Practice Inbox folder.

The contents of the SBS Practice Inbox folder are displayed in the Items list. Your screen should look similar to the following illustration.

To insert more than one e-mail message file, repeat steps 2 through 4 until all the files you want are attached.

❸ In the Insert As area, be sure that Attachment is selected.

❹ In the Items list, double-click the Thanks For A Job Well Done! message.

The Insert Items dialog box closes, and an icon for the e-mail message is added to the New Sales Initiative message.

Embed a hyperlink in your message

The finishing touch is to add a hyperlink to your message so that your client has ready access to your firm's Web site. To visit the Web site, all your client has to do is to click the hyperlink.

The hyperlink will be easily identified by your e-mail recipients, because the address will be underlined and colored.

❶ Type the following sentence and Internet address for your firm's Web site at the end of your message:

You can also access our homepage on the Internet at http://microsoft.com

The sentence appears in the message area, and the Internet address is formatted as a hyperlink.

❷ On the Message form Standard toolbar, click the Save button.

The message is saved.

Close

❸   On the Message form, click the Close button.

The message closes.

Customizing the Appearance of Your E-mail Messages

Outlook provides three formatting options for sending your e-mail messages—plain text, rich text, and HTML. Plain text, the simplest of the three options, is readable by all e-mail recipients, but does not enable you to use standard word processing formatting features in your messages, such as bold type, italics, font variations, and bulleted lists. Rich text and HTML enable you to use these standard formatting features, maximizing the impact of your e-mail messages and making them look as professional as your other business communications; but not all e-mail recipients can read this format. HTML format is becoming the formatting standard for e-mail messages and provides the richest set of formatting options for users.

You can also choose to use Microsoft Word as your *e-mail editor*. By using Word to help create your e-mail messages, you can use many of Word's features such as automatically checking your spelling as you type, adding bullets and numbering, and more. If the message recipient is not using Word, however, some formatting may be converted to plain text.

In addition to formatting, you can customize the appearance of your e-mail messages and save typing time by automatically adding a *signature*. A personal signature is a predefined block of text that appears at the end of your e-mail messages. It may include information such as your name, title, and company name, or anything else that you want to include. You can create multiple signatures to choose from, such one for formal and another for informal e-mail messages, and, if you are using rich text or HTML formatting, you can format the signature to look professional.

Format e-mail using
Outlook 2000 rich text, HTML, or plain text

In this exercise, you set your messages to use HTML format.

❶   On the Tools menu, click Options.

The Options dialog box appears.

Your screen should look similar to the following illustration.

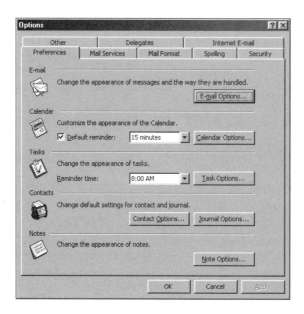

2   In the Options dialog box, click the Mail Format tab, and then, in the Send In This Message Format drop-down list, select HTML.

important

In the Message Format area, select the Use Microsoft Word To Edit E-mail Messages check box to use Word as your e-mail editor.

Use steps 1 through 3 to select the Microsoft Outlook rich text or plain text formats.

3   Click OK.

The Options dialog box closes.

Add your electronic signature

In this exercise, you create an electronic personal signature and add it to the Signature list so that all new messages will automatically include your name and contact information.

1   On the Tools menu, click Options.

The Options dialog box opens with the Preferences tab active.

2   In the Options dialog box, click the Mail Format tab.

The Mail Format tab becomes active.

3 On the Mail Format tab, in the Signature area, click the Signature Picker button.

The Signature Picker dialog box opens.

4 In the Signature Picker dialog box, click the New button.

The Create New Signature dialog box opens.

5 In the Create New Signature dialog box, in the Enter A Name For Your New Signature box, type **Formal Signature** and then click the Next button.

The Edit Signature dialog box opens.

6 In the Edit Signature dialog box, type and format the information that you would like to include as your personal signature.

Your screen should look similar to the following illustration.

7 In the Edit Signature dialog box, click the Finish button, and then in the Signature Picker dialog box, click OK.

The Edit Signature dialog box and the Signature Picker dialog box closes.

8 In the Options dialog box, click OK.

The Options dialog box closes.

Your signature will appear by default in newly created e-mail messages. Because this message is in draft form, you must insert your signature into it.

9 On the Outlook Bar, click the My Shortcuts button, and then click the Drafts shortcut.

The Drafts Information viewer appears.

10 In the Drafts Information viewer, double-click the New Sales Initiative message.

The New Sales Initiative message opens.

11 Position the insertion point in the message box, press Ctrl+End to move to the end of the text, and then press the Enter key.

⑫   On the Insert menu, point to Signature, and then click Formal Signature. Your electronic signature is added to the bottom of your message.

> **tip**
>
> If you are using Word as your e-mail editor, type and select your desired signature on a message form. On the Insert menu, point to AutoText and then click New In the Create AutoText dialog box. Type a name for the signature and click OK. To insert the signature at the end of your message, on the Insert menu, point to AutoText, point to Normal, and then click the signature you want.

Setting Your Send Options

Outlook 2000 provides several options for *flagging* or *marking* your messages to let the recipient know the message content's status at a glance. You can mark a message as private, personal, or confidential, or you can mark the importance level as high or low. You can flag a message with a variety of flags to indicate the type of response needed. Since the message you need to send contains sensitive pricing information, you flag your message as both urgent and confidential by changing the default send options.

Set the importance level

Because your client must see this message as soon as possible, you mark it as urgent. This way, it arrives flagged and listed at the top of his new messages.

Importance: High

●   On the Message form Standard toolbar, click the Importance: High button. Your client will now be able to see that the message is urgent because the Importance: High symbol will appear next to the message in his Inbox.

Importance: Low

>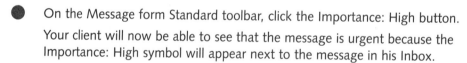
> **tip**
>
> To send the message with low importance, on the Message form Standard toolbar, click the Importance: Low button.

Set the sensitivity level

Because the message contains proprietary company information that you do not want shared with your competitors, you also mark the message as confidential.

1 On the Message form Standard toolbar, click the Options button.

The Message Options dialog box appears.

2 In the Message Settings area, in the Sensitivity drop-down list, select Confidential. Your screen should look similar to the following illustration.

Close

3 In the Message Options dialog box, click the Close button.

The Message Options dialog box closes and the sensitivity setting will appear in the recipient's Comment area of the message.

important

Selecting one of the enhanced sensitivity features alerts the recipient to the special nature of the message content. It does not prevent the recipient from forwarding, printing, or otherwise disclosing the content. To set enhanced security options, such as encryption and digital signatures, see "Sending Secure E-mail Messages" in Lesson 10, "Managing and Protecting Your Files."

Sending Your E-mail Messages

Now that your message is complete, you send it over the Internet to your client, and over your company's network to the support staff on your Cc list. Unfortunately, moments after you send the message, a message appears on your own screen telling you that your e-mail was not delivered because of a faulty e-mail address. After correcting the address, you resend the message.

Send a message over the Internet and within your workgroup

In this exercise, you send your message to your client over the Internet and to the internal staff through your firm's network.

important

Throughout this book, you send e-mail to fictitious people. After you send the message, you will receive a screen message telling you that your message is non-deliverable. You can ignore this message and continue with the lesson.

1   On the Message form Standard toolbar, click the Send button.

If you work in a Workgroup or if you work in an Internet only environment and are connected to the Internet, your message is sent automatically.

2   If you are not connected to the Internet, your message is placed in the Outbox. To send the message, on the Standard toolbar, click the Send/Receive button. Complete the instructions from your Internet service provider to access the Internet.

Your message is sent.

tip

To track your e-mail correspondence and other communications with a contact, you can use Journal. See the One Step Further section, "Using Journal to Log Your Business Activities" in Lesson 10 to learn how to set up and maintain a contact journal.

Retracting an E-mail Message That You've Sent by Mistake

You're having a tough day. The message you sent to Dale Carter contains an error in the content. If Dale Carter hasn't already opened it, you can retrieve the message.

Recall an e-mail message

To correct your error, you quickly retrieve the message.

1   In the Folder List, click the Sent Items folder.

The contents of the Sent Items folder appears in the Information viewer.

2   In the Sent Items Information viewer, double-click the New Sales Initiative message.

The message appears.

3   On the Message form Standard toolbar, click the Actions menu, and then click Recall This Message.

The Recall This Message dialog box appears.

4   In the Are You Sure You Want To area, click Delete Unread Copies Of This Message, and click OK.

The dialog box closes.

Close

⑤ On the Message form, click the Close button.

important

You must act quickly, because the message can be retrieved only if the recipient has not yet received it.

One Step Further

Routing Files to Contacts and Coworkers for Feedback

Workgroup

In this exercise, you work in a Workgroup environment and have finished a draft of your new sales initiative outline. You want feedback from three key people in operations and sales. You also want to be able to identify the person making the comments so that you can follow up with them later. To do this, you set up a routing file.

Create a routing file

To route your document to the appropriate staff members, you need to set up a routing file so that Peter Stout, Susan Warrian, and Sue Kennedy each receive the document in that order.

① On the Windows taskbar, click Start, point to Programs, and then click Microsoft Word.

Microsoft Word opens.

Open

② On the Microsoft Word Standard toolbar, click the Open button.

The Open dialog box appears.

③ Locate the Outlook 2000 SBS Practice folder and open it.

The contents of the folder are displayed.

④ Open the Lesson03 folder, and then double-click the New Sales Initiative document.

The New Sales Initiative Word document opens.

⑤ Click the File menu, point to Send To, and then click Routing Recipient.

The Routing Slip dialog box appears.

⑥ Click the Address button.

The Address Book dialog box appears.

Your screen should look similar to the following illustration.

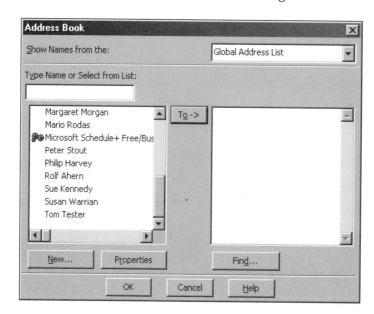

7 In the Show Names From The drop-down list, select Contacts.

8 In the name list, click Peter Stout, the first person to receive the document, and then click the To button.

The name appears in the To box.

9 Repeat this process with Susan Warrian and Sue Kennedy, and click OK.

The Routing Slip dialog box appears, listing all three names in the To box.

10 In the Message Text box, type the following:

Please review the attached report and return your feedback to me by next Wednesday.

11 At the bottom of the Routing Slip dialog box, in the Route To Recipients area, be sure that the One After Another option is selected and that the Return When Done and Track Status check boxes are also selected.

12 In the upper-right corner of the dialog box, click the Add Slip button.

The Routing Slip dialog box closes.

13 On the File menu, click Exit.

The Route Document dialog box appears, prompting you to begin routing the document.

14 In the Route Message dialog box, click No, and then in the message box prompting you to save your changes, click No.

Word closes and Outlook reappears.

important

Because this exercise was not a real scenario, you clicked No in the dialog boxes in step 14. To actually route the document, you must click Yes in the Route Document dialog box.

Finish the lesson

1 To continue to the next lesson, click the SBS Practice Inbox shortcut on the Outlook Bar.

2 If you have finished using Outlook for now and are working in a workgroup environment, click File, and then click Exit And Log Off. If you are working in an Internet only environment, click File, and then click Exit.

Lesson 3 Quick Reference

To	Do this	Button
Create a new e-mail message	On the Standard toolbar, click the New Mail Message button, and then complete the heading and message areas.	New
Save an e-mail draft	On the Standard toolbar, click the Save button, and then on the Message form, click the Close button.	
Check spelling	On the Tools menu, click Spelling. If a word or group of words is highlighted in the dialog box, correct as appropriate. When the spelling check is complete, click OK.	
Add a new contact to the Address Book	On the Standard toolbar, click the Address Book button, and then click the New Entry button. In the New Entry dialog box, be sure New Contact is selected, click OK, and then on the Contact form, type the contact information for each tab.	

Lesson 3 Quick Reference

To	Do this
Update an Address Book entry	On the Standard toolbar, click the Address Book button. In the Address Book dialog box, in the Show Names From The drop-down list, select Contacts. In the name list, double-click the contact that you want to change. In the Contact form, click the tab containing the information that you want to change, make the change, and then on the Contact Standard toolbar, click the Save And Close button.
Create a distribution list in the Address Book	On the Standard toolbar, click the Address Book button and then click the New Entry button. In the New Entry dialog box, select New Distribution List, and click OK. In the Distribution List form, type the group name. Click the Select Members button, and then in the Select Members dialog box, select Contacts. Select the name you want from the list, and then click the Add button, repeating this process for each name you want to add to the distribution list. Click OK, and then click the Save And Close button.
Enter an e-mail address from the Address Book	On the Message form Standard toolbar, click either the To, Cc, or Bcc button, as necessary. In the Select Names dialog box, select either Global Address List or Contacts, as necessary. Select the name you want from the list, and then click either the To, Cc, or Bcc button. When all names have been added, click OK.

Lesson 3 Quick Reference

To	Do this	Button
Attach a file to an e-mail message	Open an e-mail message. Position the insertion point in the message area. On the Message form Standard toolbar, click the Insert File button and then select the correct file from the list.	
Attach an e-mail message to another e-mail message	Open an e-mail message, and then in the message area, position the insertion point at the end of the text. On the Insert menu, click Item. In the Look In drop-down list, select the Inbox (or Outbox) folder, and then double-click the e-mail mesage to be attached.	
Embed a hyperlink in an e-mail message	Type the Internet address in the body of your message where desired and a formatted hyperlink is inserted.	
Format e-mail messages using HTML, Outlook 2000 rich text, or plain text	On the Standard toolbar, click the Tools menu, and then click Options. Click the Mail Format tab and in the Send In This Format drop-down list, select the format you want. Click OK.	
Add an electronic signature	On the Tools menu, click Options, and then click the Mail Format tab. In the Signature area, click the Signature Picker button, and then click the New button. In the Create New Signature dialog box, type a name for your signature, and then click the Next button. In the Edit Signature dialog box, type and format the information for the signature, and then click the Finish button. Click OK twice to close the dialog boxes. To	

Lesson 3 Quick Reference

To	Do this	Button
	insert the signature, open the message, and then position the insertion point at the end of the text in the message area. On the Insert menu, point to Signature, and then click the signature name you want.	
Set the importance level of a message	On the Message form Standard toolbar, click either the Importance: High button or Importance: Low button as appropriate.	
Set the sensitivity level of a message	On the Message form Standard toolbar, click the Options button. In the Message Settings area, in the Sensitivity box, click the drop-down arrow and select the setting from the list.	
Recall a message	In the Folder List, click the Sent Items folder, and then double-click the message to recall. On the Actions menu, click Recall This Message, and click OK.	
Create a routing file	On the Windows taskbar, click Start, point to Programs, and then click Microsoft Word. On the Word Standard toolbar, click the Open button. Scroll as necessary to locate the file you want from the list, and then double-click the file. Click the File menu, point to Send To, and then click Routing Recipient. In the Routing Slip dialog box, click the Address button. Select the name from the list of the first person to receive the document, and then click the To button. Repeat as necessary for each additional name. In	

Lesson 3 Quick Reference

To	Do this
	the Message Text area, type a message to the recipients and then click the Add Slip button. On the File menu, click Exit. In the Routing Message dialog box, click Yes.

4

Organizing and Managing the Inbox

In this lesson you will learn how to:

✔ *Organize e-mail messages for fast reviewing.*
✔ *Set up file folders for organizing e-mail messages.*
✔ *Flag e-mail messages for follow-up.*
✔ *Create rules to handle e-mail messages automatically.*
✔ *Use the Out Of Office Assistant.*

ESTIMATED TIME
40 min.

Now that you know how to create and send e-mail messages, you can use Microsoft Outlook 2000 to organize and manage them even when you are away from your workplace. These organizational and management features help you read, store, and respond to large volumes of e-mail quickly and efficiently.

As the Impact Public Relations account manager, you have received a flood of e-mail messages from your client base, as well as some from your internal staff. You are concerned about being able to quickly sort through the e-mail messages and respond to them in a timely manner without anything falling through the cracks. In this lesson, you work with an e-mail message that you have received, setting preview options to review the e-mail message quickly, creating a file folder to organize it for future reference, and flagging it to remind you of needed follow-up actions. Next you learn how to automatically file and forward e-mail messages, identify and delete unwanted e-mail messages, and notify others that you are out of the office.

Getting Ready for the Lesson

In this exercise, you start Outlook 2000 and prepare the practice files and folders that you need.

Start Outlook and copy the practice files

Microsoft Outlook

1 On the desktop, double-click the Microsoft Outlook 2000 icon.

Outlook 2000 opens.

2 If necessary, maximize the Outlook window.

Maximize

important

Before proceeding to the next step, you must have installed this book's practice folder and created an SBS Practice Inbox folder and shortcut.

SBS Practice Inbox

3 On the Outlook Bar, click the SBS Practice Inbox shortcut.

4 Drag the practice e-mail message files, indicated by envelope icons, from the Lesson04 folder in the Outlook 2000 SBS Practice folder to your SBS Practice Inbox folder in the Folder List.

Organizing Your Inbox for Fast Review

For a detailed example of how to copy practice files to a practice folder, see the exercise "Set Up Practice E-mail" in Lesson 1.

As you open your Inbox, you see several e-mail messages from prospective clients and internal staff on a variety of topics. By default, these are sorted by the date they were received. You can quickly sift through them by clicking any of the column headings to reorder the list and view them by importance, icon, attachment, flag status, sender, subject, or date of receipt. In this lesson, you practice sorting by color-coding and conversation topic.

Sort e-mail messages

You reorganize first by subject to see how many e-mail messages are from clients replying to your mailing about the new sales initiative. Then you organize by sender to see if those same clients sent you e-mail messages on other topics that you should review before contacting them.

1 On the Outlook Bar, click the SBS Practice Inbox shortcut, and then, in the SBS Practice Inbox Information viewer, click the Subject column heading.

The arrow on the Subject column heading changes to point upward, and the files in the Information viewer are organized alphabetically in ascending order by subject.

When you click the arrow on any column heading, it changes to point upward or downward to indicate that the list is in either ascending or descending order.

② Click the Subject column heading again.

The arrow on the Subject column heading changes to point downward, and the files in the Information viewer are organized alphabetically in descending order by subject.

③ Click the From column heading.

The arrow on the From column heading changes to point upward, and the files in the Information viewer are organized alphabetically in ascending order by sender.

Sort your Inbox by topic

You want to see at a glance how many of your incoming e-mail messages pertain to your top priority project, a new sales initiative. To see this tally without viewing the individual e-mail messages on the screen, you sort your Inbox by topic.

You can also click column headings in the Information viewer to organize your Drafts, Sent Items, and Deleted Items folders.

① Be sure that the SBS Practice Inbox is open, and then on the Standard toolbar, click the Organize button.

The Ways To Organize SBS Practice Inbox panel is displayed at the top of the Information viewer.

② In the Ways To Organize SBS Practice Inbox panel, click the Using Views link.

The Using Views page appears, showing the Change Your View list with a selection of options.

③ In the Change Your View list, select By Conversation Topic.

The e-mail messages are sorted by topic, based on the Subject line of the message. Your screen should look similar to the following illustration.

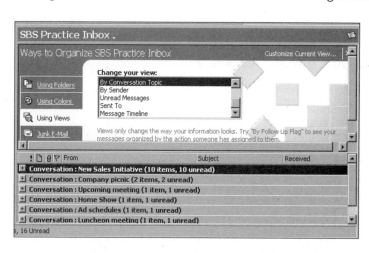

4 Locate the topic New Sales Initiative and then click the plus sign (+) in front of that line.

The topic category expands to list all the e-mail messages with that topic.

5 In the Ways To Organize SBS Practice Inbox panel, with the Change Your View list, scroll to select Messages, and then click the Organize button.

The Ways To Organize SBS Practice Inbox panel closes and the Information viewer is restored to its original setting.

---

tip

The Using Views feature enables you to sort and filter the items in your Inbox in several different ways, including: unread e-mail messages, e-mail messages (date received), sent to, sent from, e-mail message timeline (date sent), e-mail messages flagged for follow-up, and e-mail messages that arrived during the past seven days.

Organizing Your E-mail Messages into Folders

To delete an e-mail message, click the e-mail message, and then click the Delete button on the Standard toolbar.

Once you have read your e-mail messages, you might want to keep some of them for future reference. Because retaining them in your Inbox would lead to a disorganized accumulation of unrelated e-mail messages, you create folders to better manage them. In this exercise, because you handle several clients, you decide to organize client e-mail messages by company name. Then once you have filed your e-mail messages in folders, you find a message misfiled in a folder.

Create a folder in the Folder List

In this exercise, you create a file folder for Miller Textiles and move Dale Carter's e-mail messages into the Miller Textiles folder.

1 On the Outlook Bar, click the SBS Practice Inbox shortcut.

2 In the SBS Practice Inbox Information viewer, click the RE: New Sales Initiative e-mail message from Dale Carter.

3 If the Folder List is not displayed, on the View menu, click Folder List.

4 Click the Organize button.

The Ways To Organize SBS Practice Inbox panel is displayed with the Using Folders page open. Your screen should look similar to the following illustration.

New Folder button

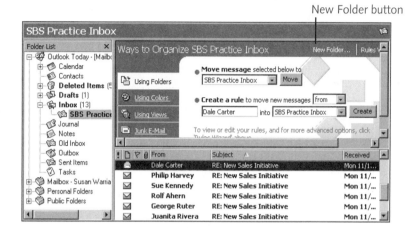

⑤ On the Ways To Organize SBS Practice Inbox panel, click the New Folder button located in the upper-right corner of the screen.

The Create New Folder dialog box appears.

Your screen should look similar to the following illustration.

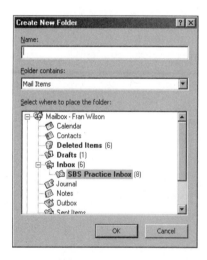

Right-click the folder in the Folder List, and then select the action that you want from the shortcut menu.

⑥ Be sure that the Folder Contains box displays Mail Items, and then in the Name box, type **Miller Textiles** and click OK.

A message appears on your screen, prompting you to add a shortcut to the Outlook Bar.

⑦ Click No.

In the Folder List, a new folder named Miller Textiles appears as a subfolder of the SBS Practice Inbox folder. In the Ways to Organize SBS Practice Inbox panel, Miller Textiles appears in the Move Message Selected Below To box.

Organizing the Inbox

4

8   In the Information viewer, click the From column heading to sort by sender.

All of Dale Carter's e-mail messages are now grouped together.

9   Select the first e-mail message in the group of Dale Carter's e-mail messages. Hold down the Shift key, and then click the last e-mail message in the group of Dale Carter's e-mail messages.

All of Dale Carter's e-mail messages are now selected.

10   In the Ways to Organize SBS Practice Inbox panel, click the Move button.

Dale Carter's e-mail messages are moved to the Miller Textiles folder.

11   Click the Organize button.

The Ways to Organize SBS Practice Inbox panel closes.

tip

To view the contents of the new folder, in the Folder List, click the plus sign (+) to the left of the SBS Practice Inbox folder, and then click the folder name.

Move an e-mail message into a folder

Now when you receive an e-mail message from another client at Miller Textiles, George Ruter, you transfer it directly into the Miller Textiles folder.

To view the SBS Practice Inbox subfolders, in the Folder List, click the plus sign (+) to the left of the SBS Practice Inbox folder.

1   Be sure that the SBS Practice Inbox is open, and that the Folder List is displayed on your screen with the Miller Textiles subfolder showing.

2   In the SBS Practice Inbox Information viewer, drag the e-mail message titled Upcoming Meeting from George Ruter to the Miller Textiles folder in the Folder List.

The e-mail message from George Ruter is moved from the SBS Practice Inbox folder to the Miller Textiles folder.

tip

To be sure that the e-mail message has been moved to the correct folder, click the folder in the Folder List to review the contents. If the e-mail message does not appear in the Information viewer for the correct folder, try checking the contents of the folder directly above or below to see if you dragged the file to the wrong folder. If you did, simply drag it from the incorrect folder into the correct one.

Find a missing e-mail message

Unable to find an e-mail message in your file, in this exercise you use Outlook 2000's Find and Advanced Find features to locate the missing e-mail message.

1 Be sure that the SBS Practice Inbox is open.

2 On the Standard toolbar, click the Find button.

The Find Items In SBS Practice Inbox panel is displayed. Your screen should look similar to the following illustration.

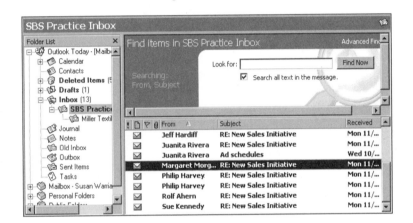

3 In the Look For box, type **Urban League**

4 Be sure that the Search All Text In The Message check box is not selected, and then click the Find Now button.

Outlook 2000 searches the From and Subject areas of all of the e-mail messages in your SBS Practice Inbox folder. In the Information viewer, the message No Items Found appears.

5 In the upper-right corner of the Find Items In SBS Practice Inbox panel, click the Advanced Find button.

The Advanced Find dialog box opens, with the Messages tab active.

To open the e-mail message, double-click the message.

6 In the Advanced Find dialog box, in the Look For box, be sure Messages is displayed, and then, in the Search For The Word(s) box, type **Urban League**

7 In the In box, click the drop-down arrow, select Subject Field And Message Body, and then click the Find Now button.

The Upcoming Meeting e-mail message from George Ruter is listed in the Information viewer.

Close

8 In the Advanced Find dialog box, click the Close button.

The Advanced Find dialog box closes and the Find panel appears.

9   In the Find Items In SBS Practice Inbox panel, click the Close button.

The Find panel closes and the Information viewer appears.

Flagging E-mail Messages for Follow-up

Some e-mail messages in your Inbox might require follow-up action on your part, such as placing a phone call, replying to the e-mail message, or checking further on information presented in the e-mail message. To note and track follow-up activities, you use the flag feature.

In this exercise, you practice flagging an e-mail message from George Ruter to remind yourself to call him. When you place the call, you then mark the flag as complete, enabling you to track it with your other completed flags to assist you in preparing your weekly report.

Flag an e-mail message for follow-up

In this exercise, you flag George Ruter's e-mail message with a note to call him tomorrow.

1   Be sure the Folder List is displayed, and then click the Miller Textiles subfolder.

The contents of the Miller Textiles subfolder are displayed in the Information viewer.

2   In the Miller Textiles Information viewer, double-click the Upcoming Meeting message from George Ruter.

The Upcoming Meeting e-mail message opens.

3   On the Message form Standard toolbar, click the Flag For Follow Up button.

The Flag For Follow Up dialog box appears.

Flag For Follow Up

4   In the Flag For Follow Up dialog box, in the Flag To box, click the drop-down arrow, and then select Call.

To change the time, select the time in the Due By box and type the desired time.

5   In the Due By box, click the drop-down arrow, and then click the next day on the calendar.

The Due By entry is changed to tomorrow's date.

> ## tip
> You can scroll through the Due By calendar by clicking one of the arrows next to the month title, using the right arrow to move to future months and the left arrow to move to the preceding months.

⑥   In the Flag For Follow Up dialog box, click OK.

   The reminder to call tomorrow appears in the Comment area below the
   Message form Standard toolbar. Your screen should look similar to the following illustration.

Reminder   Comment area

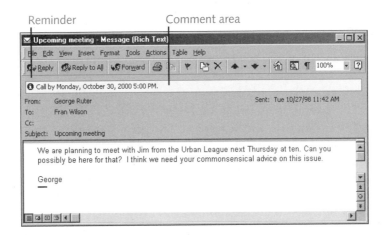

⑦   On the Message form, click the Close button.

Close

   The e-mail message closes. In the Miller Textiles Information viewer, a red
   flag appears in the Flag Status column to the left of the e-mail message
   Upcoming Meeting from George Ruter.

Mark a flagged e-mail message as completed

Having completed the call to George Ruter, you mark the flag as complete,
intending to use your list of completed flags to prepare your weekly activity report.

❶   Be sure that the Miller Textiles folder is open, and then in the Information viewer, double-click the Upcoming Meeting e-mail message from
   George Ruter.

   The Upcoming Meeting from George Ruter opens.

❷   On the Message form Standard toolbar, click the Flag For Follow Up button.

   The Flag For Follow Up dialog box appears.

❸   In the Flag For Follow Up dialog box, select the Completed check box, and
   click OK.

   On the Message form, the completion date is added to the Comment area
   below the Message form Standard toolbar.

❹   On the Message form, click the Close button.

   In the Miller Textiles information viewer, the flag next to the Upcoming Meeting e-mail message from George Ruter has been changed from red to gray.

tip

To clear the flag, right-click the e-mail message in the Information viewer and then on the shortcut menu, click Clear Flag.

Creating Rules to Automatically Organize and Manage Your Inbox

For a demonstration of how to create rules to organize the SBS Practice Inbox, in the Multimedia folder on the Microsoft Outlook 2000 Step by Step CD-ROM, double-click the Rules icon.

Although the sorting, filing, and flagging techniques described in the preceding exercises are helpful, you soon realize that you can use Outlook's sophisticated organizing tools to better manage your steady stream of incoming e-mail messages. In addition, sometimes you receive unsolicited and unwanted e-mail messages that only add clutter to your Inbox. Outlook enables you to handle these routine and repetitive tasks automatically. For example, you can:

- File e-mail messages automatically upon receipt into the appropriate folder.

- Forward e-mail messages automatically from a particular sender to another person or group, such as your boss or project team.

- Delete adult content or junk e-mail e-mail messages automatically before they ever enter your Inbox.

- Empty the Deleted Items folder automatically.

When you delete an item, it is moved to the Deleted Items folder. Unless you empty the folder regularly, these unwanted items take up valuable space on your hard disk.

As account manager at Impact Public Relations, some e-mail message activities are recurring or predictable. In the following exercise, automate some of these repetitive tasks.

Move e-mail messages to a separate folder immediately upon receipt

In this exercise, you create a rule to automatically move incoming mail from Lee Wong of Miller Textiles to the Miller Textiles folder.

1. On the Outlook Bar, click the SBS Practice Inbox shortcut.

2. In the SBS Practice Inbox Information viewer, click Lee Wong's RE: New Sales Initiative e-mail message.

3 On the Standard toolbar, click the Organize button.

The Ways To Organize SBS Practice Inbox panel appears, with the Using Folders page open.

4 In the Create A Rule To Move Messages area, be sure that From is selected in the first box, and that Lee Wong's name appears in the second box.

Your screen should look similar to the following illustration.

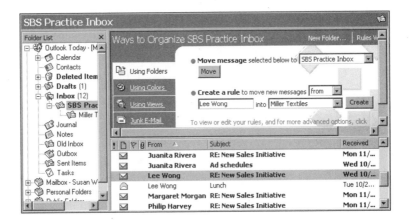

You can add any number of names at once, separating each by a semicolon.

5 If necessary, in the third box, click the drop-down arrow, and then select Miller Textiles.

6 Click the Create button.

A message box appears, telling you that the rule will be applied to new e-mail messages and prompting you to apply the same rule to other e-mail messages in your Inbox from Mr. Wong.

If you do not see the Done! message, you may need to close the Folder List.

7 Click Yes.

Next to the Create button, *Done!* appears on the screen. Now all existing e-mail messages from Lee Wong are moved to the Miller Textiles folder and all new e-mail messages from him will automatically be moved to the folder.

8 In the Ways To Organize SBS Practice Inbox panel, click the Close button.

Close

tip

To check if you have e-mail messages in a subfolder, display the Folder List and then click the plus sign (+) next to the Inbox to display the subfolders. The number of unread e-mail messages is displayed in parentheses after the subfolder name, and the name of the subfolder is in bold.

Organizing the Inbox

Forward e-mail messages to another person immediately upon receipt

In this exercise, you create a rule to forward all e-mail messages from Sue Kennedy at Miller Textiles to your manager, Peter Stout.

1 Open the Miller Textiles folder, and then on the Tools menu, click Rules Wizard.

The Rules Wizard dialog box appears.

2 In the Rules Wizard dialog box, click the New button.

The next Rules Wizard dialog box appears.

3 In the Which Type Of Rule Do You Want To Create? list, select Check Messages When They Arrive, and then click the Next button.

The next Rules Wizard dialog box appears.

4 In the Which Condition(s) Do You Want To Check? list, select the From People Or Distribution List check box.

5 In the Rule Description box, click the People Or Distribution List link.

The Rule Address dialog box appears.

6 In the Rule Address dialog box, in the Show Names From The box, be sure that Contacts is selected.

7 In the Type Name Or Select From List list, select the entry for Sue Kennedy, click the From button, and click OK.

The Rules Wizard dialog box appears again with Sue Kennedy's name listed in the Rule Description box. Your screen should look similar to the following illustration.

8   Click the Next button.

The next Rules Wizard dialog box appears.

9   In the What Do You Want To Do With The Message? list, select the Forward It To People Or Distribution List check box, and then in the Rule Description box, click the People Or Distribution List link.

The Rule Address dialog box appears.

10   In the Rule Address dialog box, be sure that Contacts is selected in the Show Names From The box.

11   In the Type Name Or Select From List box, type or select the entry for Peter Stout, click the To button, and click OK.

The Rules Wizard dialog box appears.

12   Click the Finish button, and click OK to close the dialog boxes.

Mail from Sue Kennedy will automatically be sent to Peter Stout's Inbox.

tip

The Rules Wizard enables you to set rules to automate many functions in Outlook 2000, such as automatically flagging an e-mail message from someone, automatically filing an e-mail message based on content, and automatically notifying you when important e-mail messages arrive. The Rules Wizard also enables you to specify exceptions to rules. For more details on how the Rules Wizard can assist you in your message handling, on the Tools menu, click Rules Wizard, and then scroll through the many options.

Delete junk mail or other unwanted e-mail messages immediately upon receipt

In this exercise, you create a rule to automatically delete all incoming junk e-mail messages and adult content e-mail messages.

important

To identify junk or adult content mail, Outlook 2000 checks e-mail messages for certain key words. This feature does not, however, guarantee 100 percent accuracy because some junk and adult mail may not contain these key words.

Organizing the Inbox

4

1 Be sure that the SBS Practice Inbox is open, and then on the Standard toolbar, click the Organize button.

The Ways To Organize SBS Practice Inbox panel opens.

2 In the Ways To Organize SBS Practice Inbox panel, click the Junk E-mail link.

The Junk E-mail page appears. Your screen should look similar to the following illustration.

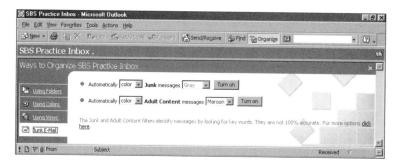

3 On the Junk Messages line of the Junk E-mail page, in the first box, click the drop-down arrow, and then select Move.

4 Be sure that the second box reads Deleted Items, and then click the Turn On button.

The line is modified to reflect your changes, and the Turn On button is changed to a Turn Off button.

5 On the Adult Content Messages line of the Junk E-mail page, in the first box, click the drop-down arrow, and then select Move.

6 Be sure that the second box reads Deleted Items, and then click the Turn On button.

The line is modified to reflect your changes, and the Turn On button is changed to a Turn Off button.

Close

7 In the Ways To Organize SBS Practice Inbox panel, click the Close button.

Outlook 2000 automatically places all incoming junk and adult content e-mail messages in the Deleted Items folder.

Automatically empty the Deleted Items folder

In this exercise, you set Outlook to automatically empty the Deleted Items folder each time you quit Outlook 2000.

1 On the Tools menu, click Options.

The Options dialog box appears.

2 In the Options dialog box, click the Other tab.

3 On the Other tab, in the General area, select the Empty The Deleted Items Folder Upon Exiting check box, and then click the Advanced Options button.

The Advanced Options dialog box appears.

4 In the General Settings area, be sure that the Warn Before Permanently Deleting Items check box is selected, and click OK.

The Advanced Options dialog box closes, and the Options dialog box reappears.

5 In the Options dialog box, click OK.

The Options dialog box closes. The Deleted Items folder will now be emptied each time you quit Outlook 2000 after first providing a warning and requesting confirmation.

One Step Further Using the Out Of Office Assistant

Workgroup

You work in a Workgroup environment using Microsoft Exchange Server and plan to be out of the office for a few days with no access to your e-mail messages. To alert those in your workgroup who might send you e-mail messages during the time that you are away, you use the Outlook 2000 Out Of Office Assistant. Once activated, the Out Of Office Assistant automatically replies with your personal out-of-office message to anyone who sends you an e-mail message during that time. So that people receive only one message from you while you are away, you can specify that the message be sent to each recipient only once.

In this exercise, you first turn on the Out Of Office Assistant to create your out-of-office message, and then you turn it off.

Turn on the Out Of Office Assistant

In this exercise, you activate the Out Of Office Assistant to notify others that you will be away.

1 On the Tools menu, click Out Of Office Assistant.

The Out Of Office Assistant dialog box appears.

Organizing the Inbox

4

Your screen should look similar to the following illustration.

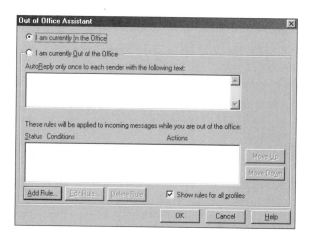

2 Select the I Am Currently Out Of The Office option button.

3 In the AutoReply Only Once To Each Sender With The Following Text box, type:
**I will be away from the office and unable to access e-mail from Monday,
October 19, through Wednesday, October 21.**

4 Click OK.

The Out Of Office Assistant is now activated and will send this response
once to the sender of any e-mail message until you deactivate the feature.

tip

To turn off the Out Of Office Assistant when you return to the office, open Outlook and when the message prompting you to turn it off appears, click Yes.

Finish the lesson

1 If you want to continue to the next lesson, on the File menu, click Close
All Items.

2 If you have finished using Outlook for now and are working in a Workgroup
environment, click File, and then click Exit And Log Off. If you are working
in an Internet only environment, click File, and then click Exit.

Lesson 4 Quick Reference

To	Do this	Button
Sort e-mail messages	In the Inbox Information viewer, click the column heading to sort. Click the column heading again to sort in the reverse order.	
Sort your Inbox by topic	On the Standard toolbar, click the Organize button, and then click the Using Views link. Select the sort option that you want to use.	
Create a folder in the Folder List	On the Standard toolbar, click the Organize button, and then click the Using Folders link. Click the New Folder button, and then enter the folder name to be created.	
Move an e-mail message into a folder	Be sure the Inbox Information viewer is open and that the Folder List and Inbox sub-folders are displayed. Drag the e-mail message in the Information viewer from the Inbox to the correct subfolder in the Folder List.	
Find a missing e-mail message	On the Standard toolbar, click the Find button, type a key word to identify the e-mail message, and then click Find Now. If the e-mail message is still not found, click the Advanced Find button. Search again using additional criteria.	
Flag an e-mail message for follow-up	With the Inbox open, double-click the e-mail message to be flagged, and then on the Message form Standard toolbar, click the Flag For Follow Up button. Select the action and due date that you want, and click OK.	

Organizing the Inbox

4

Lesson 4 Quick Reference

To	Do this
Mark a flagged e-mail message as completed	With the Inbox open, double-click the flagged e-mail message, and then on the Message form Standard toolbar, click the Flag For Follow Up button. Select the Completed check box, and click OK.
Move e-mail messages to a separate folder immediately upon receipt	With the Inbox open, on the Standard toolbar, click the Organize button. In the Ways To Organize Inbox panel, on the Using Folders page, select the appropriate options to define the filing rule, and then click the Create button.
Forward e-mail messages to another person immediately upon receipt	On the Tools menu, click Rules Wizard, and then click the New button. In the Rules Wizard dialog box, select Check Messages When They Arrive, click the Next button, and in the next Rules Wizard dialog box, select the From People Or Distribution List check box. In the Rule Description box, click the People Or Distribution List link. In the Rule Address dialog box, be sure that Contacts is selected, select the name you want, and then click the From button. Click OK.
Delete junk and adult content e-mail messages immediately upon receipt	With the Inbox open, on the Standard toolbar, click the Organize button, and then click the Junk E-mail link. On the Junk E-mail page, in the first Junk Messages box, click the drop-down arrow, and then select Move. In the second box, be sure Deleted Items is selected. Click the Turn On button. In the first Adult Content Messages box for the Adult Content Messages, click the drop-down arrow, and then select Move. In the second box, be sure Deleted Items is selected. Click the Turn On button.
Automatically empty the Deleted Items folder	On the Tools menu, click Options, and then click the Other tab. Select the Empty The Deleted Items Folder Upon Exiting check box. Click the Advanced Options button, and then select the Warn Before Permanently Deleting Items check box.

Lesson 4 Quick Reference

To	Do this
Turn on the Out Of Office Assistant	On the Tools menu, click Out Of Office Assistant, and then select the I Am Currently Out Of The Office button. Type a reply in the AutoReply text box, and click OK.

LESSON
5

Organizing Your Contacts

ESTIMATED TIME 40 min.

In this lesson you will learn how to:

✔ *Add and change contact information.*

✔ *Import contacts from other programs.*

✔ *View contact lists.*

✔ *Sort and organize contacts.*

✔ *Print contact information.*

✔ *Use your Contact list to mail merge with Word.*

The cornerstone of a powerful communication system is an accurate and versatile contact information base. Microsoft Outlook 2000 makes it easy to build and maintain a wealth of contact information and to view it, sort it, and print it in a variety of different ways to meet your special needs. In addition, Outlook's contact database is integrated easily with other programs, enabling you to import contacts from other sources, export contacts for mail merging, and even link directly to your contact's Web site.

As account manager for Impact Public Relations, you are in contact with clients, suppliers, internal staff, and a host of other people every day—placing telephone calls, exchanging e-mail messages, attending meetings, and sending mailings. You need accurate contact information at your fingertips, both when you are in the office and when you are on the road. In this lesson, you learn how to build a contact list by adding new contacts and importing contacts from other databases.

You then learn a variety of ways to view, sort, and print contact information, as well as how to access Web sites for contact information. Finally, you learn how to use the contact database to send mass mailings.

Getting Ready for the Lesson

In this exercise, you start Outlook 2000 and prepare the practice files and folders needed for this lesson. This keeps the lesson materials separate from your own daily work.

Start Outlook

Microsoft Outlook

❶ On the desktop, double-click the Microsoft Outlook 2000 icon.

Outlook 2000 opens.

❷ If necessary, maximize the Outlook window.

Maximize

Create a practice Contacts folder and shortcut and copy the practice files

In this exercise, you create a practice Contacts folder, add a shortcut to the Outlook Bar for your practice Contacts folder, and then copy the files to the folder.

Contacts

New Contact

For a detailed example of how to copy practice files to a practice folder, see the exercise "Set Up Practice E-mail" in Lesson 1.

❶ On the Outlook Bar, click the Contacts shortcut.

The Contact list is displayed in the Information viewer.

❷ On the Standard toolbar, click the New Contact button drop-down arrow, and then click Folder.

The Create New Folder dialog box appears.

❸ Be sure that the Folder Contains box displays Contact Items.

❹ In the Name box, type **SBS Practice Contacts** and click OK.

❺ If you get the message Add Shortcut To Outlook Bar? click No. You'll create the shortcut to it in step 7.

For the purposes of this lesson, a Contacts folder called SBS Practice Contacts is created.

❻ On the Standard toolbar, click the New Contact button drop-down arrow, and then click Outlook Bar Shortcut.

The Add To Outlook Bar dialog box appears.

❼ Click the plus sign (+) next to the Contacts folder, click the SBS Practice Contacts folder, and click OK.

An SBS Practice Contacts shortcut is added to the bottom of the Outlook Bar.

8 On the Outlook Bar, click the SBS Practice Contacts shortcut.

The Contact list appears in the Information viewer.

9 Drag the practice Contacts files, indicated by address card icons, from the Lesson05 folder in the Outlook 2000 SBS Practice folder to your SBS Practice Contacts folder in the Folder List. Do not copy the Extras folder, which contains the Mailing.doc and Contact.mdb files. These will be used later in the lesson.

10 In the Folder list, right-click SBS Practice Contacts, and then click Properties.

SBS Practice Contacts

The SBS Practice Contacts Properties dialog box appears.

11 In the SBS Practice Contacts Properties dialog box, click the Outlook Address Book tab, and be sure that the Show This Folder As An E-mail Address Book box is selected. Click OK.

The SBS Practice Contacts Properties dialog box closes.

Steps 12 through 15 ensure that the SBS Practice Contacts folder is checked first for address information to use in this lesson.

12 On the Tools menu, click Services.

The Services dialog box appears.

13 In the Services dialog box, click the Addressing tab, and then click the Add button.

The Add Address List dialog box appears.

14 In the Add Address List dialog box, in the Address Lists box, select SBS Practice Contacts, click the Add button, and then click the Close button.

The Add Address List dialog box disappears. The SBS Practice Contacts folder is added to the list of addresses in the Services dialog box.

15 In the Services dialog box, click the up arrow until SBS Practice Contacts moves to the top of the list. Click OK.

Adding Contact Information

For more information about the Address Book, see the exercise "Using the Address Book to Enter E-mail Recipients" in Lesson 3.

Outlook gives you up to three separate resources to organize contact information in your Address Book.

- If you work in a Workgroup environment, the Global Address Book contains the list of people on your network. Your system administrator maintains this list.

- For either a Workgroup or Internet only environment, the Outlook Address Book contains your contacts. You add the contacts to your Contact list.

- The Personal Address Book is used for the Internet only environment and functions similarly to the Outlook Address Book. It can be added as a service to the Workgroup environment.

To better manage your contact information, you can assign one or more *categories* to a contact. Categories group related contacts by a common characteristic that you assign. You can choose meaningful category names such as *holiday card list*, *business*, *personal*, or you can create your own category. You can also modify a Contact form to include a new *field*, such as a text box, for noting information not already on the contact form. For instance, you could add a field for the name of a contact's child or even a favorite restaurant. Finally, you can use the Flag For Follow Up feature as a visual reminder that a contact needs further attention.

In the next exercises, you practice adding basic and detailed information for new contacts directly to the Contact list.

Add a new contact

You add Rolf Ahern of Hay Buy Toys to your Contact list and assign him to your business, holiday card list, and key customer categories.

1   On the Outlook Bar, click the SBS Practice Contacts shortcut.

The Contact list is displayed in the Information viewer.

2   On the Standard toolbar, click the New Contact button.

A blank Contact form appears with the General tab active. Your screen should look similar to the following illustration.

New Contact

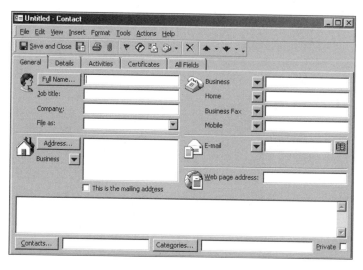

To be sure that the name components are recorded properly, click the Full Name button, and click OK.

3   In the Full Name box, type **Mr. Rolf Ahern** and then press Tab.

The title bar of the form now reads Rolf Ahern—Contact, and the File As box displays Ahern, Rolf.

4 In the Job Title box, type **Marketing Manager** and then press the Tab key.

5 In the Company box, type **Hay Buy Toys** and then press the Tab key three times.

To be sure that the address components are recorded properly, click the Address button, and click OK.

6 In the Business box, type **3045555624** and then press the Tab key four times.

The telephone number is automatically formatted.

7 In the Business Fax box, type **3045554245** and then press the Tab key four times.

8 In the Address box (next to the Address button), type **11 Parkrose Pl.** and press Enter to move the insertion point to a new line. Finish entering the address by typing **Hazelgreen, WV 26367** and be sure that the This Is The Mailing Address check box is selected.

9 In the E-mail box, type **rolf@haybuytoys.haybuytoys** and then in the Web Page Address box, type **microsoft.com**

10 At the bottom of the form, click the Categories button.

The Categories dialog box appears.

11 In the Available Categories list, select the Business, Holiday Cards, and Key Customer check boxes, and click OK.

The Categories dialog box closes and the Rolf Ahern—Contact form appears, with Business, Holiday Cards, and Key Customer is displayed in the Categories box in the lower-right corner of the form. Your screen should look similar to the following illustration.

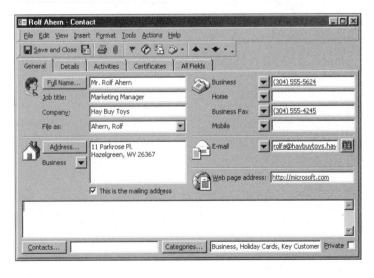

To delete the contact, on the toolbar, click the Delete button.

12 On the Contact form Standard toolbar, click the Save And Close button.

The Rolf Ahern—Contact form closes and Rolf Ahern's Contacts card appears in the SBS Practice Contacts Information viewer.

Save And New

> ## tip
>
> If you have another contact to add and the contact is not from the same company, instead of clicking the Save And Close button, you can click the Save And New button on the Contact form Standard toolbar to save the first contact and open a new Contact form. If the new contact is from the same company, on the Actions menu, click New Contact From Same Company. A new Contact form appears, with the Company Name, Address, and Business boxes already completed.

Add detailed information for a contact

You now add more detailed information about Rolf Ahern, including his department, manager's name, assistant's name, and birthday.

1. In the SBS Practice Contacts Information viewer, on the Contacts card, double-click Rolf Ahern's name.

   The Rolf Ahern—Contact form appears.

2. In the Rolf Ahern—Contact form, click the Details tab.

   The Details tab becomes active.

3. On the Details tab, type the following information in the boxes provided.

In this box	Type
Department	Marketing
Manager's Name	Rachel Briggs
Assistant's Name	Parker Evans

To learn how to view detailed information in your Contact list, see "Viewing Contact Information" later in this lesson.

4. On the Details tab, in the Birthday box, click the drop-down arrow and scroll through the monthly calendar to locate next month, and then click 28.

   The calendar closes and Mr. Ahern's birthday is displayed in the Birthday box.

5. On the Contact form Standard toolbar, click the Save And Close button.

   The Rolf Ahern—Contact form closes and Rolf Ahern's Contacts card appears in the SBS Practice Contacts Information viewer.

Add a new field

In this exercise, you add a new field to the Rolf Ahern—Contact form to record his child's name.

1 In the SBS Practice Contacts Information viewer, double-click Rolf Ahern's name.

The Rolf Ahern—Contact form appears.

2 Click the All Fields tab.

The All Fields tab becomes active.

3 On the All Fields tab, next to the Select From box, click the drop-down arrow, and then select Personal Fields from the list.

A table appears listing Personal Fields, with any values previously entered displayed in the table.

Your screen should look similar to the following illustration.

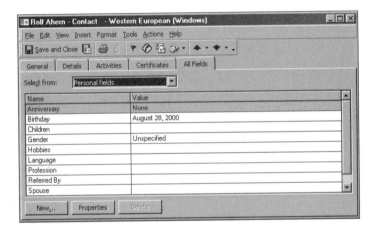

To learn how to view fields that are not in the default settings, see "Create a Custom Contact List View," later in this lesson.

4 In the Value column, click the blank cell next to Children, type **Cynthia Butterworth** and then click the Save And Close button.

The Rolf Ahern—Contact form closes. Because the Children field does not appear in the default view, his child's name does not appear in the Contact list.

Flag a contact for follow-up

In this exercise, you flag Rolf Ahern's Contacts card to remind yourself to call him later today.

1 In the SBS Practice Contacts Information viewer, double-click Rolf Ahern's name.

The Rolf Ahern—Contact form appears.

*Flag For
Follow Up*

2 On the Contact form Standard toolbar, click the Flag For Follow Up button.

The Flag For Follow Up dialog box appears.

To delete a flag, in the Flag For Follow Up dialog box, click Clear Flag.

3 In the Flag To box, click the drop-down arrow, and then select Call.

4 In the Due By box, click the drop-down arrow, and then on the calendar, click the Today button.

5 Click OK.

The Flag For Follow Up dialog box closes and the Rolf Ahern—Contact form appears.

6 On the Contact form Standard toolbar, click the Save And Close button.

The Rolf Ahern—Contact form closes and his Contacts card appears in the SBS Practice Contacts Information viewer. The notation *Follow Up Flag: Call* appears in the line immediately below Rolf's name.

Importing Contact Files from Other Programs

If you have contact information in other database programs, you can import the information into the Outlook Contact list. Outlook can import contact databases from all Microsoft applications, as well as from many other applications (provided that you installed the Full version of Outlook). Also, you can transfer your Contact list from your office computer to your laptop computer so that you have the same information with you as you travel. In this exercise, you practice importing contacts from a Microsoft Access database.

Import contact information from Microsoft Access

1 On the File menu, click Import And Export.

The Import And Export Wizard dialog box appears.

2 In the Import And Export Wizard dialog box, in the Choose An Action To Perform list, select Import From Another Program Or File, and then click the Next button.

The Import A File dialog box appears.

3 In the Import A File dialog box, in the Select File Type To Import From list, select Microsoft Access, and then click the Next button.

The next page of the dialog box appears.

4 Next to the File To Import box, click the Browse button.

The Browse dialog box appears.

5 In the Look In box, click the drop-down arrow, and then select your hard disk.

The contents of your hard disk are displayed.

6 Double-click the Outlook SBS Practice folder, and then double-click the Lesson05 folder.

The contents of the Lesson05 folder are displayed.

7 Double-click the Extras folder.

The contents of the Extras folder are displayed.

8 In the list of files, double-click the file named Contacts.

The full path and name of the file are displayed in the File To Import box.

9 In the Options area, select the Do Not Import Duplicate Items option, and then click the Next button.

10 In the Select Destination Folder box, select the SBS Practice Contacts folder, and then click the Next button.

11 In The Following Actions Will Be Performed area, be sure that the Import Contacts Into The SBS Practice Contacts Folder check box is selected, and then click the Finish button.

The contacts are imported into the SBS Practice Contacts folder from the Access database.

Viewing Contact Information

For a demonstration of how to view, sort, and customize contact information, in the Multimedia folder on the Microsoft Outlook 2000 Step by Step CD-ROM, double-click the Custom Contact icon.

Outlook enables you to view your contacts in address card views and table views. In the address card views, the contact information is presented vertically, similar to how it would appear on a business card. An alphabetical index bar located on the right side of the Information viewer assists you in finding specific contacts. In the table views, the contact information is presented horizontally, similar to how it would appear on a spreadsheet, with a scroll bar to help you find specific contacts.

Outlook provides two address card views and five table views. You can also create a variety of customized views to meet your specific needs. When you open Contacts, the Address Cards view appears by default.

This view	Provides this information
Address Cards	Contact name, address, telephone, fax, e-mail, and notation of follow up action, if applicable.
Detailed Address Cards	Same information as in Address Cards view, plus company name, job title, and department.
Phone List	Contact name, company name, file as, all phone information, journal, contact categories, flag status, and attachments.
By Category	Contact name, company name, file as, all phone information, contact categories, flag status, and attachments, grouped by contact category.

This view	Provides this information
By Company	Same information as in By Category view, plus contact's job title and department, grouped by company name.
By Location	Same information as in By Category view, plus state and country, grouped by country.
By Follow Up Flag	Same information as in By Category view, grouped by flag status (flagged, completed, or normal).

In the next exercises, you practice various ways of viewing and finding contact data. Then you use hyperlinks stored in a Contact form to view a client's Web page and a map of the client's office location.

View the list of address cards

You need the address and phone number for Jeff Hardiff of East Indonesia Coffee Company. To find the information, you check the Address Cards view.

1   On the Outlook Bar, click the SBS Practice Contacts shortcut.

The SBS Practice Contacts Information viewer displays a list of Contacts cards, with an alphabetical index bar on the right side of the Information viewer. Your screen should look similar to the following illustration.

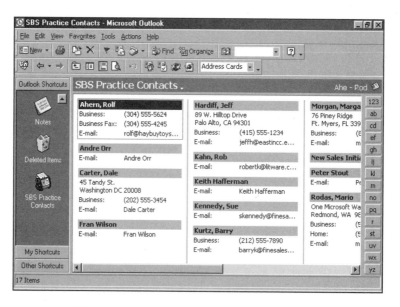

2   On the alphabetical index bar, click the H button.

*To view all
information
entered for
a contact,
double-click
the contact
name, and the
Contact form
appears.*

The list automatically scrolls to display contact Jeff Hardiff with his address, phone, and e-mail information.

tip

To view more detailed information for your Contact list, on the View menu, point to Current View, and then click Detailed Address Cards. The list expands to include the company name, job title, and department, if you provided them in the Contact form. To view empty fields, on the View menu, point to Current View, and then be sure that Address Cards is selected. Click Customize Current View, and then click the Other Settings button. In the Card Body area, select the Show Empty Fields check box. Click OK twice to close the dialog boxes.

View the phone list

For a quick check of a client's phone number, you switch to Phone List view and locate Jeff Hardiff.

*If names do
not appear in
alphabetical
order by last
name, click the
File As column
heading.*

1 On the View menu, point to Current View, and then click Phone List.

The list is instantly reformatted into a table, with names appearing in alphabetical order. In addition to phone numbers, the list also contains three columns headed by icons.

Your screen should look similar to the following illustration.

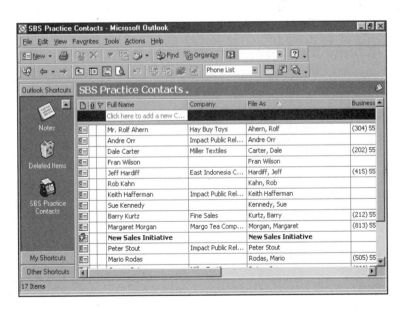

In this column	This icon	Means that
🗋	📇	The contact is an individual.
	📇	The contact is a distribution list.
📎	📎	The Contact form has an attachment, such as an e-mail message, Word document, or security certificate.
⛝	⛝	The contact has been flagged for follow-up action.
	⛝	Follow-up action for this contact has been completed.

2 Double-click the Jeff Hardiff entry.

The Jeff Hardiff—Contact form appears with the address and phone number you need.

3 On the Contact form, click the Close button.

Close

tip

Similarly, to view your Contact list by category, company, follow-up action or geographic location, on the View menu, point to Current View, and then click By Category, By Company, By Follow Up Flag, or By Location.

Create a custom Contact list view

You can customize any of the default views in a variety of different ways. In this exercise, you customize the Address Cards view to add the company name to the display.

1 On the View menu, point to Current View, and then click Address Cards.

The Address Cards view appears in the Information viewer.

important

Be sure that you are in the view you want to customize before clicking Customize Current View.

2 On the View menu, point to Current View again, and then click Customize Current View.

The View Summary dialog box appears.

3 In the View Summary dialog box, click the Fields button.

The Show Fields dialog box appears.

4 In the Show Fields dialog box, in the Available Fields list, select Company Main Phone, and then click the Add button.

The company field is added to the bottom of the Show These Fields In This Order list. Your screen should look similar to the following illustration.

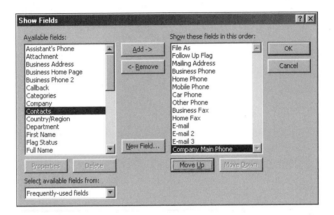

You can display a field in another position by clicking either the Move Down button or the Move Up button.

5 Click the Move Up button repeatedly until the Company Main Phone field appears above the Business Phone field, and then click OK.

The Show Fields dialog box closes and the View Summary dialog box is displayed.

6 In the View Summary dialog box, click OK.

The View Summary dialog box closes and the Information viewer displays the company name for each contact.

tip

You can use a filter to view only those contacts that meet a condition that you specify. On the View menu, point to Current View, and then click Customize Current View. Click the Filter button, and in the Filter dialog box select from various filter options, such as keywords, e-mail address, company name, or category, to identify the group that you want to view.

View a contact's Web site

Because you entered the Hay Buy Toys Web site link as part of Rolf Ahern's contact information, you decide to access the Web page directly from the Contact form.

> ## important
>
> To complete this exercise, you need an Internet connection.

1 On the View menu, point to Current View, and then click Address Cards.

The Information viewer displays the list of Contacts cards.

2 Double-click Rolf Ahern's name.

The Rolf Ahern—Contact form appears.

For the purposes of this exercise, you will be connected to the Microsoft home page.

3 On the Contact form, click the Web Page Address box containing the Web page link.

If you are presently connected to the Internet, your default Web browser starts and the Web site appears.

4 If you are not presently connected to the Internet, you might be prompted to connect. If you are prompted, click the Connect button, and then enter the information requested by your Internet service provider. Once you are connected to the Internet, the Web site appears.

5 If you are continuing to the next exercise, do not disconnect from the Internet. Otherwise, close your browser and disconnect from the Internet.

6 On the Rolf Ahern—Contact form, click the Close button.

Close

View a contact's address on a map

If you have a contact's address in the Contact form, you can locate it on a map by using a link in the Contact form that connects to Microsoft's Expedia Maps Web site. In this exercise, you locate the business address for Mario Rodas on a map.

> ## important
>
> To complete this exercise, you need an Internet connection and you must have entered an address for the contact in the Contact form.

1 Be sure that you are connected to the Internet. Double-click Mario Roda's name.

The Mario Rodas—Contact form appears.

*Display Map
Of Address*

❷   On the Contact form Standard toolbar, in the Mario Rodas—Contact form, click the Display Map Of Address button.

   If you are presently connected to the Internet, your Web browser starts and the Microsoft Expedia Maps site appears on your screen. The location of Mario Rodas's office is indicated on the map with a push pin icon.

❸   If you are not presently connected to the Internet, you might be prompted to connect. Click the Connect button and enter any information required by your Internet service provider.

   Once you are connected to the Internet, the Microsoft Expedia Maps site appears on your screen. The location of Mario Rodas's office is indicated on the map.

❹   Close your browser, disconnect from the Internet, and then close the Mario Rodas—Contact form.

Sorting Contacts

In addition to viewing your contacts in a variety of ways, Outlook 2000 also enables you to sort your Contact list. In any view, you can sort by a field, in either ascending or descending order.

Sort contacts in Address Cards view

In this exercise, you sort your contacts by location in Address Cards view.

❶   On the View menu, point to Current View, and then click Address Cards.

   The Information viewer displays the list of Contacts cards.

❷   Right-click the vertical gray line between any Contacts card column.

   A shortcut menu appears.

❸   On the shortcut menu, click Sort.

   The Sort dialog box appears.

❹   In the Sort Items By box, click the drop-down arrow, select State, and click OK.

   A message box appears, prompting you to show the state field.

❺   In the message box, click No.

   The message box closes and the Information viewer displays the contacts sorted by state in the list of Contacts cards.

❻   To restore the SBS Practice Contacts Information viewer to its original appearance, right-click the vertical gray line between any Contacts card column, and on the shortcut menu, click Sort. Then in the Sort Items By box, click the drop-down arrow, select File As, and click OK.

   Contacts are now sorted in the same order in which you filed them.

Organizing Your Contacts   5

Sort contacts in table views

Next you sort contacts in the By Category view.

1 On the View menu, point to Current View, and then click By Category.

The Information viewer displays several categories in alphabetical order by category name with the number of items in the category shown in parentheses.

2 In the Information viewer, click the plus sign button (+) on each category bar to expand the category.

All contacts within each category are displayed in alphabetical order according to the way you filed them (usually by the contact last name or company name).

When you click the arrow on any column heading, it changes to point upward or downward to indicate either ascending or descending order.

3 Click the Company column heading.

The Contacts are now sorted within each category alphabetically by company. The arrow on the Company heading is pointing upward, indicating that the list is in ascending order. Your screen should look similar to the following illustration.

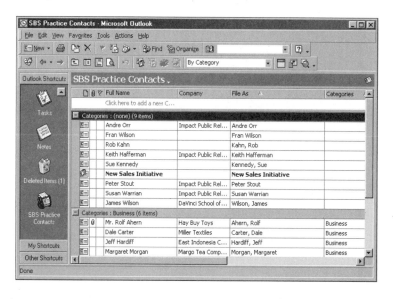

Printing Contact Information

Just as you have a vast number of ways to view and sort your contacts, you also have many ways to print your contact information, including the ability to print any view you select, either as is or in other formats, such as in Phone Directory

Style or Booklet Style. As you prepare for an out-of-town meeting with Rolf Ahern, you print his Contacts card to take with you. Because you need to make other calls while you are away, you also print your complete Contact list. Then you print your Holiday Card list to review on the airplane.

Print an individual Contacts card

In this exercise, you print Rolf Ahern's Contacts card.

Print

Close

① On the View menu, point to Current View, and then click Address Cards.

The Information viewer displays the list of Contacts cards.

② Double-click Rolf Ahern's name.

The Rolf Ahern—Contact form appears.

③ On the Contact form Standard toolbar, click the Print button.

All the information that you entered for Rolf Ahern is printed in the Address Card format.

④ On the Rolf Ahern—Contact form, click the Close button.

The Rolf Ahern—Contact form closes and the Address Cards view is displayed.

Print a list of Contacts cards

You decide to print your complete list of Contacts cards in Card Style format, and then reprint the list in Phone Directory Style format.

Print

To preview a print style, click the Preview button in the Print dialog box. Click the Close button to return to the Print dialog box.

① Be sure that the Address Cards view is displayed in the Information viewer.

② If the Welcome To Contacts heading appears in the Information viewer, double-click the heading, and then click the Delete button.

The Welcome To Contacts heading is removed from the Information viewer.

③ On the Standard toolbar, click the Print button.

The Print dialog box appears.

④ In the Print dialog box, in the Print Style area, be sure that Card Style is selected, and click OK.

The Print dialog box closes, and a complete list of contacts is printed in the Card Style format.

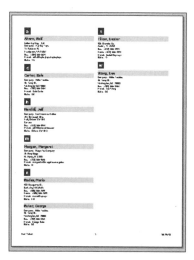

5 On the Standard toolbar, click the Print button again.

The Print dialog box appears.

6 In the Print Style area, select Phone Directory Style, and click OK.

The Print dialog box closes, and a complete list of contacts is printed in Phone Directory Style format.

tip
You can print address booklets in two sizes by selecting either of the two booklet styles in the Print Style area in the Print dialog box.

Print a table list

In this exercise, you print the Contact list by category, with the contacts in the Holiday Cards category itemized.

1 On the View menu, point to Current View, and then click By Category.

The Information viewer displays the Contact list by category.

2 Close all open categories except Holiday Cards by clicking the minus sign (-) on each category bar.

3 In the Holiday Cards category, click the first entry, hold down the Shift key, and then select the last entry.

4 On the Standard toolbar, click the Print button.

The Print dialog box appears.

Print

5 In the Print dialog box, be sure that Table Style is selected in the Print Style area.

6 In the Print Style area, click the Page Setup button.

The Page Setup: Table Style dialog box appears.

7 In the Page Setup: Table Style dialog box, click the Paper tab, and then in the Orientation area, select the Landscape option, and click OK.

The Page Setup: Table Style dialog box closes, and the Print dialog box appears.

8 In the Print dialog box, click OK.

The Print dialog box closes, and the Contact list is printed with the Holiday Cards category itemized by contact. Your printout should look similar to the following illustration.

			Full Name	Company	File As	Categories
Categories : (none) (9 items)						
Categories : Business (6 items)						
Categories : Holiday Cards (6 items)						
	0		Mr. Rolf Ahern	Hay Buy Toys	Ahern, Rolf	Holiday Cards
			Dale Carter	Miller Textiles	Carter, Dale	Holiday Cards
			Jeff Hardiff	East Indonesia Co...	Hardiff, Jeff	Holiday Cards
			Margaret Morgan	Margo Tea Comp...	Morgan, Margaret	Holiday Cards
			George Ruter	Miller Textiles	Ruter, George	Holiday Cards
			Lee Wong	Miller Textiles	Wong, Lee	Holiday Cards
Categories : Key Customer (1 item)						
Categories : Personal (1 item)						
			Mario Rodas		Rodas, Mario	Personal

Filing Contact Information in Folders

As your Contact list grows, it might be helpful to separate certain types of contacts from the main Contacts folder into another folder. For example, it could be useful to have a separate folder for your personal contacts, or for your contacts from a community organization with which you serve. This avoids having to repeatedly remove these unrelated categories of contacts each time you view or print the Contact list. It also enables you to more quickly view the specific type of Contact list you want to see.

Create a new folder

Another way to create a new folder is to right-click the Contacts folder in the Folder List and then click New Folder.

In this exercise, you create a folder for your personal contacts.

1 On the Outlook Bar, click the SBS Practice Contacts shortcut.

2 On the View menu, click Folder List.

3 On the File menu, point to New, and then click Folder.

The Create New Folder dialog box appears.

④ In the Create New Folder dialog box, be sure that the Folder Contains box displays Contact Items, and then in the Name box type **Personal Contacts** and click OK.

The Create New Folder dialog box closes, and the Add A Shortcut To Outlook Bar dialog box appears.

⑤ In the Add A Shortcut To Outlook Bar dialog box, click No.

The Add A Shortcut To Outlook Bar dialog box closes, and the Personal Contacts folder is added to the Folder List under the SBS Practice Contacts folder.

Move contacts to a folder

In this exercise, you move the Contacts cards for Lester Tilton and Mario Rodas to the Personal Contacts folder.

① In the Folder List, click the SBS Practice Contacts folder.

② On the View menu, point to Current View, and then click Phone List.

The Information viewer displays the Phone List.

Alternatively, you can right-click Lester Tilton and drag the entry to the Personal Contacts folder. On the shortcut menu, select Move.

③ In the Phone List, select Lester Tilton.

④ On the Standard toolbar, click the Organize button.

The Ways To Organize SBS Practice Contacts panel appears.

⑤ In the Ways To Organize SBS Practice Contacts panel, click the Using Folders link.

The Using Folders page appears.

⑥ In the Move Contacts Selected Below To box, click the drop-down arrow and select Personal Contacts.

⑦ In the Information viewer, click Lester Tilton, press and hold down the Ctrl key, and then click Mario Rodas.

⑧ In the Ways To Organize panel, click the Move button.

The Lester Tilton and Mario Rodas cards are moved from the SBS Practice Contacts folder to the Personal Contacts folder.

Close

⑨ In the Ways To Organize panel, click the Close button in the upper-right corner.

⑩ In the Folder List, click the Personal Contacts folder.

The Lester Tilton and Mario Rodas information is displayed in the Personal Contacts Information viewer.

⑪ To return to the SBS Practice Contacts Information viewer, in the Folder List, click the minus sign (-) next to the SBS Practice Contacts folder.

Organizing Your Contacts

One Step Further

Using Your Contact List with Mail Merge in Microsoft Word

Mail merge is a handy way to use the personal information in your Contact list to create form letters, print mailing labels, or even address envelopes without the tedium of retyping or pasting. You need to send a mailing to your contacts. You use the information in your Contact list to create an address list for mail merging with a Microsoft Word letter.

Create a form letter with the Office Assistant

For more information about the Office Assistant, see the Lesson 1 sidebar, "Meet the Office Assistant."

1 On the Standard toolbar, on the Help menu, click Show The Office Assistant.

The Office Assistant appears on your screen.

2 On the Tools menu, click Mail Merge.

The Mail Merge Contacts dialog box appears.

3 In the Mail Merge Contacts dialog box, in the Document File area, click the Browse button.

The Open dialog box appears.

4 In the Open dialog box, in the Look In drop-down list, click your hard disk.

The contents of your hard disk are displayed.

5 Double-click first the Outlook SBS Practice folder, then the Lesson05 folder, the Extras folder, and the file named Mailing.doc.

In the Mail Merge Contacts dialog box, the Mailing.doc file appears in the Existing Document box.

6 Click OK.

The Office Assistant appears, notifying you that the list contains a distribution list that will not be included in the mail merge.

7 Click OK.

The Merge document appears in Word, and the Office Assistant shows three options.

8 In the Office Assistant dialog box, click Merge Now.

The Merge dialog box appears.

9 In the Merge dialog box, click the Merge button.

The merge file is created in Word.

10 In Word, click the Close button to exit, and then in the warning box, click No.

Close

Finish the lesson

1 If you want to continue to the next lesson, click the SBS Practice Contacts shortcut on the Outlook Bar.

2 If you have finished using Outlook for now and are working in a workgroup environment, click File, and then click Exit And Log Off. If you are working in an Internet only environment, click File, and then click Exit.

Lesson 5 Quick Reference

To	Do this	Button
Add a new contact	On the Standard toolbar, click the New Contacts button, complete the Contact form, and then click the Save And Close button.	
Add detailed information for a contact	In the Contacts Information viewer, double-click the Contacts card. In the Contact form, click the Details tab, enter the appropriate information, and then click the Save And Close button.	
Add a new field	In the Contacts Information viewer, double-click the Contacts card. In the Contact form, click the All Fields tab, and then select the fields to be added from the list. Click the Save And Close button.	
Flag a contact for follow-up	In the Contacts Information viewer, double-click the Contacts card. On the Contact form Standard toolbar, click the Flag For Follow Up button. Select the activity you want to flag and a due date.	

Lesson 5 Quick Reference

To	Do this
Import contact information from other programs	On the File menu, click Import And Export. In the Import And Export Wizard, select Import From Another Program Or File, and then click the Next button. In the Select File Type To Import From list, select your program, and click the Next button. In the File To Import box, type the filename or browse to find and select the file to be imported. In the Options area, select the Do Not Duplicate Items option, and then click the Next button. Select the appropriate Contacts destination folder, and then click the Next button. Be sure that the Import Contacts check box is selected and lists the correct destination folder, and then click the Finish button.
View the list of address cards	On the View menu, point to Current View and then click Address Cards.
View a phone list	On the View menu, point to Current View and then click Phone List.
Create a custom Contact list view	On the View menu, point to Current View, and then click the view you want to customize. On the View menu, point to Current View again, and then click Customize Current View. In the View Summary dialog box, click the appropriate buttons to modify fields and other settings.

Lesson 5 Quick Reference

To	Do this	Button
View a contact's Web site	In any view, double-click the Contacts card, and then click the Web Page Address box. (The contact's Web site address must have been entered for this feature to work.)	
View a contact's address on a map	On the Contact form Standard toolbar, click the Display Map Of Address button. (The contact's street address must have been entered for this feature to work.)	
Sort contacts in Address Cards view	In the Address Cards view, right-click the vertical gray line between any Contacts card column. In the Sort dialog box, in the Sort Items By list, select the category you want to sort by. Click either the Ascending or Descending option.	
Sort contacts in table views	In any table view, click the column heading for the field by which you want to sort.	
Print an individual Contacts card	On the View menu, point to Current View, and then click Address Cards. In the Contact list, select the contact name, and then on the Standard toolbar, click the Print button.	
Print a list of Contacts cards	On the View menu, point to Current View, and then click Address Cards. On the Standard toolbar, click the Print button, and then select the style and format that you want to use.	
Print a table list	On the View menu, point to Current View, and then click any table view. On the Standard toolbar, click the Print button, and then select the style and format that you want to use.	

Lesson 5 Quick Reference

To	Do this
Create a new folder	On the View menu, click the Folder List. On the File menu, point to New, and then click Folder. Type the name of the new folder, and click OK.
Move contacts to a folder	In any view, click the Organize button, and then click the Using Folders link. Select the folder to which you want to move the contacts, select the contacts to move, and then click the Move button.
Use your Contact list with mail merge in Microsoft Word	On the Help menu, click Show The Office Assistant. On the Tools menu, click Mail Merge. In the Mail Merge Contacts dialog box, in the Document File area, browse to find and select the document you intend to merge. Click OK. In the Mail Merge warning, click OK. Click the Merge button to create the merged file.

Organizing Your Contacts

5

6

Working with Your Contacts

**ESTIMATED
TIME
35 min.**

In this lesson you will learn how to:

✔ *Send e-mail messages and faxes to contacts.*

✔ *Send letters and vCards to contacts.*

✔ *Place telephone calls using Outlook 2000.*

✔ *Conduct a survey or vote among your contacts.*

In the preceding lessons, you learned how to use your Microsoft Outlook Inbox to send e-mail messages and your Outlook Contact list to manage contact information. In this lesson, you learn how to use your Contact list to communicate directly with your contacts. You learn how to send e-mail messages, faxes, and electronic copies of your Contacts cards.

Imagine that as Fran Wilson, account manager at Impact Public Relations, you are responsible for gathering feedback from your client base on a new sales initiative. You want to send an introductory e-mail message that includes your business card so that your contacts have all the information they need to easily get in touch with you. You need to fax a copy of the product data sheet for the sales initiative to a contact who is on the road and unable to access e-mail. You also need to draft and send a letter to one key client regarding potential interest in the initiative.

Getting Ready for the Lesson

In this exercise, you start Outlook 2000 and prepare the practice files and folders that you need.

Start Outlook and copy the practice files

Microsoft Outlook

1. On the desktop, double-click the Microsoft Outlook 2000 icon.

   Outlook 2000 opens.

2. If necessary, maximize the Outlook window.

Maximize

important

Before proceeding to the next step, you must have installed the Outlook 2000 SBS Practice folder and created a SBS Practice Contacts folder and shortcut. See Lesson 5, "Organizing Your Contacts."

SBS Practice Contacts

For a detailed example of how to copy practice files to a practice folder, see the exercise "Set Up Practice E-mail" in Lesson 1.

3. On the Outlook Bar, click the SBS Practice Contacts shortcut.

4. Drag the practice Contacts files, indicated by address card icons, from the Lesson06 folder in the Outlook 2000 SBS Practice folder to your SBS Practice Contacts folder in the Folder List. The Microsoft Word practice document, Product Data Sheet.doc, should remain in the Lesson06 folder.

Sending E-mail Messages to Contacts

If you entered a contact's e-mail address in the Contacts card, you can create and send e-mail messages directly from your Outlook Contact list. You can also send a virtual business card, or *vCard*, to any contact who uses Outlook or a compatible program by attaching it to your e-mail message. The vCard can then be read and transferred directly into the recipient's Contact list, which eliminates data entry time and errors.

Send an e-mail message

In this exercise, you send an e-mail message to Jeff Hardiff from your Contact list.

1. On the Outlook Bar, click the SBS Practice Contacts shortcut.

   The SBS Practice Contacts Information viewer opens.

2. On the View menu, point to Current View, and then click Address Cards.

   The Information viewer displays the Contact list.

③ In the Contact list, double-click Jeff Hardiff's name.

The Jeff Hardiff—Contact form appears.

*New Message
To Contact*

④ On the Message form Standard toolbar, click the New Message To Contact button.

A blank Message form appears, with Jeff Hardiff's e-mail address in the To box.

⑤ On the Message form, in the Subject box, type **New Sales Initiative** and press Enter.

The title of the Message form changes to New Sales Initiative—Message.

⑥ In the message area, type **Jeff—We are planning a new sales initiative that I would like to discuss with you soon. I'll give you a call tomorrow. Fran**

Your screen should look similar to the following illustration.

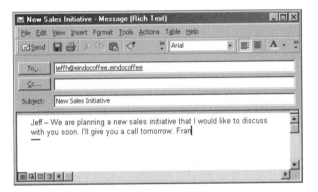

important

Throughout this book, you send e-mail to fictitious people at fictitious e-mail addresses. After you send the message, you will receive a screen message telling you that your message is nondeliverable. You can ignore this message and continue with the lesson.

⑦ On the Message form Standard toolbar, click the Send button.

If you are connected to the Internet, your message is sent automatically. If you are not presently connected to the Internet, your message is placed in the Outbox.

Internet only

⑧ To send the message, on the Standard toolbar, click the Send/Receive button. If you are not already connected to the Internet, complete the instructions from your Internet service provider to access the Internet.

Your message is sent.

Send a Contacts card (vCard)

For more information about creating a Contacts card, see the exercise "Add a New Contact " in Lesson 5.

To send your own vCard with your e-mail, you must first create a Contacts card for yourself and save it in the SBS Practice Contacts list. In this exercise, you forward your vCard to Rolf Ahern.

1 On the Outlook Bar, click the SBS Practice Contacts shortcut. On the View menu, point to Current View, and be sure that Address Cards is selected.

The Information viewer displays the Address Card list.

To create a custom vCard for yourself, see "Redesigning an Existing Form" in Lesson 12.

2 In the Information viewer, select Rolf Ahern's Contacts card.

3 On the Actions menu, click New Message To Contact.

A blank Message form appears with Rolf Ahern's e-mail address automatically displayed in the To box.

4 On the Message form, in the Subject box, type **New Sales Initiative—Follow Up** and press Enter.

5 In the message area, type **I look forward to meeting with you next week. My contact information is on the attached card.** Press Enter twice.

The message is now ready to have the attachment inserted.

6 On the Message form, on the Insert menu, click Item.

The Insert Item dialog box appears.

7 In the Insert Item dialog box, in the Look In list, click the plus sign (+) next to Contacts, and then select SBS Practice Contacts.

The contacts listed in the SBS Practice Contacts folder are displayed in the Items area.

8 In the Items box, click your name.

9 In the Insert As area, be sure that Attachment is selected, and click OK.

The Insert Item dialog box closes and an icon representing your Contacts card is inserted in the message area.

10 On the Message form Standard toolbar, click the Send button.

If you are connected to the Internet, your message is sent automatically. If you are not presently connected to the Internet, your message is placed in the Outbox.

11 To send the message, on the Standard toolbar, click the Send/Receive button. If you are not already connected to the Internet, complete the instructions from your Internet service provider to access the Internet.

Internet only

Your message is sent.

Sending Faxes to Contacts

If you use Outlook in an Internet only environment and have a contact's fax number in the Contact form, you can create and send a fax directly from your Contact list.

A fax enables you to send a file electronically, which then is printed on the recipient's fax machine, saving you the time of printing the file, going to a fax machine, and waiting while the pages are transmitted. Compared with sending the same file via e-mail, sending by fax offers several unique features:

If you work in a Workgroup environment, you can only fax using the faxing software set up to work on the server. Contact your system administrator.

- It enables the recipient to have a hard copy of your file without relying on computer and printer availability.

- It eliminates the need for the recipient to have compatible software to read or print the file.

- It prevents the transmission of an active file that the recipient could then use without your consent.

If you are working in the Internet only environment, you send a fax from your computer over the telephone line.

Send a fax over the Internet (Internet only users)

In this exercise, you fax Rolf Ahern a product data sheet on the new sales initiative.

Internet only

important

Be sure that your fax is installed and working before installing Outlook 2000. Outlook will automatically update your fax setup.

1 Be sure that the SBS Practice Inbox Information viewer is open, and then on the Actions menu, click New Fax Message.

If you are sending your first fax, a dialog box appears prompting you to install Symantec Fax Starter Edition.

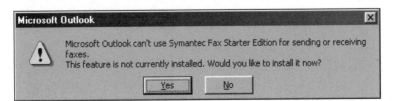

2 In the dialog box, click Yes. Insert the Office 2000 CD-ROM in your CD drive and follow the onscreen instructions.

To design your own fax cover sheet, click Options, and then click the Fax tab and select the options you would like.

3 After restarting Outlook 2000, repeat step 1.

A blank FAX form appears.

4 On the FAX form, click the To button.

The Select Names dialog box appears.

5 In the Show Names From The box, click the drop-down arrow, and then select SBS Practice Contacts.

6 In the names list, select Rolf Ahern (Business Fax), click the To button, and then click OK.

Rolf Ahern's contact information is imported into the Fax form.

7 In the Subject box, type **Product Data Sheet** and then press the Tab key.

The Insert File dialog box appears.

Insert File

8 On the FAX form Standard toolbar, click the Insert File button.

The Insert File dialog box appears.

9 In the Look In drop-down list, select the Lesson06 folder located in the Outlook 2000 SBS Practice folder. In the list of files that appears, double-click Product Data Sheet.doc.

The product data sheet is attached to your fax.

Since this exercise uses a fictitious fax number, a Fax Status Report e-mail message will inform you that the fax was undeliverable.

10 On the FAX form standard toolbar, click the Send button.

The Symantec WinFax Starter Edition dialog box appears containing Rolf Ahern's name and fax number imported from his Contact form.

11 Click the Send button.

The Symantec WinFax Starter Edition dialog box shows the dialing progression.

One Step Further   Conducting a Vote

For a demonstration of how to conduct a survey, in the Multimedia folder on the Microsoft Outlook 2000 Step by Step CD-ROM, double-click the Survey icon.

If you work in a workgroup environment, you might need to canvas a group of people for their input on a particular topic, such as their availability to attend a national sales meeting. While you could send an e-mail message to the group and await individual responses, this method would result in your need to open, read, and tally each person's response, as well as increased e-mail traffic in your Inbox. Instead, if you use Outlook in a workgroup environment, Outlook can conduct the survey for you, tally the results, and record each person's response, all in one e-mail message file.

important

To complete the exercises in this section, you need to request help from at least two other people on your network who are willing to respond to your message.

Add voting buttons to your e-mail message

Workgroup

New Mail Message

In this exercise, you create an e-mail message to your sales team and add voting buttons to enable the recipients to respond more easily.

① On the Outlook Bar, click the SBS Practice Inbox.

② On the Standard toolbar, click the New Mail Message button.

A blank Message form appears.

③ Click the To button.

The Select Names dialog box appears.

④ In the Select Names dialog box, in the Show Names From The drop-down list, select Global Address List.

⑤ In the name list, scroll to select the names of the people in your network who agreed to participate in this exercise, click the To button for each name, and click OK.

The Select Names dialog box closes and the participants' names are listed in the To box on the Message form.

⑥ In the Subject box, type **National Sales Meeting** and then in the message area, type the following:

Would you prefer donuts or bagels for the morning session?

⑦ On the Message form Standard toolbar, click the Options button.

The Message Options dialog box appears.

⑧ In the Message Options dialog box, in the Voting And Tracking Options area, click the Use Voting Buttons check box.

In the box next to Use Voting Buttons, Approve;Reject appears.

⑨ In the Use Voting Buttons box, type **Donuts;Bagels**

⑩ In the Delivery Options area, be sure that the Save Sent Messages To check box is selected, and that Sent Items appears in the box.

Your screen should look similar to the following illustration.

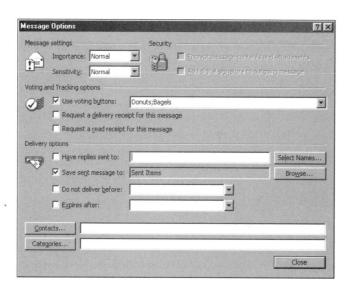

⓫   Click the Close button, and then, on the Message form Standard toolbar, click the Send button.

The Message Options dialog box closes, and the National Sales Meeting message is sent to the recipients, with Donuts and Bagels voting buttons in each message.

E-mail responses will now be tracked on your copy of the original message located in your Sent Items folder. Although the voting buttons do not appear on your message form, they appear in the e-mail message that your recipients view. A recipient's screen should appear similar to the following illustration.

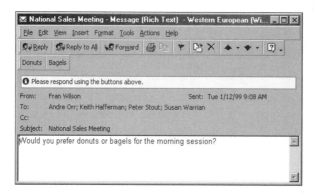

Review survey responses

As recipients respond to your e-mail message, the responses are delivered to your Inbox, with each recipient's answer displayed in the Subject column so that you can view responses at a glance, without having to open the message. In this exercise, you check your Inbox folder.

1   Be sure that the SBS Practice Inbox Information viewer is displayed.

2   On the View menu, point to Current View, and then click By Conversation Topic.

     The messages in your Inbox are arranged by conversation topic, with the topic Conversation: National Sales Meeting appearing in the Information viewer.

3   Click the plus sign (+) next to Conversation: National Sales Meeting.

     The Conversation: National Sales Meeting topic opens and all responses that have been received are shown.

4   Open and close each response.

     This action records the results in the tracking feature in your copy of the original message located in your Sent Items folder.

Track survey results

The responses you have opened are tracked automatically in your copy of the original message in your Sent Items folder. This tracking feature is particularly helpful if you sent your survey to several people and would otherwise have to manually tally the results. In this exercise, you check the survey results in your Sent Items folder.

1   On the Outlook Bar, click the My Shortcuts button, and then click the Sent Items shortcut.

     The message items in the Sent Items folder are displayed.

2   Double-click the National Sales Meeting message.

     The National Sales Meeting message opens.

The Message form displays the Message and Tracking tabs after the recipients respond.

3   On the Message form, click the Tracking tab.

     The Tracking tab becomes active, with the total replies summarized in the Comment area and the response from each respondent listed.

Your screen should look similar to the following illustration.

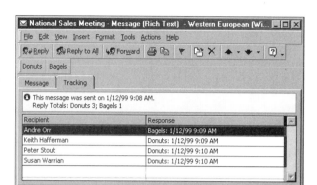

Close

④   Click the Close button.

The National Sales Meeting message closes.

Finish the lesson

①   To continue to the next lesson, on the File menu, click Close.

②   If you have finished using Outlook for now and are working in a workgroup environment, click File, and then click Exit And Log Off. If you are working in an Internet only environment, click File, and then click Exit.

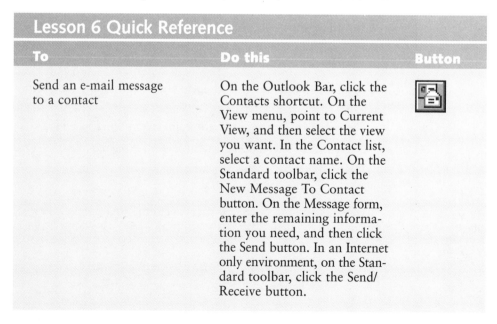

Lesson 6 Quick Reference

To	Do this	Button
Send an e-mail message to a contact	On the Outlook Bar, click the Contacts shortcut. On the View menu, point to Current View, and then select the view you want. In the Contact list, select a contact name. On the Standard toolbar, click the New Message To Contact button. On the Message form, enter the remaining information you need, and then click the Send button. In an Internet only environment, on the Standard toolbar, click the Send/ Receive button.	

Lesson 6 Quick Reference

To	Do this
Send a Contacts card (vCard)	On the Outlook Bar, click the Contacts shortcut. On the View menu, point to Current View, and then click Address Cards. In the Contact list, select the contact name you want. On the Actions menu, click New Message To Contact. On the Message form, enter the appropriate address and message information. On the Insert menu, click Item. In the Insert Item dialog box, in the Look In box, click the drop-down arrow, and then select Contacts. In the Items box, click the name of your contact. In the Insert As area, be sure that Attachment is selected, and click OK. On the Message form Standard toolbar, click the Send button. In an Internet only environment, on the Standard toolbar, click the Send/Receive button.
Send a fax (Internet only users)	On the Outlook Bar, click the Contacts shortcut, and then on the Actions menu, click New Fax Message. On the FAX form, click the To button. In the Select Names dialog box, select either Global Address List or Contacts, as necessary. Select the name you want from the list, and click OK. Fill in the Subject and Message boxes, and on the FAX form Standard toolbar, click the Send button. In the Symantec WinFax Starter Edition dialog box, verify the information, and click the Send button.

Lesson 6 Quick Reference

To	Do this
Add voting buttons to an e-mail message	On the Outlook Bar, click the Inbox shortcut. On the Standard toolbar, click the New Mail Message button. On the Message form, click the To button, and then in the Show Names From The drop-down list, select Global Address List. Select the names of the voters on the network, click the To button, and click OK. On the Message form, enter the additional address and message information you need. In the message area, position the insertion point, and then on the Message form Standard toolbar, click the Options button. In the Voting And Tracking Options area, click the Use Voting Buttons check box. Then either type the voting options you want to use or click the drop-down arrow and select the voting button option. In the Delivery Options area, be sure that Save Sent Messages To is selected and that Sent Items appears in the next box. Click Close and then click Send. In an Internet only environment, on the Standard toolbar, click the Send/Receive button.
Review voter responses	On the Outlook Bar, click the Inbox shortcut. On the View menu, point to Current View, and then click By Conversation Topic. Click the plus sign (+) next to the conversation topic that contains your voting request message. Open and then close each response.
Track survey results	Be sure that you have opened all the responses to the voting request in your Inbox. On the Outlook Bar, click the My Shortcuts button, and then click the Sent Items shortcut. Double-click your original voting request message, and then click the Tracking tab.

Review & Practice

**ESTIMATED
TIME
20 min.**

You will review and practice how to:

✔ *Send an e-mail message with an attachment.*

✔ *Flag a message for follow-up.*

✔ *Add a contact to your Contact list.*

✔ *Send a fax to a contact.*

Before you move on to Part 3, which covers ways to master your scheduling, you can practice the skills you learned in Part 2 by working through this Review & Practice section. You send e-mail messages, flag messages for follow-up, add contacts to your Contact list, and send faxes to contacts.

important

Before beginning the following exercises, drag the practice e-mail message file, indicated by an envelope icon, from the RP02 folder in the Outlook 2000 SBS Practice folder to your SBS Practice Inbox folder in the Folder List. Drag the practice Contacts files, indicated by address card icons, from the same folder to your SBS Practice Contacts folder in the Folder List. The Microsoft Word file Agenda.doc should not be copied or moved. (See the exercise "Set Up Practice E-mail" in Lesson 1 for detailed instructions.)

Scenario

As the account manager for Impact Public Relations, you are continuing preparation for the national sales meeting. You send an e-mail message containing the agenda to your sales team. When a few sales people respond with comments, you flag their e-mail messages for follow-up discussions. Next, you add a potential speaker to your Contacts list, and then you fax the speaker the meeting agenda and information on the company.

Step 1:   ### Send an E-mail Message with an Attachment

Before finalizing the date and the agenda, you send an e-mail message to your sales team with the draft agenda and request their comments.

1. On the Outlook Bar, click the SBS Practice Inbox shortcut.
2. Open a blank Message form.
3. Use the Address Book to address the message to Peter Stout, Susan Warrian, Keith Hafferman, and Andre Orr. Type the following as the message title: **Draft Agenda for National Sales Meeting**
4. Type a message inviting them to the national sales meeting scheduled for May 6 through 8, and then locate the file called Agenda.doc in the RP02 subfolder of the Outlook 2000 SBS Practice folder on your hard disk and attach it to your e-mail message. Include your vCard, and send the message.

For more information about	See
Using the Address Book	Lesson 3
Sending a Contacts card (vCard)	Lesson 6
Adding attachments to messages	Lesson 3

Step 2:   ### Flag a Message for Follow-up

Peter Stout's e-mail response to your message contains several ideas that you would like to discuss further with him, so you flag his message for follow-up.

1. Open the message from Peter Stout titled RE: Draft Agenda for National Sales Meeting.
2. Flag the message for a follow-up phone call tomorrow.

For more information about	See
Flagging a message for follow-up	Lesson 4
Viewing flagged messages	Lesson 4
Marking a flagged message as completed	Lesson 4

Step 3:   Add a Contact to Your Contacts List

Your colleague gave you the business card of Gilles Ratia, who is a potential speaker at the national sales meeting. You add the contact to your Contacts list.

1 On the Outlook Bar, click the SBS Practice Contacts shortcut.

2 Open a blank Contact form.

3 Complete the Contact form for Gilles Ratia, entering his address as **89 Forks Place, Santa Clara, CA 95050**, his phone number as **(209) 555-7689**, and his fax number as **(209) 555-2965**.

4 Print the contact information in the Address Card format.

For more information about	See
Adding contact information	Lesson 5
Viewing contact information	Lesson 5
Printing contact information	Lesson 5

Step 4:   Send a Fax to a Contact

After talking with Gilles Ratia, you send him a fax of the agenda for the national sales meeting.

Internet only

1 If you work in an Internet only environment, use Gilles Ratia's Address Card to open a FAX form.

2 Complete the address information, type a brief message on the cover page thanking him for his interest in speaking at the sales meeting, and fax Agenda.doc to him.

For more information about	See
Faxing in an Internet only environment	Lesson 6

Finish the Review & Practice

Follow these steps to delete the practice files that you created in this Review & Practice, and then quit Outlook 2000.

❶ Delete the Draft Agenda for National Sales Meeting message in the Sent Items folder.

❷ Delete the RE: Draft Agenda for National Sales Meeting message in the SBS Practice Inbox.

❸ Delete the Gilles Ratia contact form in the Contact list in the SBS Practice Contacts folder.

❹ If you are finished using Outlook for now and are working in an Internet only environment, on the File menu, click Exit. If you are finished using Outlook and are working in a Workgroup environment, on the File menu, click Exit And Log Off.

PART 3

Mastering Your Schedule with Outlook 2000

LESSON

7

Managing Your Calendar

ESTIMATED TIME
45 min.

In this lesson you will learn how to:

✓ *Schedule different types of appointments and events.*

✓ *Move and edit appointments.*

✓ *Manage appointments by setting reminders and assigning categories.*

✓ *Save an appointment in vCalendar format to share on the Internet.*

✓ *Customize your Calendar to meet your personal needs.*

✓ *Export Outlook data to the Timex Data Link Watch.*

In Lesson 2, "Learning the Basics of Scheduling," you learned how to enter appointments in your Calendar. In this lesson, you learn about meetings and events and practice using advanced techniques to organize your schedule to meet specific work and personal needs.

The Outlook Calendar provides a variety of ways to manage your schedule. You can enter details about an appointment to help you remember important information, such as what you are to discuss and with whom you are meeting. You can set up reminders to alert you about upcoming meetings or attach documents, such as an agenda or background material, to an appointment. Appointments can be organized by the same categories you use to manage your messages, tasks, and contacts. You can also block out time for all-day events and create appointments that recur at specified intervals.

If you use Outlook in a Workgroup environment, you can share your Calendar with whichever coworkers you choose at various viewing levels. For example, at the default viewing level, your colleagues are able to see just the times when you are busy or free without seeing the details of your schedule. Viewing your colleagues' availability in this way is useful for efficiently scheduling meetings and is covered in Lesson 8, "Managing Meetings and Events." Higher permission levels can be delegated to allow another person, such as an administrative assistant, to work in Calendar on your behalf. Depending on the type of permissions you set up, another person can create, revise, or delete items from your Calendar. Delegating permissions is covered in Lesson 11, "Using Outlook with Other Connections."

To share your Calendar with colleagues who use different scheduling programs or who use Outlook in another organization, you can save your appointments as a *vCalendar*, a technology standard for the exchange of scheduling information. The vCalendar format creates a file that others can import into any scheduling program that supports the vCalendar standard.

As Fran Wilson, Impact Public Relations account manager, one of your responsibilities is to attend trade shows for such clients as Awesome Computers and Ramona Publishing. In this lesson, you block out time for a trade show and set it as a recurring event. You save an appointment in vCalendar format to share with a colleague. You also organize your Calendar information by category and create your own categories so that you can manage your time as efficiently as possible.

Getting Ready for the Lesson

In this exercise, you start Outlook 2000 and prepare the practice files and folders that you need.

Start Outlook and copy the practice files

Microsoft Outlook

❶ On the desktop, double-click the Microsoft Outlook 2000 icon.
Outlook 2000 opens.

❷ If necessary, maximize the Outlook window.

Maximize

important

To continue with this lesson, you must have installed this book's practice folder on your hard disk and created an SBS Practice Calendar folder and shortcut, and an SBS Practice Contacts folder and shortcut. If you have not yet done so, see Lesson 2, "Learning the Basics of Scheduling."

SBS Practice Calendar

For a detailed example of how to copy practice files to a practice folder, see the exercise "Set Up Practice E-mail" in Lesson 1.

3 On the Outlook Bar, click the SBS Practice Calendar shortcut.

4 Drag the practice Calendar files, indicated by calendar icons, from the Lesson07 folder in the Outlook 2000 SBS Practice folder to your SBS Practice Calendar folder in the Folder List.

5 Drag the practice Contacts file, indicated by an address card icon, from the Lesson07 folder in the Outlook 2000 SBS Practice folder to your SBS Practice Contacts folder. The Microsoft Word document should remain in the Lesson07 folder.

Scheduling Appointments

In Lesson 2, you practiced how to enter an appointment directly into your Calendar by typing it in a time slot. Outlook provides other ways to enter more complex appointments into your Calendar. For example, you can schedule:

- Recurring appointments for activities such as weekly staff meetings. You can easily set your appointments to recur automatically by defining a number of recurrences or until a given date.

- Appointments that contain detailed information to help you stay on top of your commitments. Outlook enables you to create such a record by entering information such as the location and duration of an appointment and comments describing the purpose on the Appointment form.

- Private appointments that appear on your Calendar but which hide the details of the appointment, even from those with permission to view your schedule.

In this section, you enter detailed information about an appointment, schedule an appointment classified as private, schedule an event, create a recurring appointment and delete one occurrence, move an appointment to a new date, and edit appointment information that has changed.

Appointments, Meetings, and Events

For optimum use of Outlook, you need to know how the terms *appointment*, *meeting*, and *event* are defined in Calendar.

Appointments are activities that you can schedule in Outlook that do not involve inviting other people or reserving resources, such as a conference room.

(continued)

Managing Your Calendar

7

continued

Meetings are activities to which you invite other people or for which you reserve resources. When you create a meeting, you identify the people to invite and the resources to reserve, and you pick a meeting time. Then you send meeting requests via Outlook for a face-to-face or online meeting. Responses to your meeting requests appear in your Inbox.

Events are activities that last 24 hours or longer. Events can include conventions, holidays, birthdays, or the company picnic. Events do not occupy blocks of time in the Appointment area of Calendar; rather, the name of the event appears in a banner above the time slots on the specified date.

Schedule a detailed appointment

You need to call Juanita at Ramona Publishing in preparation for the American Booksellers Association meeting. To be sure that you don't forget any of the details of the meeting, you enter complete information on the Appointment form.

New Appointment

1 On the Outlook Bar, click the SBS Practice Calendar shortcut, and then on the Standard toolbar, click the New Appointment button.

A blank Appointment form appears.

tip

You can open a blank form for a new appointment, contact, task, journal entry, or message from any window in Outlook 2000. For example, you do not have to be in a Calendar folder to open a new Appointment form. From any window you have open, on the File menu, point to New, and then click Appointment.

2 On the Appointment form, in the Subject box, type the following:

Call Juanita at Ramona Publishing

3 In the Location box, type **My office**

4 In the Start Time boxes, select the contents and type **Mon 5/23/2005** and **9 am**

5 In the End Time boxes, select the contents, type the same date, and type **10 am**

6 In the Comment area, type the following:

Finalize plans for the ABA: how many posters should we bring?

7 Click the Save And Close button.

The new appointment appears in the 9:00 A.M. to 10:00 A.M. time slots on your Calendar for May 23, 2005.

> **tip**
> To see the comments about your appointments, on the Standard toolbar, click the View menu, point to Current View, and then click Day/Week/Month View With AutoPreview. The entry for the appointment will display the location and comments from the Appointment form.

Schedule a private appointment

There are some appointments that you do not want others in your organization to know about. In this exercise, you schedule an appointment and flag it as private, for your eyes only.

1 In the Date Navigator, scroll to December 2004, and then click December 9.

December 9, 2004, is displayed in the Appointment area.

2 In the Appointment area, select the 9:00 A.M. to 10:00 A.M. time slots.

3 On the Standard toolbar, click the New Appointment button.

The Appointment form appears. The date and time boxes are already filled in.

4 On the Appointment form, in the Subject box, type **See Dr. White**

5 In the Location box, type **His office**

6 In the Comment area, type **Annual physical exam**

7 On the Appointment form, in the lower-right corner, select the Private check box.

Private

8 On the Appointment form Standard toolbar, click the Save And Close button.

The Appointment form closes. Your Calendar reappears, displaying the new appointment entry with a key icon to indicate that the appointment is private.

Schedule an event

A trip to the annual convention of the American Booksellers Association will keep you out of the office for about a week. You need to enter this event in your Calendar to be sure that it does not conflict with commitments to your other clients.

1 Be sure that the SBS Practice Calendar Appointment area is displayed.

To schedule events lasting more than one day, clear the All Day Event check box. Then complete the End Time information you want.

2 On the Actions menu, click New All-Day Event.

A blank Event form appears.

3 On the Event form, in the Subject box, type **American Booksellers Association**

4 In the Location box, type **Miami**

5 In the Start Time box, select the current text and type **May 27, 2005**

6 In the End Time box, select the current text and type **May 31, 2005**

7 In the Comment area, type the following:

Distribute Ramona Publishing posters to press, TV, reviewers, and readers

8 On the Event form Standard toolbar, click the Save And Close button.

The Event form closes.

To indicate that you are out of the office, in the Show Time As drop-down list, select Out Of Office.

9 On the View menu, point to Go To, and then click Go To Date. In the Go To Date dialog box, in the Date box, select the current text and type **May 27, 2005**

In the Show In drop-down list, select Week Calendar, and click OK.

The days dedicated to the convention are now entered as events in your Calendar. They appear on your Calendar as a banner above the other appointments for each day. Your time during those days is flagged as free. You can still enter any appointments you might have while at the convention. In Week view, your screen will look similar to the following illustration.

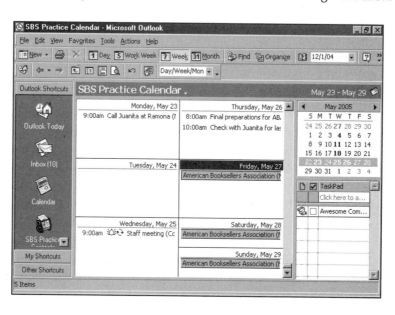

Free and Busy Time

On the Appointment form, you can designate whether your time is free or busy by selecting one of several options (Free, Tentative, Busy, or Out Of Office). The option you choose is important for others who have access to your Calendar and may want to schedule a meeting with you. Events are automatically designated as free time, since you might want to schedule appointments or meetings at the event. To block out an entire day during which you are unavailable, you would enter it in Calendar as an all-day appointment, since appointment time is designated as busy.

Schedule an all-day appointment

To prepare for the American Booksellers Association convention, you schedule an appointment for an entire day during which you do not want to be disturbed.

You can also open an Appointment form by selecting and then right-clicking the time slot. On the shortcut menu, click New Appointment.

1 On the Standard toolbar, click the Day button.

The Appointment area displays the time slots for a single day.

2 In the Date Navigator, scroll to May 2005, and then click May 26.

May 26, 2005, is displayed in the Appointment area.

3 Double-click the 8:00 A.M. time slot.

The Appointment form appears with the date and times filled in.

4 In the Subject box, type **Final preparations for ABA**

5 On the Appointment form, in the second End Time box, select the text and type **5:00 p.m.**

6 On the Appointment form Standard toolbar, click the Save And Close button.

The appointment now fills the Appointment area.

7 Select and double-click the 10 A.M. time slot.

An Appointment form opens.

8 In the Subject box, type **Check with Juanita for last-minute problems** and then click Save And Close.

The Appointment area is now divided into two columns.

Your screen should look similar to the following illustration.

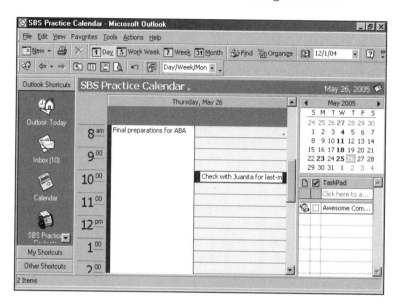

tip

To change your appointment status from free to busy or busy to free, open the Appointment form for the item, and in the Show Time As box, click the drop-down arrow, and then select the option that you prefer.

Schedule a recurring appointment

Because you attend the American Booksellers Association convention every year, you decide to enter a recurring appointment in your Calendar for a day of preparation prior to the event.

1. In the Date Navigator, click May 16, and then double-click any time slot.

    A new Appointment form appears, with the date and times filled in.

2. On the Appointment form Standard toolbar, click the Recurrence button.

    The Appointment Recurrence dialog box appears.

3. In the Appointment Time area, in the Duration box, click the drop-down arrow, and then select 1 Day.

4. In the Appointment Recurrence dialog box, in the Recurrence Pattern area, select Yearly, and then click the option that displays Third, Monday, and May in the three side-by-side boxes.

    The option now reads The Third Monday Of May.

5 Click OK.

The Appointment Recurrence dialog box closes. The Appointment form appears with the recurrence pattern listed below the location.

6 On the Recurring Appointment form, in the Subject box, type **Preparations for the ABA**

7 In the Location box, type **Varies**

8 On the Appointment form Standard toolbar, click the Save And Close button.

You now have a preparation day scheduled to occur two weeks before every Memorial Day weekend.

9 To view the next occurrence of your ABA preparation day, in the Date Navigator, scroll to May 2006, and then double-click the third Monday.

Your ABA preparation day appears in the Appointment area. The appointment is displayed with a circular arrow icon to indicate a recurring appointment.

Recurring

Make an existing appointment recurring

In this exercise, you decide to make an existing appointment to call Juanita Rivera into a series of recurring appointments that occur monthly for five months prior to the ABA convention.

1 In the Date Navigator, scroll to May 2005, click May 23, and then double-click the 9:00 A.M. appointment to call Juanita.

The Call Juanita at Ramona Appointment form appears.

2 On the Appointment form Standard toolbar, click the Recurrence button.

The Appointment Recurrence dialog box appears.

3 In the Appointment Recurrence dialog box, in the Recurrence Pattern area, select Monthly, and then click the option that displays Fourth, Monday, and 1 in the three side-by-side boxes.

The option reads The Fourth Monday Of Every 1 Month(s).

4 In the Range Of Recurrence area, select the existing Start date and type **1/24/05**

5 In the Range Of Recurrence area, click the End After option, and then in the box, select the current text, and then type **5**

6 Click OK.

The Appointment Recurrence dialog box closes, and the recurrence pattern appears on the Appointment form below the location.

7 On the Appointment form, in the Subject box, change the text to read: **Annual Preparations for the ABA: monthly phone conference with Ramona Publishing**

If you get a warning message at this point, you can ignore it.

8 Click the Save And Close button.

Five monthly phone conferences are now scheduled prior to the ABA trade show (scheduled for late May) on your Calendar.

9 On Date Navigator, scroll to January 2005, and then click the fourth Monday.

The first monthly appointment appears in the 9:00 A.M. time slot. The fourth Mondays in February, March, April, and May show the same appointment.

Move or copy an appointment

You sometimes have to change your appointments. But with Outlook you don't have to delete them in one place and then retype them in another; instead, you can move or copy appointments to their new times. In this exercise, you reschedule your physical exam with Dr. White.

1 In the Date Navigator, scroll to December 2004, and then click December 9.

December 9, 2004, is displayed in the Appointment area.

2 Click the left border (the move bar) of the Dr. White appointment scheduled for 9:00 A.M. to 10:00 A.M.

The pointer becomes a four-headed arrow.

To move an appointment to another time on the same date, click its left border and drag it to the new time slot.

3 Drag the appointment to December 16 in the Date Navigator.

The date changes to December 16. The Appointment area for that day appears, with Dr. White's rescheduled appointment retaining its original start and end times.

Edit a recurring appointment

Sometimes people's schedules change so much that the time of a regular, recurring meeting becomes inconvenient and must be rescheduled. Because of a new conflict, you decide to change your weekly meetings with Chris from 9:00 A.M. on Wednesday to 10:00 A.M. on Monday.

1 In the Date Navigator, scroll to January 2005, and then click January 26.

January 26, 2005, appears in the Appointment area of your Calendar.

2 Double-click the appointment Review Meeting With Chris appointment at 9:00 A.M.

Because this is a recurring appointment, the Open Recurring Item dialog box appears, prompting you to open either the single occurrence of the meeting or the series of meetings.

3 In the Open Recurring Item dialog box, click the Open The Series option, and click OK.

The Recurring Appointment form appears.

④ On the Recurring Appointment form Standard toolbar, click the Recurrence button.

The Appointment Recurrence dialog box appears.

⑤ In the Appointment Recurrence dialog box, in the Appointment Time area, change the Start Time box to 10:00 A.M., and then in the Recurrence Pattern area, change the day from Wednesday to Monday.

If you get a warning message at this point, you can ignore it.

⑥ Click OK.

The Appointment Recurrence dialog box closes.

⑦ On the Appointment form Standard toolbar, click the Save And Close button.

Now during the first five months of 2005, your monthly conference will occur on the fourth Monday of the month at 10:00 A.M., rather than on the fourth Wednesday at 9:00.

tip

If you want to change only one appointment in a series of recurring appointments, in the Open Recurring Item dialog box, select the Open This Occurrence option, and then make your changes on the Appointment form.

Delete a recurring appointment

Juanita Rivera has phoned and reported that she may not always be available for a phone conference at 9:00 A.M. on the fourth Monday of every month to prepare for the ABA convention, so you decide to delete the series of meetings.

① In the Date Navigator, scroll to January 2005, and then click January 24.

January 24, 2005, is displayed in the Appointment area.

② In the Appointment area, click the 9:00 A.M. appointment.

The 9:00 A.M. time slot is selected.

Delete

③ On the Standard toolbar, click the Delete button.

The Confirm Delete dialog box appears, prompting you to delete either the entire series or only this one occurrence.

④ In the Confirm Delete dialog box, click the Delete All Occurrences option, and click OK.

The series of appointments is deleted.

Managing Your Calendar

Delete

> **tip**
> Pressing the Delete key on the keyboard erases only the text for the selected appointment, but the appointment still remains on your Calendar. To delete the appointment itself, you must click the Delete button on the Standard toolbar.

Managing Appointments

Effective time management depends on knowing when you need to be somewhere and exactly how you are spending your time. Outlook provides features that help you manage your time better, such as finding appointments, setting reminders, attaching documents to appointments, sharing appointments electronically with others, and categorizing appointments.

- You can easily find when an appointment is scheduled to occur by using Find to search for words or other data that appear in your Outlook Calendar.

- You can set up a reminder for a single appointment as far ahead as you choose, and you can even have Outlook routinely remind you of all of your upcoming commitments. A reminder notice is a small box that pops up on your screen, even if you're using another application, alerting you to the appointment.

- You can electronically attach documents for an appointment to the appointment itself so that they will be instantly available when you need them.

- You can share your schedule with others who do not use the same scheduling program by saving an appointment in vCalendar format. If your colleagues are using Outlook or another scheduling program compatible with vCalendar technology, they will be able to import the files directly into their schedules.

- You can assign your appointments to several default categories or to customized categories that you create to better understand how you are allocating your time. This allows you to view appointments in only certain categories.

Find an appointment

In this exercise, you practice finding an appointment dealing with preparations for the American Booksellers Association convention.

1 On the Standard toolbar, click the Find button.

The Find Items In SBS Practice Calendar panel appears.

2 In the Find Items In SBS Practice Calendar panel, in the Look For box, type **ABA** and click the Find Now button.

The items containing the term *ABA* are displayed in a table under the Find Items In SBS Practice Calendar panel.

Close button

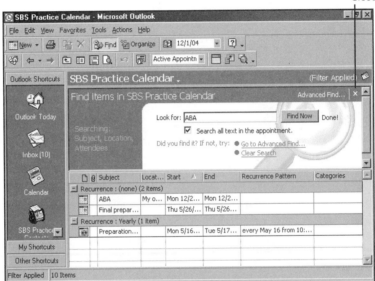

Close

3 In the Find Items In SBS Practice Calendar panel, click the Close button.

The panel closes.

Set up a reminder notice

Some appointments are so important that you want to be sure that you don't miss them. You can set up a reminder to alert you about all your appointments as far ahead of time as you choose.

1 On the View menu, point to Current View, and be sure that Day/Week/ Month is selected.

2 In the Date Navigator, scroll to December 2004, and then click December 16.

December 16 appears in the Appointment area.

3 In the Appointment area, double-click the Dr. White appointment.

The See Dr. White Appointment form appears.

④ On the Appointment form, select the Reminder check box.

⑤ In the Reminder box, click the drop-down arrow and select 30 minutes.

The reminder is now set to pop up on your screen 30 minutes prior to the appointment with Dr. White.

⑥ On the Appointment form Standard toolbar, click the Save And Close button.

Since reminders will not function in subfolders such as the SBS Practice Calendar folder, a message box prompts you for an OK.

⑦ In the message box, click Yes.

The message box closes and then the Appointment form closes. An alarm icon appears in the See Dr. White appointment, indicating a reminder notice has been set.

Alarm

Reminder Notices

When a reminder notice appears on your screen, you can perform one of three actions:

■ Click the Dismiss button to close the Reminder dialog box.

■ Click the Snooze button to reschedule the reminder. If you click the Snooze button, the reminder will be repeated in another five minutes, unless you change the amount of time in the Click Snooze To Be Reminded Again drop-down list.

■ Click the Open Item button to open the Appointment form and review its contents.

When a Reminder dialog box appears, you screen will look similar to the following illustration.

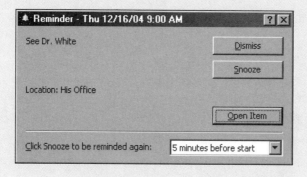

Set reminder options for all new appointments

Rather than decide case-by-case which appointments should have reminders, you can set up Calendar to always remind you of upcoming commitments.

1 On the Tools menu, click Options.

The Options dialog box appears.

2 On the Preferences tab, in the Calendar area, select the Default Reminder check box, and then in the Default Reminder box, select 10 Minutes.

A reminder will automatically appear on your screen 10 minutes before any appointment is scheduled to start.

3 Click OK.

tip

If you do not want to be reminded of items in your Calendar, in the Options dialog box, on the Preferences tab, in the Calendar area, clear the Default Reminder check box.

Attach a document to an appointment

Outlook allows you to electronically "staple" any documents you need to the appointment. In this exercise, you attach the promotional literature that will be considered at a meeting to the appointment for that meeting.

1 On the View menu, point to Current View, and be sure that Day/Week/Month is selected.

2 In the Date Navigator, scroll to January 2005, and then click January 24.

January 24, 2005, is displayed in the Appointment area.

3 In the Appointment area, select the 1:00 P.M. to 2:00 P.M. time slots.

New Appointment

4 On the Standard toolbar, click the New Appointment button.

A blank Appointment form appears with the start and end times filled in.

5 On the Appointment form, in the Subject box, type **Five Lakes promotional campaign** and then in the Location box, type **Conference room**

Insert File

You can attach any type of file to an appointment.

6 On the Appointment form Standard toolbar, click the Insert File button.

The Insert File dialog box appears.

7 In the Look In drop-down list, browse to find the Outlook 2000 SBS Practice folder and then double-click it.

The contents of the folder are displayed.

8 Double-click the Lesson07 folder, and then double-click the Five Lakes Promotion document.

The Five Lakes Promotion icon is inserted in the Comment area on the Appointment form. Your screen should look similar to the following illustration.

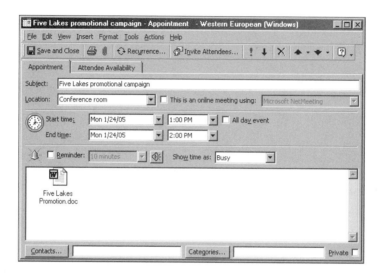

9 On the Appointment form, click the Save And Close button.

The Appointment form closes.

Save an appointment in vCalendar format

Now that you've set up your Five Lakes appointment, in this exercise you save it in vCalendar format. Once it is in this format, you send the appointment as an e-mail attachment to your colleagues so that they know your schedule.

1 In the Appointment area, click the Five Lakes appointment.

2 On the File menu, click Save As.

The Save As dialog box appears.

3 In the Save As dialog box, in the Save In drop-down list, locate the folder where you want to save the file.

4 In the File Name box, type a name for the file.

5 In the Save As Type box, click the drop-down arrow, and then select vCalendar Format.

6 Click the Save button.

Your appointment is saved in vCalendar format.

Organizing with Categories

To help organize and keep track of your appointments, meetings, and events, you can assign them to various *categories*. Categories are assigned to all types of Outlook items from the *Master Category List,* an alphabetical list of categories that includes the set of default categories provided by Outlook in addition to categories you create to suit your particular needs. After assigning one or more categories to an appointment, meeting, or event, you can use the categories in two ways.

You can organize different types of Outlook items, such as messages, contacts, tasks, and your appointments, into related groups while still maintaining them in separate Outlook folders. For example, the messages, contacts, tasks, and appointments related to your international customers can be stored in separate folders but grouped by assigning them to the International category found in the Master Category List.

You can organize similar items, such as appointments, into different groups without having to store them in different folders. For example, you may want to view only those appointments related to your activities with a community group with which you volunteer. You can create a custom category to group these appointments and view them separately from the rest of your Calendar.

Assign appointments to categories

You decide to organize your Calendar so that you can view your personal and business appointments separately. In this exercise, you assign several appointments to the Business category and an appointment to the Personal category.

> ## tip
> Assigning an appointment to the Personal category is not the same as selecting the Private check box on the Appointment form. The Private check box prevents others who might have access to your Calendar from seeing the details of the appointment. You might select a Business appointment as Private if it dealt with sensitive matters, such as a personnel problem.

1 In the Date Navigator, scroll to December 2004, and then click December 8. December 8, 2004, is displayed in the Appointment area.

2 On the Standard toolbar, click the Organize button. If it is not visible, click the More Buttons drop-down arrow, and then click the Organize button.

The Ways To Organize SBS Practice Calendar panel appears.

More Buttons

Managing Your Calendar   **7**

For a demonstration of how to assign appointments to categories and view related groups, in the Multimedia folder on the Microsoft Outlook 2000 Step by Step CD-ROM, double-click the Categories icon.

3 On the Ways To Organize SBS Practice Calendar panel, click the Using Categories link.

The Using Categories page opens.

4 On the Using Categories page, in the Add Appointments Selected Below To list, select Business.

5 In the Appointment area, select the 9:00 A.M. staff meeting, press and hold down the Ctrl key, and then select the 2:00 P.M. End Of Year Report Planning meeting.

6 In the Ways To Organize SBS Practice Calendar panel, click the Add button.

Done! is displayed next to the Add button.

7 In the Add Appointments Selected Below To list, select Personal.

8 In the Appointment area, scroll to December 2004, click December 10, select the 10 A.M. Holiday Shopping appointment, and then click the Add button.

Done! is displayed next to the Add button.

9 On the Ways To Organize SBS Practice Calendar panel, click the Using Views link.

The Using Views page opens.

10 On the Using Views page, in the Change Your View list, select By Category.

The headings for the groups of appointments are displayed in the Information viewer. Your screen should look similar to the following illustration.

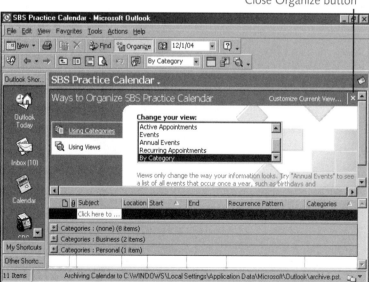

Close Organize button

⑪ In the Information viewer, click the plus sign (+) next to the Business and Personal categories.

The appointments in each group are displayed.

Close

⑫ On the Ways to Organize SBS Practice Calendar panel, click the Close button.

Personalizing Your Calendar

Unlike that of a desk calendar, the format of Outlook's Calendar can be changed to suit your needs. It provides five basic *views* or formats, each of which can be further modified to let you see your time commitments and tasks in the way most useful to you. Each view, except Day/Week/Month, displays the subject, start and end times, the location, and categories. Each view can also display symbols to show whether there's an attachment and whether the item is a recurring appointment.

About Calendar Views

Outlook provides a variety of ways to view your Calendar.

Click this view	To see
Day/Week/Month	Appointments, events, and meetings for days, weeks, or a month. Also includes a list of tasks. This view looks like a paper calendar or planner.
Day/Week/Month With AutoPreview	Same as the Day/Week/Month view, except that the first lines of the text appear in each Calendar item.
Active Appointments	A list of all appointments and meetings beginning today and going into the future, with details.
Events	A list of all events, with details.
Annual Events	A list of events that happen once a year, with details.
Recurring Appointments	A list of recurring appointments, with details.
By Category	A list of all Calendar items grouped by category, with details.

(continued)

Managing Your Calendar

7

continued

Change the period of time that is displayed

You can choose how much time is displayed in the Day/Week/Month Calendar views.

1   On the View menu, point to Current View, and then click Day/Week/Month.

2   On the Standard toolbar, click the button for the amount of time that you want to view.

To view Calendar items for	Do this	
One day	Click the Day button.	1
Seven days	Click the Week button.	7
Five days, Monday through Friday	Click the Work Week button.	5
One month	Click the Month button.	31

Set the days and hours for your work week

Not everyone works the same hours, days, or weeks. Your schedule at Impact Public Relations is to work four 10-hour days. In this exercise, you set up your Calendar to reflect your actual work schedule, a four-day work week.

1   On the View menu, point to Current View, and be sure that Day/Week/Month is selected.

2   On the Tools menu, click Options.

The Options dialog box appears.

3   On the Preferences tab, click the Calendar Options button.

The Calendar Options dialog box appears.

4   In the Calendar Options dialog box, be sure that the check boxes next to only Monday, Tuesday, Wednesday, and Thursday are selected.

5   In the Start Time box, click the drop-down arrow, and then select 7:00 A.M.

6   In the End Time box, click the drop-down arrow, and then select 6:00 P.M.

7   In the First Day Of Week box, click the drop-down arrow, and then select Monday.

8   In the Calendar Options dialog box, click OK, and then in the Options dialog box, click OK.

9   On the Standard toolbar, click the Work Week button.

The Appointment area displays a four-day week, beginning with Monday, with daily work hours from 7 A.M. to 6 P.M.

Display appointments with end times and as clocks

Some people like to see when their appointments both begin and end. Also, some people can visualize their schedules more easily if their appointments are presented in the form of a clock. In this exercise, you customize your Calendar by adding end times in your appointment entries and by displaying both start and end times in the form of a clock.

1   In the Date Navigator, scroll to December 2004, and then click December 6.

December 6, 2004, is displayed in the Appointment area.

2   On the View menu, point to Current View, and then click Customize Current View.

The View Summary dialog box appears.

3   In the View Summary dialog box, click the Other Settings button.

The Format Day/Week/Month View dialog box appears.

4   In the Format Day/Week/Month View dialog box, in the Week and Month areas, be sure that the Show End Time check boxes are selected.

5   In the Week and Month areas, select the Show Time As Clocks check boxes.

6   In the Format Day/Week/Month View dialog box, click OK, and in the View Summary dialog box, click OK.

7   On the Standard toolbar, click the Week button.

A seven-day week is displayed in the Appointment area. The start and end times for your appointments are indicated to the left of each entry by clock graphics.

Your screen should look similar to the following illustration.

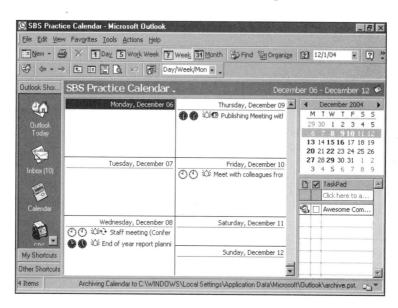

Change the current time zone

When you travel across times zones, reconciling your schedule can be tricky. In this exercise, you change your current time zone in Outlook.

> # important
>
> Changing your current time zone in Outlook is equivalent to changing it in Microsoft Windows Control Panel. Any change in Outlook affects the time displayed in other Windows-based programs.

① On the Tools menu, click Options.

The Options dialog box appears.

② In the Options dialog box, click the Preferences tab, and then click the Calendar Options button.

The Calendar Options dialog box appears.

If you already work in New York, substitute Los Angeles, and choose Pacific time.

③ In the Calendar Options dialog box, in the Calendar Options area, click the Time Zone button.

The Time Zone dialog box appears.

④ In the Time Zone dialog box, in the Label box, type **New York**

⑤ In the Time Zone box, click the drop-down arrow, and then select Eastern Time.

⑥ To set your computer clock to automatically adjust for Daylight Saving Time changes, select the Adjust For Daylight Saving Time check box.

⑦ In the Time Zone dialog box, click OK; in the Calendar Options dialog box, click OK; and then in the Options dialog box, click OK.

The three dialog boxes close. The Appointment area reappears, displaying the label *New York* above the time bar. Your appointment times have now been adjusted to reflect the new time zone.

tip
To quickly change the time zone on your computer, on the Standard toolbar, click the Day button. In the Appointment area, right-click anywhere on the gray time bar, and then on the shortcut menu, click Change Time Zone.

Show an additional time zone in Calendar

In this exercise, you add a second time zone, Greenwich Mean Time, next to the original time zone in the Appointment area.

① On the Standard toolbar, click the Day button.

② On the Tools menu, click Options.

The Options dialog box appears.

③ On the Preferences tab, click the Calendar Options button.

The Calendar Options dialog box appears.

④ In the Calendar Options dialog box, click the Time Zone button.

The Time Zone dialog box appears.

⑤ In the Time Zone dialog box, select the Show An Additional Time Zone check box.

⑥ In the Label box, type **Greenwich Mean Time**

⑦ In the Time Zone box, click the drop-down arrow, and then select Greenwich Mean Time: Dublin, Edinburgh, Lisbon.

⑧ In the Time Zone dialog box, click OK; in the Calendar Options dialog box, click OK; and then in the Options dialog box, click OK.

The three dialog boxes close. Greenwich Mean Time appears as a second time bar.

Managing Your Calendar

7

Your screen should look similar to the following illustration.

tip

To remove the second time zone, right-click the time bar on the left edge of the Appointment area. Click Change Time Zone, and then clear the Show An Additional Time Zone check box. Click OK to close the dialog box.

You can quickly switch between the two time zone columns displayed in your daily Appointment area. For example, if you regularly commute between Seattle and Dublin, set your current time zone to Seattle time and your second time zone to Dublin time. When you fly to Dublin, click Swap Time Zones so that the Dublin time zone column is located next to your appointments. To switch your current time zone with the second time zone, on the Tools menu, select Options, and then on the Preferences tab, click the Calendar Options button. In the Calendar Options dialog box, click the Time Zone bar, click the Swap Time Zones button, and then click OK three times to close the dialog boxes. The second time zone column will appear in the Appointment area next to the time slots, adjusting the times for your appointments.

Add a country's holidays to your Calendar

Holidays are considered all-day events or appointments.

To keep up with the holidays that might be important to a key Canadian client, you decide to add Canadian holidays to your Calendar.

1 On the Tools menu, click Options.

The Options dialog box appears.

2 On the Preferences tab, click the Calendar Options button.

The Calendar Options dialog box appears.

You can add holidays for most of the major countries and religious communities of the world.

❸ In the Calendar Options dialog box, click the Add Holidays button.

The Add Holidays To Calendar dialog box appears.

tip

Individual holidays can be copied to Calendar by opening a holiday folder and then dragging each appointment to Calendar.

❹ In the Add Holidays To Calendar dialog box, in the list of countries, select the check box next to Canada.

❺ In the Add Holidays To Calendar dialog box, click OK.

An Import-Holidays dialog box appears while the holidays are added.

❻ In the Calendar Options dialog box, click OK; and then in the Options dialog box, click OK.

The dialog boxes close. Calendar is now set up to display Canadian holidays on the appropriate dates.

❼ In the Date Navigator, scroll to July 2001, and then click July 1.

Canadian Independence Day is displayed for that date in the Appointment area.

tip

To remove holidays for a country from your Calendar, on the View menu, point to Current View, and then click Events. A list of events in your Calendar is displayed in a table view. In the list of events, select the holiday that you want to remove, and then on the Standard toolbar, click the Delete button. Repeat until each holiday that you want to remove is deleted.

One Step Further **Using the Timex Data Link Watch**

The Timex Data Link Watch produced by Timex Corporation receives information exported from Outlook and other similar programs, including Microsoft Schedule+. The Outlook Timex Data Link Watch Wizard makes it easy to export any of the following to the watch: appointments, tasks, phone numbers, anniversaries, reminders, and current time and time zone information.

Copy Outlook information to the Timex Data Link Watch

> # important
>
> Before you can follow this procedure, you must have the Timex Data Link Watch and have installed the Timex Data Link Watch files from your Outlook 2000 installation CD-ROM or from the network location that you used to set up the program. If you didn't install Outlook from a CD-ROM, you can download the files you need over the Internet. To access the Internet, in Outlook, click the Help menu, and then click Office On The Web.

1 Install the software included with your Timex Data Link Watch onto your hard disk.

2 Start Outlook, and then on the File menu, click Import And Export.

The Import And Export Wizard dialog box appears.

3 In the Choose An Action To Perform box, select Export To The Timex Data Link Watch, and then click the Next button.

The Timex Data Link Watch Wizard dialog box appears. The default check boxes for the data to be exported are selected. Your screen should look similar to the following illustration.

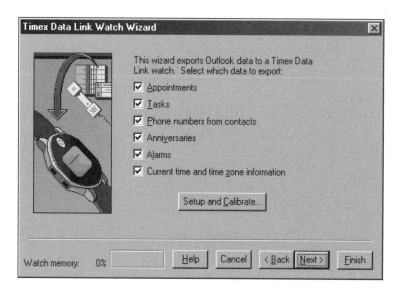

4 Continue to click the Next button to move through the Import And Export Wizard and specify more export options.

⑤ Click the Finish button.

The Export To Watch dialog box appears.

⑥ Hold the watch in front of the screen as directed, and click OK.

The data is exported to the watch, and a message appears asking if the export was successful.

⑦ If the export was successful, click Yes.

The message and the Timex Data Link Watch Wizard dialog box close.

⑧ If the export was unsuccessful, try again or see the Timex Data Link Watch troubleshooting instructions.

Finish the lesson

① To continue to the next lesson, on the File menu, click the Close button.

② If you have finished using Outlook for now and are working in a Workgroup environment, on the File menu, click Exit And Log Off. If you are working in an Internet only environment, on the File menu, click Exit.

Lesson 7 Quick Reference

To	Do this	Button
Schedule a detailed appointment	On the Outlook Bar, click the Calendar shortcut, and then click the New Appointment button. On the Appointment form, type information in the appropriate boxes, select options, and then on the Appointment form Standard toolbar, click the Save And Close button.	New ▾
Schedule a private appointment	Select and double-click the time slot you want. On the Appointment form, type information in the appropriate boxes. In the lower-right corner, select the Private check box, and then click the Save And Close button.	
Schedule an event	On the Actions menu, click New All-Day Event. On the Event form, type information in the boxes, and then click the Save And Close button.	

Lesson 7 Quick Reference

To	Do this
Schedule an all-day appointment	Select and double-click the time slot you want. On the Appointment form, change the start and end times to show a full workday. Type any additional information, and then click the Save And Close button.
Schedule a recurring appointment	Select the appropriate time slot. Double-click the time slot. On the Appointment form, click the Recurrence button. On the Appointment Recurrence form, select the options that you want, and click OK. On the Appointment form, type additional information in the boxes, and then click the Save And Close button.
Make an existing appointment recurring	Double-click an appointment. On the Appointment form, click the Recurrence button. On the Appointment Recurrence form, select the options that you want, and click OK. On the Appointment form, type additional information in the boxes, and then click the Save And Close button.
Move or copy an appointment	Click the left border of the appointment that you want to move, and then drag the appointment to a new date in the Date Navigator. If the appointment needs to be on the same date at a different time slot, drag it to the new time slot.

Lesson 7 Quick Reference

To	Do this	Button
Edit or move a recurring appointment	Open the appointment that you want to edit or move. In the Open Recurring Item dialog box, select Open The Series. On the Recurring Appointment form, click the Recurrence button. Change the time and date as needed, and click OK. On the Appointment form, click the Save And Close button.	
Delete a recurring appointment	Select the appointment to delete. On the Standard toolbar, click the Delete button. In the Confirm Delete dialog box, click Delete All Occurrences, and click OK.	
Find an appointment	On the Standard toolbar, click the Find button. In the Look For box, type a keyword, and then click the Find Now button.	
Set up a reminder notice	Double-click the appointment you want to be reminded about. On the Appointment form, select the Reminder check box, and then in the next box, click the drop-down arrow and select the amount of time prior to the appointment that you want the reminder to appear. Click the Save And Close button.	
Set reminder options for new appointments	On the Tools menu, click Options, and then click the Preferences tab. In the Calendar area, select the Default Reminder check box, and then enter how long before the appointment you want the reminder to occur. Click OK.	

Managing Your Calendar

7

Lesson 7 Quick Reference

To	Do this	Button
Attach a document to an appointment	Double-click the time slot you want for the appointment. On the Appointment form, type the appropriate information. On the Appointment form Standard toolbar, click the Insert File button. Locate and double-click the file that you want to attach. Click the Save And Close button.	
Save an appointment in vCalendar format	Select the appointment that you want to save in vCalendar format. On the File menu, click Save As. In the Save As dialog box, in the Save In drop-down list, locate the folder where you want to save the file. In the File Name box, type the filename. In the Save As Type box, click the drop-down arrow, select vCalendar, and then click the Save button.	
Add appointments to categories	On the Standard toolbar, click the Organize button, and then click the Using Categories link. In the Add Appointment Selected Below To drop-down list, select a category. In the Appointment area, select an appointment, and then click the Add button. Select other categories or appointments as needed, and click the Add button each time. To view related groups of appointments, on the Ways to Organize Your Calendar panel, click the Using Views link. On the Using Views page, in the Change Your View list, select By Category. Click the plus sign (+) next to the category you want to view.	

Lesson 7 Quick Reference

To	Do this
Set up your work week days and hours	On the Tools menu, click Options, and then click the Preferences tab. Click the Calendar Options button, and select the options for days and times that you want. Click OK twice to close the dialog boxes.
Display appointments with end times and as clocks	On the View menu, point to Current View, and then click Customize Current View. Click the Other Settings button, and then in the Week and Month areas, be sure that the Show End Time and the Show Time As Clock check boxes are selected. Click OK twice to close the dialog boxes.
Change the current time zone	On the Tools menu, click Options, and then click the Preferences tab. Click the Calendar Options button, and then click the Time Zone button. In the Current Time Zone area, type a description in the Label box, then in the Time Zone box, click the drop-down arrow, and select the time zone that you want to view. To adjust your computer clock to automatically adjust for Daylight Saving Time changes, select the Adjust For Daylight Saving Time check box. Click OK three times to close the dialog boxes.
Add an additional time zone in Calendar	On the Tools menu, click Options, and then click the Preferences tab. Click the Calendar Options button, and then click the Time Zone button. Select the Show An Additional Time Zone check box. In the Label box, type a description. In the Time Zone box, click the drop-down arrow, and then select the time zone that you want to add. Click OK three times to close the dialog boxes.
Add a country's holidays to your Calendar	On the Tools menu, click Options, and then click the Preferences tab. Click the Calendar Options button, and then click the Add Holidays button. Select the check box next to each country whose holidays you want to add, and click OK three times to close the dialog boxes.

Managing Your Calendar

7

Lesson 7 Quick Reference

To	Do this
Copy Outlook information to the Timex Data Link Watch	Install the software included with the Timex Data Link Watch on your hard disk. Start Outlook, and then on the File menu, click Import And Export. In the Choose An Action To Perform box, select Export To The Timex Data Link Watch, and then click the Next button. Continue to click the Next button to move through the Import And Export Wizard and specify export options. Click the Finish button. Hold the watch in front of the screen as directed, and click OK. If the export was successful, in the message box that appears, click Yes. If the export was unsuccessful, try again or see the Timex Data Link Watch troubleshooting instructions.

LESSON

8

Managing Meetings and Events

ESTIMATED TIME
30 min.

In this lesson you will learn how to:

- ✔ *Plan and schedule meetings.*
- ✔ *Respond to meeting requests.*
- ✔ *Verify attendee responses.*
- ✔ *Reschedule or modify a meeting already on your Calendar.*
- ✔ *Respond to meeting requests automatically.*
- ✔ *Set up events.*
- ✔ *Set up a NetMeeting.*

Planning and managing meetings can be a time-consuming process. You need to contact attendees, determine their availability, find a location, and coordinate logistical details such as projection equipment, refreshments, and handouts. Outlook helps you organize and manage all these activities, allowing you to concentrate on the content of the meeting.

As an account manager at Impact Public Relations, you plan and manage numerous meetings with your clients. In this lesson, you learn how to set up one-time, all-day, and recurring meetings, and how to update meeting information, respond to meeting requests, and create new events.

Getting Ready for the Lesson

In this exercise, you start Outlook 2000 and prepare the practice files and folders that you need.

Start Outlook and copy the practice files

1 On the desktop, double-click the Microsoft Outlook 2000 icon.

Outlook 2000 opens.

2 If necessary, maximize the Outlook window.

Maximize

> # important
>
> Before proceeding to the next step, you must have installed this book's practice folder on your hard disk from the Outlook 2000 Step by Step CD-ROM and created practice Calendar, Contact, and Inbox folders and shortcuts.

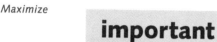

Calendar

3 Click the SBS Practice Calendar shortcut.

4 Drag the practice Calendar files, indicated by calendar icons, from the Lesson08 folder in the Outlook 2000 SBS Practice folder to your SBS Practice Calendar folder in the Folder List.

For a detailed example of how to copy practice files to a practice folder, see the exercise "Set Up Practice E-mail" in Lesson 1.

5 Drag the practice Contacts files, indicated by address card icons, from the Lesson08 folder in the Outlook 2000 SBS Practice folder to your SBS Practice Contacts folder in the Folder List.

6 Drag the practice meeting request file (Plans For The Next Millennium), indicated by an envelope icon, from the Lesson08 folder in the Outlook 2000 SBS Practice folder to your SBS Practice Inbox folder in the Folder List.

Using E-mail to Plan a Meeting

To display the Folder List, on the View menu, click Folder List.

E-mail is an important tool for planning meetings. Whether you are communicating within a Workgroup environment on a company intranet or externally over the Internet, you can use e-mail to invite meeting attendees from a variety of different locations, as well as to schedule a room and other meeting resources.

When you plan a meeting with Outlook, you send a *meeting request*, a special type of e-mail message, to each invited attendee or resource. As you receive the responses in your Inbox, they are automatically tallied by Outlook for a quick summary of the results. In your work as an Impact Public Relations account manager, you often need to hold meetings with colleagues and clients who are scattered across the United States and sometimes around the world. In this section, you organize a meeting, schedule a location, turn an appointment into a meeting, and create a meeting request from a Contacts card.

important

In the next exercises, you have been provided with the names of several fictitious people to help you practice planning a meeting. You can also use coworkers and plan an actual meeting. If you do, use the Global Address List or the Contacts list rather than the SBS Practice Contacts list to find contact names.

Organize a meeting

A meeting is an appointment to which you invite other people.

In this exercise, you organize a meeting to plan a promotional campaign strategy. You select who will attend and describe the subject.

1 On the Outlook Bar, click the SBS Practice Calendar shortcut.

The SBS Practice Calendar appears in the Information viewer.

2 On the Actions menu, click Plan A Meeting.

The Plan A Meeting dialog box appears. Your screen should look similar to the following illustration, except that your name will appear on the form instead of Fran Wilson's name.

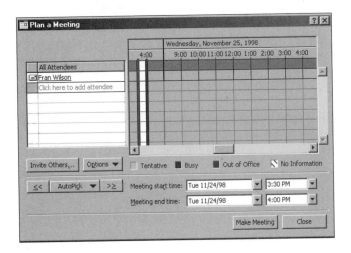

3 In the Plan A Meeting dialog box, click the Invite Others button.

The Select Attendees And Resources dialog box appears, with Global Address List listed in the Show Names From The box.

Your screen should look similar to the following illustration.

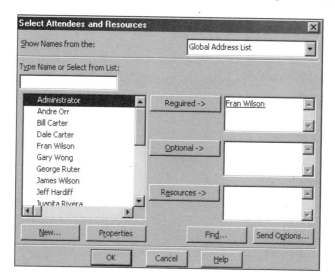

❹ In the Select Attendees And Resources dialog box, in the Show Names From The box, click the drop-down arrow, and then select SBS Practice Contacts.

important

If SBS Practice Contacts is not an available option in the Show Names From The drop-down list, see steps 10 through 15 in the exercise "Getting Ready" in Lesson 5 to learn how to designate the SBS Practice Contacts folder as an Outlook Address Book.

❺ In the Type Name Or Select From List, select Juanita Rivera. Hold down the Ctrl key and select Bill Carter. Click the Required button.

In addition to your own name (Fran Wilson in the above illustration), Juanita Rivera and Bill Carter have now been added to the Required box.

Workgroup

6   In the Type Name Or Select From List box, select Gary Wong, and then click the Optional button.

Gary is added to the Optional box.

7   Click OK.

The Select Attendees And Resources dialog box closes, and the Plan A Meeting dialog box reappears.

8   In the Plan A Meeting dialog box, click the Make Meeting button.

A new Meeting form appears with your attendee selections already filled in. Your screen should look similar to the following illustration.

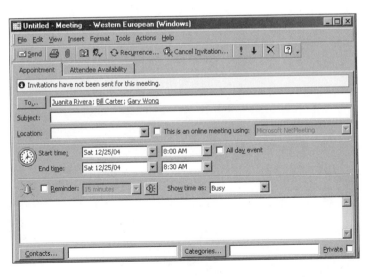

9   On the Meeting form, in the Subject box, type **Strategy Planning**

Determine attendee availability and send a meeting request

In this exercise, you review attendee availability for the promotional campaign strategy meeting, decide on the best time for everyone to attend, and send a meeting request.

Because you are working with fictitious characters, their schedules won't appear. If you invite colleagues in your office workgroup to help you with this lesson, their schedules will appear here.

❶ On the Attendee Availability tab, click the Show Attendee Availability option.

Your screen should look similar to the following illustration. Diagonal lines in the rows next to some names indicate schedules that are not available for viewing.

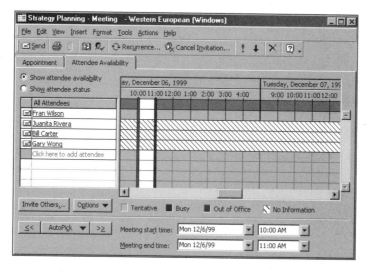

If attendees are located in another time zone, their busy times are adjusted to be displayed correctly in your time zone.

❷ On the Attendee Availability tab, click the scroll arrows to scroll through the invitees' schedules to find a free time that is convenient for everyone.

A person's busy times are indicated by a blue bar in the appropriate time slot next to his or her name. If a person is planning to be out of the office, a purple bar is displayed during the time he or she will be away. A light blue box indicates that a tentative meeting is planned for that time.

tip

AutoPick is a feature that automatically compares available free time in the schedules of meeting invitees and then finds the first time slot when all are free to attend. To use AutoPick, on the Meeting Request form, click the Attendee Availability tab, and then click the AutoPick button.

③ Click the Appointment tab, and in the Meeting Start Time box, click the drop-down arrow, scroll to December 2004, and then click December 6.

④ In the Start Time box, select 10:00 A.M., and then in the End Time box, select 12:00 P.M.

⑤ In the Location box, type **Conference Room** and then click the Send button.

A message appears, stating that meeting responses will not be tallied since the meeting is not in your main Calendar folder. In your actual use of Outlook, you would place meetings in your main Calendar folder, and responses would be tallied for a quick summary of results.

important

Throughout this book, you send e-mail messages to fictitious people. After you send an e-mail message, you will be notified that your message is nondeliverable. You can ignore this and continue with the lesson.

⑥ Click OK.

If you are using coworkers to practice planning a meeting, the Meeting form closes, and a meeting request is sent to each attendee. If you are using fictitious people, the meeting request cannot be sent, and you will have to click the Close button to return to the SBS Practice Calendar Information viewer. If a message box appears prompting you to save the changes, click Yes. If a message box appears, prompting you to send the message, click No. Click the Close button on any other message as they appear.

Turn an appointment into a meeting

For a demonstration of how to organize a meeting, in the Multimedia folder on the Microsoft Outlook 2000 Step by Step CD-ROM, double-click the Organize icon.

You invite Juanita Rivera to a luncheon you've arranged with Bill Carter to discuss publishing possibilities. In this exercise, you convert an appointment with Bill into a meeting with Juanita as well.

① In the Date Navigator, scroll to December 2004, click December 9, and then double-click the Lunch With Bill Carter appointment.

The Appointment form for the Lunch With Bill Carter appointment appears.

② On the Appointment form, click the Attendee Availability tab, and then click the Invite Others button.

The Select Attendees And Resources dialog box appears.

③ In the Select Attendees And Resources dialog box, in the Show Names From The box, click the drop-down arrow and select SBS Practice Contacts.

4 In the Type Name Or Select From List box, select Juanita Rivera, and then click the Required button.

Juanita Rivera appears in the list of Required attendees on the right.

5 Click OK.

The title bar of the Appointment form changes to show that it is now a Meeting form.

6 On the Meeting form Standard toolbar, click the Send button.

A Microsoft Outlook message appears, stating that meeting responses will not be tallied since the meeting is not in your main Calendar folder. In your actual use of Outlook, you would place meetings in your main Calendar folder and responses would therefore be tallied.

7 Click OK.

If you are using coworkers to practice planning a meeting, the Meeting form closes, and a meeting request is sent to each attendee. If you are using fictitious people, the meeting request cannot be sent, and you will have to click the Close button to return to the SBS Practice Calendar Information viewer. If a message box prompts you to save the changes, click Yes. If a message box prompts you to send the message, click No. Ignore any other messages by clicking the Close button on each box as it appears.

tip

To quickly turn an appointment into a meeting, in the Appointment area, select the appointment and right-click the blue border. On the shortcut menu that appears, click New Meeting Request. On the Meeting form, type the meeting subject, and then click the To button. In the Select Attendees And Resources dialog box, select the names of attendees and choose whether they are Required or Optional, and click OK. On the Appointment form, click the Send button.

Create a meeting request from a Contacts card

You can quickly and easily schedule a meeting using a Contacts card. In this exercise, you use Juanita Rivera's Contacts card to request a meeting with her.

1 On the Outlook Bar, click the SBS Practice Contacts shortcut.

The Contacts list appears in the Information viewer.

2 In the Contacts list, double-click the Contacts card for Juanita Rivera.

The Contact form for Juanita Rivera appears.

3 On the Contact form, click the Actions menu, and then click New Meeting Request To Contact.

A Meeting form appears with Juanita Rivera's contact information already completed.

4 On the Meeting form, in the Subject box, type **Southwest Art Books** and then in the Location box, type **DaVinci Library**

5 In the first Start Time box, click the drop-down arrow and select December 17, 2004. In the second box, click the drop-down arrow and select 1:00 P.M. In the second End Meeting box, click the drop-down arrow and select 3:00 P.M.

6 On the Message form Standard toolbar, click the Send button.

The Meeting form closes. In your actual use of Outlook, the meeting request would be sent to the invitee(s).

7 Close the Contact form.

Responding to Meeting Requests

Meeting requests are a special type of e-mail message sent to you by others in your workgroup. If you accept a request electronically, Outlook automatically enters the meeting in your Calendar.

Outlook provides three options for responding to a meeting request:

- You can *accept* the meeting request, letting the sender know that you are available and plan to attend. The meeting is entered in your Calendar.

- You can send a *tentative* acceptance. Outlook also enters these meetings in your Calendar.

- If you know you are unable to attend a meeting, you can *decline*.

Because a meeting request is a special type of e-mail message, it appears in your Inbox folder, rather than in your Calendar folder.

Accepting a meeting request

In this exercise, you receive and accept a meeting request from Peter Stout.

1 On the Outlook Bar, click the SBS Practice Inbox shortcut.

2 Double-click the meeting request from Peter Stout titled Plans For The Next Millennium.

The Meeting form appears.

Calendar

3 To view the meeting in your Calendar before you respond, on the Meeting form Standard toolbar, click the Calendar button.

Your Calendar appears in a new window, with the requested meeting in place on the desired date.

Close

4 In the Calendar window, click the Close button.

The Calendar window closes.

5 On the Meeting form, click the Accept button.

A Microsoft Outlook dialog box appears, prompting you to include comments with your response.

6 Click the Send The Response Now option, and click OK.

The Meeting form closes, and your response is sent. The meeting is automatically entered in your Calendar. (Ignore any warning messages by clicking the Close button on each message box as it appears.)

Verify attendee responses

After you send a meeting request, you can view the responses from people you have invited as they arrive in your Inbox. In this exercise, you practice verifying attendee response to your earlier Strategy Planning meeting request. (There cannot, of course, actually be responses from the fictitious persons used in these exercises.)

1 On the Tools menu, click Options.

The Options dialog box appears.

2 In the Options dialog box, click the Preferences tab, and then click the E-mail Options button.

The E-mail Options dialog box appears.

3 In the E-mail Options dialog box, click the Tracking Options button.

Your screen should look similar to the following illustration.

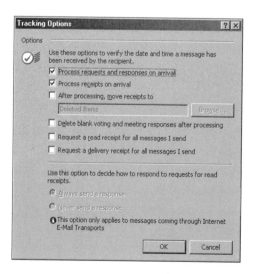

4 In the Tracking Options dialog box, select the Process Requests And Responses On Arrival check box and click OK.

Responses to your meeting request will be automatically recorded.

5 In the E-mail Options dialog box, click OK; and then in the Options dialog box, click OK.

The two dialog boxes close.

6 Click the SBS Practice Calendar shortcut. In the Date Navigator, scroll to December 2004, click December 6, and then double-click the Strategy Planning appointment in the Appointment area.

The Meeting form appears.

7 Click the Attendee Availability tab, and then click the Show Attendee Status option.

If this were an actual Meeting request, the invitee responses would be tabulated here as they arrive.

8 On the Meeting form, click the Close button. If a message box appears, prompting you to send the request, click No.

The Meeting form closes.

Changing Meeting Information After Sending the Invitation

After reviewing the responses to your initial meeting request, you might discover that in order for everyone to attend, you need to change some of the meeting parameters, such as when it will be held. Outlook makes it simple to revise your plans.

In this exercise, you reschedule a meeting and then decide to revise the list of attendees.

Reschedule a meeting

Because there is a conflict with another meeting, you reschedule a meeting with Juanita Rivera to later in the day.

1 Click the SBS Practice Calendar, and in the Date Navigator, scroll to December 2004, click December 6, and double-click the Strategy Planning meeting at 10:00 A.M.

The Meeting form for the meeting appears.

2 On the Appointment tab, in the Start Time box, select or type **2:30 P.M.** and then in the End Time box, select or type **4:00 P.M.**

Managing Meetings and Events   8

❸ On the Meeting form Standard toolbar, click the Send Update button.

A Microsoft Outlook message appears, stating that meeting responses will not be tallied since the meeting is not in your main Calendar folder. In your actual use of Outlook, you would place meetings in your main Calendar folder and responses would therefore be tallied.

❹ Click OK.

If you are using coworkers to practice planning a meeting, the Meeting form closes, and a meeting request is sent to each attendee. If you are using fictitious people, the meeting request cannot be sent, and you will have to click the Close button to return to the SBS Practice Calendar Information viewer. If a message box appears, prompting you to save the changes, click Yes. If a message box appears, prompting you to send the message, click No. Ignore any other messages by clicking the Close button on each box as it appears.

Remove or add attendees

Bill Carter can't attend your Strategy Planning meeting with Juanita Rivera. In this exercise, you remove him from the meeting list and add James Wilson in his place.

❶ In the Date Navigator, scroll to December 2004, click December 6, and double-click the Strategy Planning appointment.

The Meeting form appears.

❷ On the Meeting form, click the Attendee Availability tab, and then click the Show Attendee Status option.

A table listing each attendee name, status, and response to the meeting request appears.

❸ In the Name column, select Bill Carter, and then press the Delete key to clear his name.

To change an attendee's Required or Optional status, click the Attendance box for the name. When the drop-down arrow appears, select the status you want.

❹ Click the Click Here To Add Attendee box, and then in the Name column, type **James Wilson** and press Enter.

The Show Attendee Status table reappears. The default setting Required Attendee is displayed for James Wilson in the Attendance column.

❺ On the Meeting form Standard toolbar, click the Send Update button.

A Microsoft Outlook message appears stating that meeting responses will not be tallied since the meeting is not in your main Calendar folder. In your actual use of Outlook, you would place meetings in your main Calendar folder and responses would therefore be tallied.

❻ Click OK.

If you are using coworkers to practice planning a meeting, the Meeting form closes, and a meeting request is sent to each attendee. If you are using fictitious people, the meeting request cannot be sent, and you will have to click the Close button to return to the SBS Practice Calendar Information viewer. If a message box appears, prompting you to save the changes, click Yes. If a message box appears, prompting you to send the message, click No. Ignore any other messages by clicking the Close button on each box as it appears.

Managing Meeting Requests Automatically

Workgroup

Responding to a multitude of meeting requests can be time-consuming, but Outlook enables you to overcome this problem. You can set up your Calendar to automatically accept requests that fit into your schedule and reject requests that conflict with the commitments that you already have.

Accept or decline meeting requests automatically

In this exercise, you set Outlook to automatically accept meeting requests and decline conflicting meeting requests.

1 On the Tools menu, click Options.

The Options dialog box appears.

2 In the Options dialog box, on the Preferences tab, click the Calendar Options button.

The Calendar Options dialog box appears.

3 In the Calendar Options dialog box, click the Resource Scheduling button.

The Resource Scheduling dialog box appears.

4 In the Resource Scheduling dialog box, select the Automatically Accept Meeting Requests And Process Cancellations check box, and then select the Automatically Decline Conflicting Meeting Requests check box.

5 In the Resource Scheduling dialog box, click OK; in the Calendar Options dialog box, click OK; and in the Options dialog box, click OK.

The three dialog boxes close. If Outlook responds to a meeting request for you, you will be notified that you have new e-mail, and an e-mail message about the meeting will be in your Inbox.

See Lesson 1, "Jumping Into Your E-mail," for information on how to delete messages from your Inbox.

Delete meeting requests after responding

After you have responded to a meeting request, it will remain in your Inbox like any other message. To clear out your Inbox, you can manually delete the meeting request from your Inbox or you can have Outlook automatically delete it for you. In this exercise, you set Outlook to automatically delete meeting requests after you have responded to them.

The Options dialog box is available by clicking Options on the Tools menu when you are working in the Inbox, Calendar, Contacts, Journal, Tasks, or Notes Information viewers.

1 On the Tools menu, click Options.

The Options dialog box appears.

2 In the Options dialog box, click the Preferences tab, and then click the E-mail Options button.

The E-mail Options dialog box appears.

3 In the E-mail Options dialog box, click the Advanced E-mail Options button.

The Advanced E-mail Options dialog box appears.

4 In the Advanced E-mail Options dialog box, in the When Sending A Message area, select the Delete Meeting Request From Inbox When Responding check box.

5 In the Advanced E-mail Options dialog box, click OK; in the E-mail Options dialog box, click OK; and in the Options dialog box, click OK.

The three dialog boxes close.

Setting Up an Event

In Outlook, an *event* is defined as an activity that lasts all day, with the time flagged as free rather than busy. No one is specifically invited to it, although resources might be allocated for it. An open house is an example of an event since individual people are not invited to attend, whereas a formal cocktail party with a specific invitation list would be considered a meeting. Annual events include birthdays, holidays, days of religious observance, anniversaries, the company picnic, the annual meeting, and so on.

Create an annual event

In this exercise, you schedule an annual event for Five Lakes Publishing's annual meeting.

1 In the Date Navigator, scroll to December 2004, and then click December 17.

2 On the Actions menu, click New All Day Event.

A blank Event form appears.

3 On the Event form, in the Subject box, type **Five Lakes Publishing Annual Meeting**

4 In the Location box, type **Headquarters Auditorium**

5 On the Event form Standard toolbar, click the Recurrence button.

The Appointment Recurrence dialog box appears.

⑥　In the Appointment Recurrence dialog box, in the Recurrence Pattern area, click Yearly, and then click the option for Every December 17. Click OK.

The Appointment Recurrence dialog box closes.

⑦　On the Event form Standard toolbar, click the Save And Close button.

The Event form closes.

⑧　To view the event for the following year, in the Date Navigator, scroll to December 2005, and then click December 17.

The event now appears in your Calendar on the correct day.

tip

Events are defined as lasting from midnight to midnight, with the time flagged as free. You can change an event into an appointment, with the time blocked out in your Calendar. Double-click the event banner at the top of the appropriate date. When the Open Recurring Item dialog box appears, select Just This Occurrence, and click OK. When the Event form appears, clear the All Day Event check box. The Event form changes to an Appointment form. Complete the start and end dates and times.

One Step Further

Setting Up an Online Meeting with Microsoft NetMeeting

NetMeeting, a program that comes with Microsoft Internet Explorer, enables you to conduct online meetings via the Internet. NetMeeting expands your communication capabilities to include both video and audio conferences with one or more people. It is often used for real-time document collaboration, technical support in a Help Desk environment, training and distance learning, and remote meetings. With NetMeeting, you can see what other meeting participants are holding in their hands, share applications and documents, draw with others on an electronic whiteboard, or transfer files.

During a NetMeeting, two or more participants can confer at the same time using one or several modes of communication, including:

- Interactive e-mail, which allows each participant to see what others are typing as they type
- Audio or video, if your computer has the required hardware
- Interactive file sharing, in which others can see a Microsoft program as you work in it or use the program themselves.

important

You can use NetMeeting without the audio features. To take full advantage of the audio and video capabilities of NetMeeting, you need a camera, video card, audio card, speakers, and a microphone. Without a camera, you can view other people's video, but they cannot view yours.

Schedule an online meeting

In this exercise, you decide to take full advantage of NetMeeting's capabilities to arrange an online planning session for the Five Lakes Publishing Annual Meeting.

important

You must have NetMeeting version 2.1 or later installed for this procedure to work.

To select names from the Address Book, click the To button.

❶ Be sure that the SBS Practice Calendar is open, and on the File menu, point to New, and then click Meeting Request.

A blank Meeting form appears.

❷ On the Meeting form, select the This Is An Online Meeting Using check box.

The NetMeeting conference name will be the same as your entry in the Subject box and can be changed only on this tab.

❸ In the box next to the This Is An Online Meeting Using check box, be sure that Microsoft NetMeeting is selected.

❹ In the To box, enter one or more fictitious names, or the names of people who have agreed to help you with this exercise.

❺ In the Subject box, type **Annual Meeting Planning Session**

❻ In the Start Time box, and then in the End Time box, enter tomorrow's date and the times that you want to use for the NetMeeting.

You can get the information you need to enter in the Directory Server box from your system administrator or your Internet service provider.

❼ In the Directory Server box, enter the requested information, and then next to the Directory Server box, click the Automatically Start NetMeeting With Reminder check box.

Outlook will now provide you with a reminder prior to the NetMeeting and will automatically connect to the Internet at the scheduled time.

❽ Click the Reminder option, and in the Reminder box, enter the number of minutes prior to the meeting that you want the reminder to appear.

❾ On the Meeting form Standard toolbar, click the Send button.

A Microsoft Outlook message appears, stating that the reminder for the meeting will not appear since the meeting is not in your main Calendar folder.

❿ Click Yes.

A Microsoft Outlook message appears, stating that meeting responses will not be tallied since the meeting is not in your main Calendar folder. In your actual use of Outlook, you would place meetings in your main Calendar folder and responses would therefore be tallied.

⑪ Click the OK button.

The Meeting form closes, and a meeting request is sent to each attendee. If you are using fictitious people, the meeting request cannot be sent, and you will have to click the Close button to return to the SBS Practice Calendar Information viewer. If a message box appears, prompting you to save the changes, click Yes. If a message box appears, prompting you to send the message, click No. Ignore any other messages by clicking the Close button on each box as it appears.

Finish the lesson

❶ To continue to the next lesson, on the Outlook Bar, click the Tasks shortcut.

❷ If you have finished using Outlook for now and are working in a Workgroup environment, click File, and then click Exit And Log Off. If you are working in an Internet only environment, click File, and then click Exit.

Lesson 8 Quick Reference

To	Do this
Organize a meeting	On the Outlook Bar, click the Calendar shortcut, and then on the Actions menu, click Plan A Meeting. Click the Invite Others button. In the Select Attendees And Resources dialog box, in the Show Names From The box, click the drop-down arrow, and then select Contacts. In the Type Name Or Select From List box, enter or select contact names, and then click either the Required button, the Optional button, or the Resource button for each name. Click OK. In the Plan A Meeting dialog box, click the Make Meeting button, and then type a subject in the Subject box.
Determine attendee availability and send a meeting request	In the Appointment area, double-click a meeting. Click the Attendee Availability tab, and then select Show Attendee Availability. Scroll to find a free time for each person listed. Click the Appointment tab, enter start and end times, and enter a location. Select other preferred options, and then on the Meeting form Standard toolbar, click the Send button.

Managing Meetings and Events 8

Lesson 8 Quick Reference

To	Do this
Turn an appointment into a meeting	Double-click the appointment, and then, on the Appointment form, click the Attendee Availability tab. Click the Invite Others button. Select or type attendee names and resources, and then click the Required button, the Optional button, or the Resource button for each attendee and resource. Click OK. Change the meeting's start and end times, if necessary. Click the Appointment tab, and then type the location. Click the Send button.
Create a meeting request from a Contacts card	On the Outlook Bar, click the Contacts shortcut. In the Contacts list, double-click the name of the contact. On the Contact form, click the Actions menu, and then click New Meeting Request To Contact. In the Subject box, type a description. Enter a location and start and end times. Select other options, and then click the Send button.
Respond to a meeting request	On the Outlook Bar, click the Inbox shortcut. Double-click the meeting request. To view the meeting in your Calendar before you respond, on the Meeting form Standard toolbar, click the Calendar button. In the Appointment area, double-click the appointment, and then on the Meeting form, click either the Accept button, the Tentative button, or the Decline button. Enter comments if necessary. Click the Send The Response Now option, and click OK.
Verify attendee responses	On the Tools menu, click Options. Click the Preferences tab, and then click the E-mail Options button. In the E-mail Options dialog box, click the Tracking Options button. In the Tracking Options dialog box, select the Process Requests And Responses On Arrival check box, and click OK three times to close the dialog boxes. To view the results, click the Calendar shortcut, double-click the meeting, click the Attendee Availability tab, and then click the Show Attendee Status option.

Lesson 8 Quick Reference

To	Do this
Reschedule a meeting	Double-click the meeting. On the Appointment tab, select or type changes. On the Meeting form Standard toolbar, click the Send button, and when prompted to send updates to attendees, click Yes.
Remove or add attendees	Double-click the meeting, click the Attendee Availability tab, and select the Show Attendee Status option. To remove a name, in the Name column, select it and press the Delete key. To add a name, in the Name column, click the Click Here To Add Attendee box, type the new name, and then in the Attendance column, click the box next to the name, click the drop-down arrow that appears, and then select Required, Optional, or Resource. On the Meeting form Standard toolbar, click the Send button, and then when prompted to send updates to attendees, click Yes.
Accept or decline meeting requests automatically	On the Tools menu, click Options. Click the Preferences tab, click the Calendar Options button, and then click the Resource Scheduling button. Clear or select the appropriate check boxes. Click OK three times to close the dialog boxes.
Delete meeting requests after responding	On the Tools menu, click Options. Click the Preferences tab, and then click the E-mail Options button. In the E-mailOptions dialog box, click the Advanced E-mail Options button. Select the Delete Meeting Request From Inbox When Responding check box. Click OK three times to close the dialog boxes.
Create an annual event	On the Actions menu, click New All Day Event. On the Event form, in the Subject box, type a description, and then in the Location box, type a location. On the Event form Standard toolbar, click the Recurrence button. If the event lasts more than one day, in the Appointment time area, in the Duration box, select the correct length of time. In the Recurrence

Lesson 8 Quick Reference

To	Do this
	Pattern area, click the length of time for recurrence, and then select the date or day of the year. Click OK, and then click the Save And Close button.
Schedule an online meeting with NetMeeting	Click the Calendar shortcut. On the File menu, point to New, and then click Meeting Request. On the Meeting form, select the This Is An Online Meeting Using check box. In the next box, be sure Microsoft NetMeeting is selected, and then in the To box, enter the names of the people with whom you want to schedule a meeting. Enter the subject, start time, and end time in the appropriate boxes. In the Directory Server box, enter the appropriate information, and then select the Automatically Start NetMeeting With Reminder check box. Click the Reminder option, and then in the Reminder box, enter the number of minutes prior to the meeting that you want the reminder to appear. Click the Send button.

LESSON

9

Taking Charge of Tasks

ESTIMATED TIME
45 min.

In this lesson you will learn how to:

✔ *Create tasks.*

✔ *View your Task list.*

✔ *Find and edit a task.*

✔ *Set task reminders.*

✔ *Assign tasks to others.*

✔ *Send task information to others.*

✔ *Organize your Task list.*

✔ *Track tasks assigned to others and receive status reports.*

Taking Charge of Tasks

Before the advent of the personal computer, most people kept track of what they had to do by maintaining a to-do list in a pocket or purse. In Outlook, you can use Tasks to replace such lists. Using Tasks greatly improves your ability to manage your many duties by serving as an online project assistant. With Tasks, you can break a big project into manageable portions, assign the portions to the appropriate persons, and automatically track progress on the assignments. The time and energy that you free up can go instead into higher-level decisions, planning, and management.

In this lesson, as an Impact Public Relations account manager, you will practice managing your tasks with Outlook as you help your clients plan for the American Booksellers Association trade show. You will view your tasks, add tasks to the Task list, assign tasks to others, and add tasks to your Calendar. You will also use categories and rules to customize the way you organize tasks to better suit your own work style.

Getting Ready for the Lesson

In this exercise, you start Outlook 2000, prepare the practice files and folders that you need, and then copy the files to the appropriate folders.

Start Outlook and copy the practice files

1 On the desktop, double-click the Microsoft Outlook 2000 icon.

The Microsoft Outlook screen appears.

2 If necessary, maximize the Outlook window.

Maximize

3 On the Outlook Bar, click the SBS Practice Inbox shortcut.

important

Before proceeding to the next step, you must have installed this book's practice folder on your hard disk and created a practice Inbox and Contacts folder and shortcut. Because task requests and task updates are special forms of e-mail, all practice files for this lesson will be copied into the practice Inbox.

For a detailed example of how to copy practice files to a practice folder, see the exercise "Set Up Practice E-mail" in Lesson 1.

4 Drag the practice Contacts files, indicated by address card icons, from the Lesson09 folder in the Outlook 2000 SBS Practice folder to your SBS Practice Contacts folder in the Folder List.

5 Drag the remaining practice files, indicated by task icons and envelope icons, from the Lesson09 folder in the Outlook 2000 SBS Practice folder to your SBS Practice Inbox folder in the Folder List.

Starting a Task List

A *task* is defined as an activity that you want to track through to completion. It can occur once or it can repeat (called a *recurring task*). A recurring task can repeat at regular intervals, such as a status report that is due to your CEO on the last workday of every month. It can also repeat based on the date that you mark the task complete each time, such as an inventory that occurs six months from the date that the previous one is completed. You can create a task from either the TaskPad located on your Calendar or by entering it in the Task list, which appears when you click the Tasks shortcut or folder.

Create a recurring task

As an account manager for Impact Public Relations, you handle publicity for several publishing companies. It's time to go into high gear preparing for the American Booksellers Association trade show, and you have to prepare a booklist of all your clients' titles as part of the process. Because you expect to prepare for the ABA trade show every year, you decide to make it a recurring, annual task. In this exercise, you enter the task into your Task list.

New Task

1 On the Outlook Bar, click the Tasks shortcut, and then on the Standard toolbar, click the New Task button.

A blank Task form appears.

2 On the Task form, in the Subject box, type **Prepare booklist for exhibit**

3 In the Due Date box, select the contents, and then type **May 1, 2005**

4 On the Task form Standard toolbar, click the Recurrence button.

The Task Recurrence dialog box appears.

Do not click Regenerate New Task, or the task will not recur at regular intervals.

5 In the Task Recurrence dialog box, in the Recurrence Pattern area, select the Yearly option, and then select Every May 1 as the option for the recurrence. Click OK.

The Task Recurrence dialog box closes.

6 On the Task form Standard toolbar, click the Save And Close button.

The Task form closes. The new task appears on your Task list.

tip

To quickly add a task in the Task list, right-click a blank area of the list, and then select New Task from the shortcut menu. Type a task name, and press Enter.

Creating a detailed task allows you to record more information about the task, including subject, status, due date, priority, percent complete, and assigned categories.

Create a detailed task

An annual trade show is a complex, large-scale event requiring unwavering attention to details and deft coordination. As an account manager, you also serve as a publicist for your publishing clients, and much of this work falls to you. In this exercise, you create a detailed task to find out how many authors are bringing their families with them on their working vacations.

❶ On the View menu, point to Current View, and be sure that Detailed List is checked.

The Detailed List view is displayed.

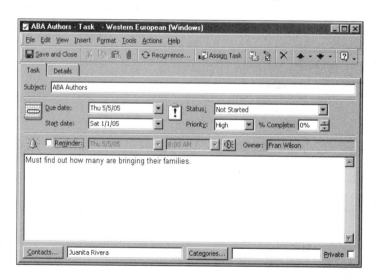

❷ On the Standard toolbar, click the New Task button.

A blank Task form appears.

❸ On the Task form, in the Subject box, type **ABA Authors**

The start date for your task specifies when you want to initiate your activities, and the due date specifies when the task is to be completed.

❹ In the Due Date box, select the contents, type **5/5/05**, and press Enter.

The date May 5, 2005, is displayed in the Due Date box.

❺ In the Start Date box, select the contents, type **1/1/05**, and press Enter.

The date January 1, 2005, is displayed in the Start Date box.

❻ In the Priority box, select High.

❼ In the Comment area, type the following:

Must find out how many are bringing their families.

❽ In the Contacts box, type **Juanita Rivera**

Your screen should look similar to the following illustration.

❾ Click the Details tab, and then in the Companies box, type **Ramona Publishing**

❿ On the Task form Standard toolbar, click the Save And Close button.

The new task appears in your Task list.

Create a recurring task based on completion date

Some tasks need to recur after a set amount of time, counting from the date on which they are completed, which can vary. In this exercise, you create a recurring task to write a report summarizing the events of the trade show. The report is due one month after the convention is over.

1 On the Standard toolbar, click the New Task button.

A blank Task form appears.

2 On the Task form, in the Subject box, type **Report on the ABA**

3 In the Due Date box, select the contents, and then type **6/27/05**

4 On the Task form Standard toolbar, click the Recurrence button.

The Task Recurrence dialog box appears.

5 In the Task Recurrence dialog box, in the Recurrence Pattern area, select the Yearly option.

6 In the Recurrence Pattern area, select the Regenerate New Task option, and then be sure that the box displays 1 for Year(s) After Each Task Is Completed.

7 Click OK.

The Task Recurrence dialog box closes.

8 On the Task form Standard toolbar, click the Save And Close button.

The Task form closes. The new task appears on your Task list.

Create a task from an e-mail message

You received an e-mail message from Juanita Rivera asking you to update her authors on the events at the ABA that they need to attend. In this exercise, you turn this message into a task and put it on your Task list.

1 On the Outlook Bar, click the SBS Practice Inbox shortcut.

The contents of the SBS Practice Inbox are displayed in the Information viewer.

2 Select the ABA Update message from Juanita Rivera, and drag it onto the Tasks shortcut on the Outlook Bar.

A Task form appears. The ABA Update is displayed in the Subject box, and the text of the e-mail message is displayed in the Comment area. A copy of the message remains in the SBS Practice Inbox.

3 On the Task form, in the Due Date box, select the contents, and then type **Next week**

Tasks

④ On the Task form Standard toolbar, click the Save And Close button.
The Task form closes.

⑤ On the Outlook Bar, click the Tasks shortcut.
The new task has been added to your Task list.

Viewing Your Tasks

You have several options for viewing your Tasks. To use any of the views
in this table, on the Outlook Bar, click the Tasks shortcut. On the View
menu, point to Current View, and then click the view that you want. All
views show the subject and due date. Some views show additional information about each task.

Click this view	To see your tasks
Simple List	In a list that shows subject, due date, and a check box to select once the task is completed.
Detailed List	In a list that shows subject, status, due date, priority, percent complete, and assigned categories.
Active Tasks	That are incomplete (including ones that are overdue).
Next Seven Days	Due in the next seven days.
Overdue Tasks	That are overdue.
By Category	Grouped by category and sorted by due date within each category.
Assignment	Assigned to others, sorted by the task owner's name and due date.
By Person Responsible	Grouped by the task owner's name and sorted by due date for each task owner.
Completed Tasks	Marked complete.
Task Timeline	Represented by icons arranged in chronological order by start date on a timeline. Tasks without start dates are arranged by due date.

Modifying Your Tasks

Because work is dynamic, your tasks may need to be modified after you add
them to your Task list. You can easily locate and revise your tasks to match your
changing needs.

For example, you can:

- Mark a task complete.
- Quickly locate specific tasks in your Task list by using the Find feature.
- Change any detail of a task.
- Create a series of recurring tasks from a single occurrence.
- Skip a single occurrence of a recurring task.
- Cancel the rest of a series of recurring tasks.
- Set task reminders to pop up on your screen before the deadline for a single task or all tasks.
- Restore deleted tasks to your Task list.
- Use a task to create an appointment on your Calendar to prepare or complete the work.

Find a task

In this exercise, you search your Task list for the ABA Authors task.

1 On the View menu, point to Current View, and be sure that Detailed List is checked.

2 On the Standard toolbar, click the Find button.

The Find Items In Tasks panel appears at the top of the Information viewer. Your screen should look similar to the following illustration.

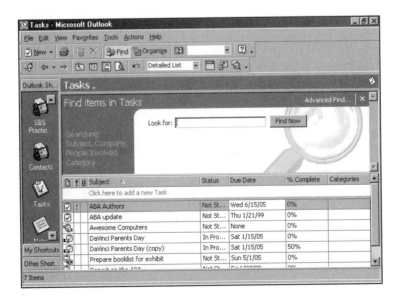

❸ In The Find Items In Tasks panel, in the Look For box, type **authors** and then click the Find Now button.

Done! appears next to the button. The ABA Authors task is displayed in the Task list along with other tasks containing the keyword *authors* as part of their contents.

❹ In the Find Items In Tasks panel, click the Clear Search option.

The entire Task list is displayed again.

Close

❺ In the Find Items In Tasks panel, click the Close button.

Edit a task

In this exercise, you change the due date for the ABA Authors task.

❶ In the Task list, click the Due Date column for the ABA Authors task.

The Due Date cell becomes active, and a drop-down arrow appears next to the entry.

❷ Click the Due Date drop-down arrow.

A calendar showing the current month appears.

❸ In the calendar, scroll until you see the next month, and then click the third Wednesday of that month.

The new due date is displayed in the Task list.

tip

A task can be attached to any other Outlook item by copying it to the appropriate folder, such as Contacts or Calendar. To quickly copy a task to another folder, in the Task list, right-click to select the task and drag it to the Outlook Bar shortcut that you want. On the shortcut menu that appears, click the appropriate Move or Copy command.

Set a reminder for a task

Because of your very busy schedule, your unaided memory may not be very dependable. In this exercise, you set a reminder for your task of preparing the ABA booklist.

❶ In the Task list, double-click the Prepare Booklist For Exhibit task.

The Task form appears.

❷ On the Task form, above the Comment area, be sure that the Reminder check box is selected, and then in the date box, click the drop-down arrow and select April 16, 2005. In the time box, click the drop-down arrow and select 9:00 A.M.

tip
When a task reminder pops up on your screen, you can respond in one of three ways. The Dismiss button closes the reminder, the Open Item button opens the Task form for review, and the Snooze button resets the reminder to appear again. If you click the Snooze button, you can determine when you want the reminder to appear again. In the Click Snooze To Be Reminded Again box, click the drop-down arrow, and then select the amount of time you want before the reminder appears again.

❸ On the Task form Standard toolbar, click the Save And Close button.

The Task form closes. A reminder has been set for 9 A.M., April 16, 2005.

Set reminder options for new tasks

You find reminders to be so useful that you want to have them on all future tasks. In this exercise, you arrange to have a default reminder automatically set for all tasks.

❶ On the Tools menu, click Options.

The Options dialog box appears.

❷ Click the Other tab, and then click the Advanced Options button.

The Advanced Options dialog box appears.

❸ Click the Advanced Tasks button.

The Advanced Options dialog box appears.

The reminder will be set only if a Due Date is entered in the Task form.

❹ Select the Set Reminders On Tasks With Due Dates check box.

Your screen should look similar to the following illustration.

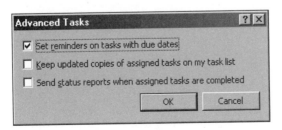

(Side tab) Taking Charge of Tasks   9

When you send a task to someone else, Outlook switches the reminder off so that the person who accepts the task can set one.

5   In the Advanced Tasks dialog box, click OK; in the Advanced Options dialog box, click OK; and then in the Options dialog box, click OK.

The three dialog boxes close, and the Task list reappears.

Change a task into a recurring task

Because you will be responsible for the ABA authors at next year's trade show, in this exercise, you create a recurring task from this year's task.

1   In the Task list, double-click the ABA Authors task.

The Task form appears.

2   On the Task form Standard toolbar, click the Recurrence button.

The Task Recurrence dialog box appears.

3   In the Task Recurrence dialog box, in the Recurrence Pattern area, click Yearly, and click OK.

The Task Recurrence dialog box closes.

4   On the Task form Standard toolbar, click the Save And Close button.

The Task form closes.

Stop a recurring task

Juanita Rivera lets you know that Ramona Publishing has decided to take over the task of coordinating its authors' travel plans for the ABA trade show, so you will not be responsible for that task in the future. In this exercise, you modify that task so that it will no longer appear in your list of future tasks.

1   In the Task list, double-click the ABA Authors task.

The Task form appears.

2   On the Task form, click the Recurrence button.

The Task Recurrence dialog box appears.

3   In the Task Recurrence dialog box, click the Remove Recurrence button.

The Task Recurrence dialog box closes.

4   On the Task form Standard toolbar, click the Save And Close button.

The Task form closes.

Taking Charge of Tasks

9

tip

To skip one occurrence of a recurring task, in the Task list, double-click the recurring task that you want to skip. On the Task form, on the Actions menu, click Skip Occurrence. On the Task form Standard toolbar, click the Save And Close button. The Task form closes, and the next occurrence of the task appears on your Task list.

If you set the recurring task to end after a specific number of occurrences, skipping the task counts as one occurrence.

Mark a task completed

The ABA authors' travel plans have been taken care of for this year and will no longer be your responsibility in the future. In the previous exercise, you stopped the task from recurring in your future Task lists. In this exercise, you mark the current ABA Authors task as completed.

1 In the Task list, right-click the ABA Authors task.

A shortcut menu appears.

2 On the shortcut menu, select Mark Complete.

The Task is marked as completed.

3 On the View menu, point to Current View, and then click Simple List.

The Task list appears with a column containing check boxes. The check box next to the ABA Authors task has been selected and a line has been drawn through the entry title, indicating it is complete.

Delete a task

To delete more than one non-adjacent task at one time, hold down the Ctrl key, select the specific tasks, and then click the Delete button.

Sometimes a task is completely done. You've already marked the ABA Authors task as complete. All that remains is to remove it from your Task list.

Delete

● In the Task list, select the ABA Authors task, and then on the Standard toolbar, click the Delete button.

tip

Deleting a task that you assigned to someone else removes it from your Task list only. The task remains in the Task list of the person who accepted it. However, if you were scheduled to receive status reports for the task, you will no longer receive them.

Retrieve a deleted task

As long as you have not emptied the Deleted Items folder on the Outlook Bar, the deleted task is still available.

Sometimes you might delete a task accidentally. In the following exercise, you retrieve the task you just deleted and restore it to your Task list.

1 On the View menu, click Folder List.

The Folder List appears.

2 On the Outlook Bar, scroll through the shortcut icons if necessary, and then click the Deleted Items shortcut.

The contents of the Deleted Items folder are displayed in the Information viewer.

Deleted items

3 Select the ABA Authors task.

4 Drag the item to the Tasks folder in the Folder List.

If you restore a deleted task that you had assigned to another person, you will not receive status reports, even if you were receiving them before.

5 Click the Tasks shortcut.

The ABA Authors task reappears in the Task list.

Create an appointment from a task

Sometimes completing a task means scheduling some time to do it. You can easily use a task to create an appointment on your Calendar. In this exercise, you schedule an hour to work on the booklist for the ABA exhibit a few days before the task is due to be completed.

1 On the View menu, point to Current View, and be sure that Detailed List is selected.

If you are working in Calendar, you can drag a task directly from the TaskPad to a time slot in the Appointment area.

2 In the Task list, select the Prepare Booklist For Exhibit task, and then drag it to the SBS Practice Calendar shortcut.

An Appointment form appears, with data from the task in the appropriate boxes.

3 On the Appointment form, in the Start Time date box, select the current text and type **April 27, 2005**

4 In the Start Time time box, select the current text and type **2 pm**, and then in the End Time time box, select the current text and type **3 pm**

5 On the Appointment form Standard toolbar, click the Save And Close button.

The Appointment form closes and the Task list reappears.

6 On the Outlook Bar, click the SBS Practice Calendar shortcut, and then on the View menu, click Go To, and then click Go To Date.

The Go To Date dialog box appears.

Your screen should look similar to the following illustration.

7 In the Date box, select the contents, type **April 27, 2005** and click OK.

The Go To Date dialog box closes. The SBS Practice Calendar Information viewer shows the correct day in the Appointment area, with the task scheduled from 2:00 P.M. to 3:00 P.M.

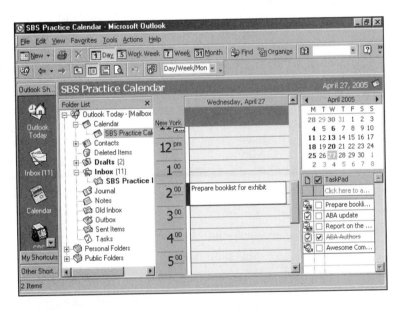

Assigning Tasks to Others

Workgroup

If you use Outlook in a Workgroup environment, task assignments can help you track the work you have assigned to other people for a project. For example, a manager might assign a task to an assistant, or an employee might assign a task to a coworker in a group effort. A task assignment requires at least two people: one to send a task request and another to respond to it.

When you send a task request, you give up ownership of the task. You can keep an updated copy of the task in your Task list and receive status reports, but you cannot change information, such as the due date for the task. Only the owner or temporary owner of a task can update it. If you own a task that was assigned to other people before you accepted it, every time you make a change, it is automatically copied to the task in their Task lists. And when you complete the task, status reports are automatically sent to the other people who were assigned the task and to those who requested reports.

If you assign a task to more than one person at a time, you cannot keep an updated copy of the task in your Task list. To assign work to more than one person and have Outlook keep you up-to-date on work progress, divide the work into separate tasks, and then assign each one individually. For example, to assign a report to three writers, create three tasks named Report: Author 1, Report: Author 2, and Report: Author 3.

Once a task is assigned, Outlook keeps track of who owns the task and when it gets updated. When the owner updates the task, Outlook updates all the copies in the Task lists of the assignees.

Create a new task request

In this exercise, you create and send a task request for your colleague Keith Hafferman to help with the planning and serve as the backup for the arrangements for DaVinci Parents Day, a major promotional and fund-raising event for the school.

1. On the Outlook Bar, click the Tasks shortcut.
2. On the File menu, point to New, and then click Task Request.

    A Task Request form appears.

3. In the To box, type **Keith Hafferman**
4. In the Subject box, type **DaVinci Parents Day**
5. In the Due Date box, select the contents, and then type **January 15, 2005**
6. In the Start Date box, select the contents, and then type **November 20, 2004**
7. In the Status box, click the drop-down arrow, and then select In Progress.
8. Select the Keep An Updated Copy Of This Task On My Task List check box and the Send Me A Status Report When This Task Is Complete check box.
9. In the Comment area, type the following:

    Keith, could you be my backup for these arrangements?

10. Click the Send button.

    Outlook automatically adds a copy of the task to your Task list when you send the task request.

For a demonstration of how to create a task request, in the Multimedia folder on the Microsoft Outlook 2000 Step by Step CD-ROM, double-click the Task-Request icon.

A declined task is indicated by an X on the task icon. It still appears in your Task list because you chose to keep an updated copy on your list.

To reclaim ownership of a declined task, on the Task form Standard toolbar, click the Return To Task List button.

---

tip

To turn an existing task into a task request, double-click the task, and then on the Task form Standard toolbar, click the Assign Task button.

Reassign a task request that was declined

Your colleague Keith cannot take on the requested assignment. In this exercise, you need to find a different person to help you with it.

1 On the Outlook Bar, click the SBS Practice Inbox, and then double-click the e-mail message from Keith Hafferman that contains the declined task request.

The Task Request form appears, with Keith's response to you.

2 On the Task form Standard toolbar, click the Assign Task button.

3 In the To box, type **Andre Orr**

4 Select the Keep An Updated Copy Of This Task On My Task List check box and the Send Me A Status Report When This Task Is Complete check box.

5 On the Task form Standard toolbar, click the Send button.

The task has now been added to your Task list, and if this were an actual situation, the task request would be sent.

important

If you assigned a task and it was accepted, but you change your mind about who should complete the assignment, create an unassigned copy of the task and assign the copy to the new person. To create an unassigned copy of a task, you must have selected the Keep An Updated Copy Of This Task On My Task List check box in the original task request that you sent.

Create an unassigned copy of a task and assign the copy

You have had second thoughts about whether Andre Orr is the right person for the Parents Day project, so in this exercise, you assign an additional person to the task.

1 In your Task list, double-click the original task assigned to Keith Hafferman for DaVinci Parents Day, and then click the Details tab.

2 On the Details tab, click the Create Unassigned Copy button, and then in the warning dialog box, click OK.

The Task form appears with a new, unassigned copy of the task.

❸ On the Task form Standard toolbar, click the Assign Task button.

❹ In the To box, type **Jeff Hardiff**

❺ Click the Send button.

The task has now been added to your Task list, and if this were an actual situation, your response would be sent.

---

tip

When you create an unassigned copy, the names of people in the Update list box on the Details tab in the Task dialog box are removed, so everyone who formerly received updates or status reports will not receive them for the newly assigned task. Also, the original task you assigned will stay in the Task list of the person to whom you first assigned it, and you will no longer be able to keep an updated copy of the original task in your Task list. But if you request a status report for that task, you will receive the report when the original owner marks the task complete.

View responses to a task request

When a recipient accepts or declines a task, his or her response automatically appears in your Inbox like an e-mail message. You can track task requests in your Task list if you ask for task updates. In this exercise, you read a response to your task request.

❶ On the Outlook Bar, click the SBS Practice Inbox shortcut.

The contents of the SBS Practice Inbox are displayed in the Information viewer. The subject line of Jeff Hardiff's response to your task request reads Task Accepted: DaVinci Parents Day.

❷ Double-click the task response.

A Task form appears, showing when the task was accepted and by whom.

❸ Circle the Close button. The Task form closes.

Close

Sending Task Information to Others

You can send information about a task to other people in the following ways:

▪ Send a status report that Outlook creates from the task.

The status report is sent in an e-mail message and contains details such as the hours worked on the task and the task owner's name.

Outlook automatically addresses a status report for an assigned task to everyone on the update list.

■ Type a comment about an assigned task in an e-mail message (to which a copy of the task can be attached) that Outlook automatically addresses.

You can address the reply to all the people who chose to keep an updated copy of the task or who chose to receive a status report when the task is completed. Or you can address the reply to a logical recipient. For example, if you own the task, you can address your reply to the person who assigned the task. If you assigned the task, you can address your reply to the owner.

Send a status report for a task

In this exercise, you send a status report about the progress of the DaVinci Parents Day task.

1 Double-click the DaVinci Parents Day task.

The Task form appears.

2 On the Task form, on the Actions menu, click Send Status Report.

A Message form appears, complete with the status report for the task.

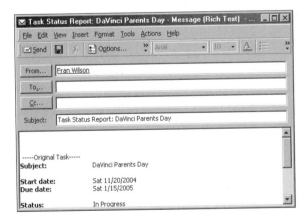

If the task was assigned to you, the names of people on the update list are automatically added.

3 Enter recipient names in the To and Cc boxes.

4 On the Message form Standard toolbar, click the Send button.

The Message form closes, and if this were an actual situation, the status report message would be sent.

important

If you are not connected to the Internet, when you click the Send button, your message is placed in the Outbox. To send the message, on the Standard toolbar, click the Send/Receive button. Complete the instructions from your Internet service provider to access the Internet.

Send a copy of a task as an attachment in an e-mail message

In this exercise, you send a copy of the DaVinci Parents Day task as an attachment to an e-mail message to Bill Carter.

1 Double-click the DaVinci Parents Day task.

The Task form appears.

2 On the Task form, on the Actions menu, click Forward.

A Message form appears, with the task attached and the subject line completed.

3 On the Message form, in the To box, type **Bill Carter**

4 On the Message form, in the Comment area, type the following:

Bill, thought you'd like to know we have backup on this.

E-mail recipients can double-click the attachment to open the task and then copy the task to their Task lists.

5 On the Message form Standard toolbar, click the Send button.

The Message form closes, and if this were an actual situation, your task would be forwarded.

tip

To send copies of more than one task, drag the additional tasks from the Task list to the message area of the e-mail message that you are forwarding.

Organizing Your Task List

A *category* is an assigned keyword or phrase that helps you keep track of items so that you can easily find, sort, or group them. You can use categories to keep track of items that are related but stored in different folders. For example, you can keep track of all the meetings, contacts, and e-mail messages for the Five Lakes project when you create a category named Five Lakes Project and assign items to it.

Categories also give you a way to track items without having to put them in separate folders. For example, you can keep business and personal tasks in the same Task list and use the Business and Personal categories to view the tasks separately.

Outlook supplies a list of categories you can use, called the Master Category List. You can use this list as it is or add your own categories to it.

Assign a new task to a category

In this exercise, you create a new task and assign it to a category you add to the Master Category List.

① Be sure that the Task list is displayed in the Information viewer.

New Task

② On the Standard toolbar, click the New Task button.

A new Task form appears.

③ On the Task form, in the Subject box, type **Install new scanner**

④ At the bottom of the form, click the Categories button.

The Categories dialog box appears. After scrolling through the Available Categories list, you decide the category you want is not available.

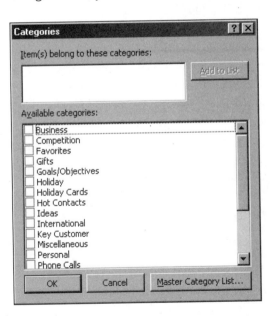

⑤ Click the Master Category List button.

The Master Category dialog box appears.

Your screen should look similar to the following illustration.

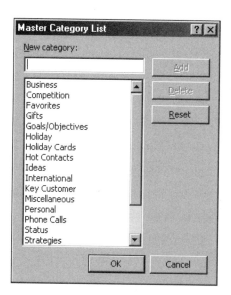

⑥ In the New Category box, type **Computer Hardware**

⑦ Click the Add button, and click OK.

The Available Categories dialog box reappears, with the new category added to the list.

⑧ In the Categories dialog box, select the check box for the Computers category, and click OK.

The Task form reappears with Computers displayed in the box next to the Categories button.

⑨ Complete the Task form, and then on the Task form Standard toolbar, click the Save And Close button.

The Task form closes.

Add a category and assign tasks

In this exercise, you create a new category and then assign existing tasks to it.

① On the Standard toolbar, click the Organize button.

The Ways To Organize Tasks panel appears.

② On the Ways To Organize Tasks panel, click the Using Categories link.

The Using Categories page appears.

③ On the Using Categories page, in the Create A New Category Called box, type **ABA trade show** and then click the Create button.

The word *Done!* is displayed next to the Create A New Category Called box, and the phrase *ABA trade show* is displayed in the Add Tasks Selected Below To box.

4 In the Task list, select the Prepare Booklist task, press and hold the Ctrl key, and then select the ABA Authors task.

Both tasks are selected.

5 On the Using Categories page, click the Add button.

The word *Done!* is displayed next to the Add Tasks Selected Below To box, and the two tasks are added to the ABA Trade Show category.

6 On the View menu, point to Current View, and be sure that Detailed List is selected.

The detailed Task list appears. The ABA Trade Show category is listed in the Categories column for each of the two tasks.

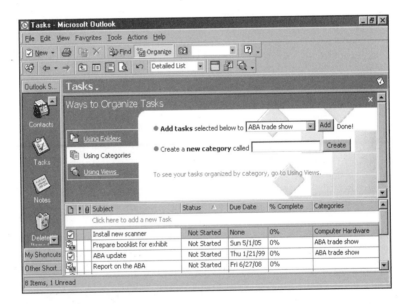

Taking Charge of Tasks 9

important

For any Outlook item except a note or a message, you can type the category name in the Categories box in the Ways to Organize Tasks panel instead of selecting it from the Available Categories list. However, if you misspell the category name, the item is assigned to the misspelled category. The new category is not in the Master Category List, so other items cannot be assigned to it later.

Move tasks up or down in the Task list

When tasks are not sorted or grouped, you can change their position in the Task list by moving individual tasks up or down. This is most useful when you want to change the order of only a few tasks—for example, to put related tasks next to each other. In this exercise, you move the DaVinci Parents Day task up in the Task list.

1 On the View menu, point to Current View, and then click Customize Current View.

The View Summary dialog box appears.

Steps 3 and 5 unlock the list so that items can be moved up or down.

2 In the View Summary dialog box, click the Sort button.

The Sort dialog box appears.

3 In the Sort dialog box, click the Clear All button, and click OK.

The View Summary dialog box reappears.

4 In the View Summary dialog box, click the Group By button.

The Group By dialog box appears.

5 In the Group By dialog box, click the Clear All button, and click OK.

The View Summary dialog box reappears.

6 In the View Summary dialog box, click OK.

The Task list appears.

7 In the Task list, drag the DaVinci Parents Day task to place it second in the list, using the red guideline to position the task.

Sort tasks and save the new order as the default

You can sort the entire Task list and save the new order as the default. This procedure is useful when you want tasks arranged by the contents of a particular field—for example, in order of priority or due date. In this exercise, you sort your Task list by due date and save the new order as the default.

1 On the View menu, point to Current View, and then click Customize Current View.

The View Summary dialog box appears.

2 In the View Summary dialog box, click the Group By button.

The Group By dialog box appears.

3 Click the Clear All button, and click OK.

The View Summary dialog box reappears.

④ In the View Summary dialog box, click the Filter button.

The Filter dialog box appears.

To change the priority level of a task, open the task and in the Priority box, click a new priority level.

⑤ In the Filter dialog box, click the Clear All button, and click OK.

The Filter dialog box closes.

⑥ In the View Summary dialog box, click OK.

The View Summary dialog box closes.

⑦ On the View menu, point to Current View, and be sure that Detailed List is checked.

A detailed Task list appears.

Sort By: Priority

⑧ In the Task list, click the Sort By: Priority column heading to sort your tasks by priority.

⑨ In the Task list, click the Due Date column heading.

The tasks are now sorted by due date.

⑩ On the Actions menu, click Save Task Order.

The next time you click the Tasks shortcut on the Outlook Bar, the Tasks Information viewer will display the Task list according to the new default criterion—in this case, by due date.

Creating a Rule to Organize Your Tasks

You can create rules to automatically move tasks into folders with other related items. For example, you could move any task request with the word *Meeting* in the Subject box to a specially created Meeting folder that contains task requests, meeting requests, and other items that meet the rule criterion. However, there are some limitations to using the Rules Wizard:

■ E-mail items, if moved to a non-mail folder, will not automatically generate a new item for that folder. For example, if a message is moved to Calendar, a new appointment is not created.

■ If a response to a meeting or task request is moved to the Deleted Items folder with a rule, the tracking in the original item is not updated.

■ You cannot flag a meeting or task request with a rule.

■ Rules that apply when you send an e-mail message are not applied to task requests and meeting requests.

Taking Charge of Tasks   9

One Step Further

Tracking Tasks Assigned to Others and Receiving Status Reports

Using Tasks in Outlook 2000 enables you to coordinate, monitor, and supervise the work that you have assigned to others. You can have Tasks automatically update you about all assignments, without others having to spend time writing separate reports on their work. Whenever a person who has accepted a task request from you updates that task, you automatically receive a report if you have requested one, and your copy of the task is automatically updated.

View a task update

In this exercise, you open a task status report e-mail message and view the status report for a task you have previously assigned—the DaVinci Parents Day task.

① On the Outlook Bar, click the SBS Practice Inbox shortcut, and then double-click the e-mail message titled Task Status Report: DaVinci Parents Day.

A Message form appears. The comment in the message area reports when the task is due, when the update was sent, the task status, the percentage complete, total and actual work, and the requester.

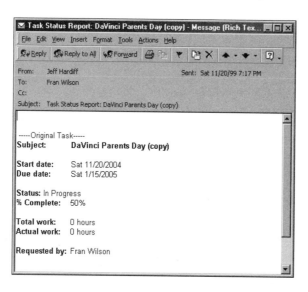

② On the Message form, click the Close button.

③ On the Outlook Bar, click the Tasks shortcut.

Close

Your Task list is displayed in the Information viewer. The status for the DaVinci Parents Day task has changed to reflect the updated contents of the task status report: In Progress in the Status column and 50% in the % Complete column.

View tasks that you have assigned to others

In this exercise, you review the list of tasks you have assigned to others.

1. Be sure the Tasks list appears in the Information viewer.
2. On the View menu, point to Current View, and then click Assignment.

   The list of tasks that you have assigned to others appears.

Receive status reports

In this exercise, you set Outlook to automatically track the progress of all new tasks you assign to others and notify you when the tasks have been completed.

1. On the Tools menu, click Options, click the Other tab, and then click the Advanced Options button.

   The Advanced Options dialog box appears.
2. In the Advanced Options dialog box, click the Advanced Tasks button.

   The Advanced Tasks dialog box appears.
3. In the Advanced Tasks dialog box, select the Keep Updated Copies Of Assigned Tasks On My Task List check box.

   You will now automatically track the progress of new tasks you assign to others.
4. Select the Send Status Reports When Assigned Tasks Are Completed check box.

   You will now automatically receive notification when an assigned task is complete.
5. In the Advanced Tasks dialog box, click OK, and in the Advanced Options dialog box, click OK. In the Options dialog box, click OK.

   The three dialog boxes close.

Finish the lesson

1. If you want to continue to the next lesson, on the Outlook Bar, click the SBS Practice Inbox shortcut.
2. Delete the tasks that you added to your Task list for this lesson.
3. If you have finished using Outlook for now and are working in a Workgroup environment, on the File menu, click Exit And Log Off. If you are working in an Internet only environment, on the File menu, click Exit.

Lesson 9 Quick Reference

To	Do this	Button
Create a recurring task	Click the Tasks shortcut. On the Standard toolbar, click the New Task button. In the Subject box, type the name of the task. In the Due Date box, select a date. Click the Recurrence button. In the Task Recurrence dialog box, in the Recurrence Pattern area, select when you want the task to re-cur, and click OK. On the Task form Standard toolbar, click the Save And Close button.	☑ New ▾
Create a detailed task	On the View menu, point to Current View, and then click Detailed List. On the Standard toolbar, click the New Task button. In the Subject box, type the name of the task. In the Due Date and Start Date boxes, select dates. In the Priority box, select a priority level. In the Comment area, type any comments. Click the Details tab, and complete the information that you want. On the Task form Standard toolbar, click the Save And Close button.	
Create a task that recurs based on completion date	On the Standard toolbar, click the New Task button. In the Subject box, type the name of the task. In the Due Date box, select a date. On the Task form Standard toolbar, click the Recurrence button, and then in the Recurrence Pattern area, select the frequency of recur-rence. Select the Regenerate New Task option, and then in the box, type a time period. Click OK, and then on the Task form Standard toolbar, click the Save And Close button.	

Lesson 9 Quick Reference

To	Do this
Create a task from an e-mail message	Click the Inbox shortcut. In the Inbox Information viewer, select the e-mail message and drag it to the Tasks shortcut on the Outlook Bar. On the Task form, in the Due Date box, type a date, and then on the Task form Standard toolbar, click the Save And Close button.
Find a task	On the View menu, point to Current View, and then click Detailed List. On the Standard toolbar, click the Find button. In the Look For box, type a word to search for, and then click the Find Now button. Click Clear Search, and then close the Find Items In Tasks panel.
Edit a task	In the Task list, double-click the task. Revise the information as necessary.
Set a reminder for a task	Double-click the task, and then select the Reminder check box. In the adjacent boxes, type or select the date and time you want the reminder to appear. Click the Save And Close button.
Set reminder options for new tasks	On the Tools menu, click Options. Click the Other tab, click the Advanced Options button, and then click the Advanced Tasks button. Select the Set Reminders On Tasks With Due Dates check box. Click OK three times to close the dialog boxes.

Taking Charge of Tasks

9

Lesson 9 Quick Reference

To	Do this	Button
Change a task into a recurring task	Double-click the task. On the Task form Standard toolbar, click the Recurrence button. In the Recurrence Pattern area, click the frequency of recurrence, and then select the options that you want. Click OK, and then click the Save And Close button.	
Stop a recurring task	Double-click the task. On the Task form Standard toolbar, click the Recurrence button, and then click the Remove Recurrence button. Click the Save And Close button.	
Mark a task completed	In the Task list, right-click the task. On the shortcut menu, select Mark Complete.	
Delete a task	In the Task list, select the task, and then on the Standard toolbar, click the Delete button.	
Retrieve a deleted task	On the View menu, click the Folder List. On the Outlook Bar, scroll through the icons if necessary and click the Deleted Items shortcut. Select the task item to be retrieved, and drag it to the Tasks folder in the Folder List.	
Create an appointment from a task	In the Task list, select a task and drag it to the Calendar shortcut. On the Appointment form, fill in the Start Time and End Time boxes, and then on the Appointment form Standard toolbar, click the Save And Close button.	

Lesson 9 Quick Reference

To	Do this
Create a new task request	On the File menu, point to New, and then click Task Request. In the To box, type the name of the person receiving the request. In the Subject box, type the name of the task. Select due date and status options. Select the options desired. If the task is recurring, click the Recurrence button, select options, and click OK. In the Comment area, type information about the task, and then click the Send button.
Reassign a task request that was declined	On the Outlook Bar, click the Inbox shortcut. Double-click the task request e-mail message. On the Task form Standard toolbar, click the Assign Task button. In the To box, enter the name of the new assignee. Select or clear the appropriate check boxes, and then click the Send button.
Create an unassigned copy of a task and assign the copy	In the Task list, double-click the task to be copied, and then click the Details tab. On the Details tab, click the Create Unassigned Copy button, and click OK. On the new copy of the Task form, on the Task form Standard toolbar, click the Assign Task button. In the To box, type the new assignee's name, and then click the Send button.
View responses to a task request	In the Inbox, double-click the task response message.
Assign a new task to a category	Be sure the Task list is displayed in the Information viewer. On the Standard toolbar, click the New Task button, and then click the Categories button. To add a new category to the Master Category List, click the Master Category List button. In the New Category box, type the category name, click the Add button, and click OK. In the Categories dialog box, select the check box for the new category, and click OK. Complete the Task form, and then on the Task form Standard toolbar, click the Save And Close button.

Lesson 9 Quick Reference

To	Do this
Add a category and assign tasks	Be sure the Task list is displayed in the Information viewer. On the Standard toolbar, click the Organize button, and then click the Using Categories link. In the Create a New Category Called box, type the name of the new category, and then click the Create button. In the Task list, select the tasks that you want to assign to the category, and then click the Add button. On the Ways To Organize Panel, click the Close Organize button.
Move tasks up or down in a Task list	On the View menu, point to Current View, and then click Customize Current View. Click the Sort button, click the Clear All button, and click OK. Click the Group By button, click the Clear All button, and click OK twice to close the dialog boxes. Click and drag a task up or down to a new position in the list.
Sort tasks and save the new order as the default	On the View menu, point to Current View, and then click Customize Current View. Clickthe Group By button, click the Clear All button, and click OK. Click the Filter button, click the Clear All button, and click OK twice to close the dialog boxes. Sort tasks by clicking the appropriate column head, and then on the Actions menu, click Save Task Order.
View a task update	Click the Inbox shortcut, and then double-click the task status report message.
View tasks assigned to others	Click the Tasks shortcut. On the View menu, point to Current View, and then click Assignment.
Receive status reports	On the Tools menu, click Options, click the Other tab, and then click the Advanced Options button. In the Advanced Options dialog box, click the Advanced Tasks button. Select the Keep Updated Copies of Assigned Tasks On My Task List and Send Status Reports When Assigned Tasks Are Completed check boxes. Click OK three times to close the dialog boxes.

Review & Practice

You will review and practice how to:

- ✔ *Create a recurring appointment.*
- ✔ *Create an annual event.*
- ✔ *Organize a meeting.*
- ✔ *Create a detailed task.*
- ✔ *Create a task request.*

ESTIMATED TIME
25 min.

Before you move on to Part 4, which covers logging your activities, using Outlook with external networks, archiving and protecting files, and customizing Outlook forms, you can practice the skills you learned in Part 3 by working through this Review & Practice section. You will reinforce your skills in handling appointments, events, meetings, tasks, and task requests.

As account manager for Impact Public Relations, you face a steady stream of meetings, messages, and tasks to be done for your client companies and sometimes for their clients as well. You need the tools provided by Outlook to stay on top of all these demands.

Step 1:   Create a Recurring Appointment

You have just received a message from Alice Abrams. An upcoming meeting for December 13 is going to be the first in a series. You must enter the meetings in your Calendar.

❶   Open your Calendar.

❷   Create a weekly recurring appointment called Tutorial for every Tuesday starting December 13, 2004. End the recurring appointment after 12 occurrences.

For more information about	See
Scheduling a recurring appointment	Lesson 7

Step 2:   Create an Annual Event

The local association of publishers and booksellers has decided that an annual local bookfair would provide valuable public exposure for the book industry. You need to add this event to your Calendar.

●   Schedule an all-day, annual event called Bookfair, to be held each year on February 15 at the local mall.

For more information about	See
Scheduling an event	Lesson 7
Scheduling recurring appointments	Lesson 7

Step 3:   Organize a Meeting

As chair of the education committee of the book publicists association in your city, you are responsible for organizing the committee's meetings. Now that it is a new year, you are free to set up meetings on an entirely new schedule.

If you can use actual colleagues to help you with this exercise, their free and busy times will be shown.

●   Set up a meeting for yourself and three other people for January 16, 2004. The meeting will be in your office from 10:00 to 11:30 A.M. Call the meeting Annual Planning, and send the meeting request.

For more information about	See
Organizing a meeting	Lesson 8
Determining attendee availability and sending a meeting request	Lesson 8

Step 4:   **Create a Detailed Task**

You face an important deadline, and the work needs to be carried out quickly and accurately. To coordinate your efforts, you create a detailed task to describe the parameters of your project.

1   Create a high-priority task called Try For The Proseware Account, with a due date of January 31, 2005.

2   Type the following comment:

Develop sales pitch for final meeting with Sarah Addison, Proseware Marketing VP.

3   Enter Sarah Addison as the contact.

4   On the Details tab, enter Proseware in the Companies box.

For more information about	See
Creating a detailed task	Lesson 9

Step 5:   **Create a Task Request**

You have so much on your hands that you need to delegate some tasks to your colleagues. Accordingly, you send out a request for help.

If you can use an actual colleague to help you with this exercise, the request can be delivered.

1   Create a task request called Bookfair Ads.

2   Enter the name of the person receiving the request, and set January 15 as the due date.

3   Type the following comment:

I need some creative help with this. How do we make books exciting to the range of people who may be at a mall?

4   Send the task request.

For more information about	See
Creating a new task request	Lesson 9

Step 6:   **Finish the Review & Practice**

Follow these steps to delete the practice messages, appointments, and tasks you created in this Review & Practice, and then quit Outlook.

1   Open your Folder List and delete the practice files created for this Review & Practice session from the SBS Practice Inbox folder, the SBS Practice Calendar folder, and your Tasks folder.

2 Open the Outbox folder and delete any practice messages in it.

SBS Practice Inbox

3 If you are continuing to the next lesson, on the Outlook Bar, click the SBS Practice Inbox shortcut.

4 If you have finished using Outlook for now and are working in a Workgroup environment, on the File menu, click Exit And Log Off. If you are working in an Internet only environment, on the File menu, click Exit.

PART 4

Managing and Protecting Your Information

10

Managing and Protecting Your Files

In this lesson you will learn how to:

**ESTIMATED
TIME
40 min.**

✔ *Export Outlook folders to use on your laptop.*

✔ *Export Outlook folders to use in other programs.*

✔ *Archive Outlook folders.*

✔ *Retrieve archived folders.*

✔ *Encrypt and digitally sign e-mail messages.*

✔ *Track activities using Journal.*

In this lesson, you learn how to use the more advanced features of Microsoft Outlook 2000 to help you manage and protect your contact information and communications. You can manage the contents in your Outlook folders by archiving items so that they are available for future reference but don't take up valuable space in your current folders. You can export folders to use on your laptop at home or to use in other applications in the office, and you can also use Journal to track your e-mail messages, phone calls, and other activities. To protect your files, you can encrypt e-mail messages and attachments, and you can digitally sign your messages.

As an account manager for Impact Public Relations, you have many old e-mail messages cluttering your Inbox and making it difficult to easily locate your newer messages in the list. So you archive the old e-mail messages and then discover later that you need to retrieve them to help write a quarterly report. You then export your Inbox folder to work on your report at home and export your

Notes folder to Microsoft Word for use in the report. Next you send a digitally signed e-mail message to the bank and an encrypted e-mail message to a coworker in another office. Finally, you use Journal to track your business activities with a key prospect.

Getting Ready for the Lesson

In this exercise, you start Outlook 2000 and prepare the practice files and folders that you need. For the archiving exercises, if you are using this book before January 1, 2000, you must reset your system clock so that the practice e-mail messages will appear to have been received after that date.

Microsoft Outlook

Start Outlook and copy the practice files

1 On the desktop, double-click the Microsoft Outlook 2000 icon.

Outlook 2000 opens.

Maximize

2 If necessary, maximize the Outlook window.

> # important
>
> Before proceeding to the next step, you must have installed this book's practice folder on your hard disk and created a practice Inbox folder and shortcut. If you have not yet created a practice folder and practice shortcut for your work, see Lesson 1, "Jumping into Your E-mail."

If you are using this book after January 1, 2000, skip steps 3 and 4.

3 To reset the clock, on the taskbar, right-click the status bar time area located in the lower-right corner of your screen, and then on the shortcut menu, click Adjust Date/Time.

The Date/Time Properties box appears with the Date & Time tab active.

SBS Practice Inbox

4 On the Date & Time tab, click the year box up arrow, and scroll to 2003. Click OK.

When you point to the status bar time area, the date now displays the current month and day for the year 2003.

For a more detailed example of how to copy practice files to a practice folder, see the exercise "Set Up Practice E-mail" in Lesson 1.

5 Click the SBS Practice Inbox shortcut.

6 Drag the practice Notes files, indicated by note icons, from the Lesson10 folder in the Outlook 2000 SBS Practice folder to the Notes folder in the Folder List.

7 Drag the practice e-mail message files, indicated by envelope icons, from the Lesson10 folder in the Outlook 2000 SBS Practice folder to the SBS Practice Inbox folder in the Folder List.

Exporting Files

Exporting enables you to move a copy of an Outlook folder and its contents to another location while retaining the original folder and its contents in Outlook.

One way to export a folder is as a personal folder file, indicated by a PST extension after the filename. Like a folder on your desktop, a personal folder file contains one or more items saved as a single file. In Outlook, personal file folders are used to store items from your Outlook folders. The PST files can then be archived or exported for other uses.

For example, you might want to back up an Outlook folder to safeguard against system crashes or to use on your laptop. In this case, you would export your folder as a personal folder file so that it can later be imported back into Outlook if necessary.

You might also want to use the contents of a folder in another program. For example, you can use your Contacts folder with Microsoft Word to create a mail merge. In this case, you export the folder directly into the other program, and not as a PST file, since you do not need to import it back into Outlook.

In the next exercises, you prepare to complete your quarterly report at home. First, you create a backup copy of your SBS Practice Inbox so that you can import it into your laptop. Next, you remember that you have some information in your Notes folder that you need to refer to in preparing the report, so you export your Notes folder to a Microsoft Word document.

Export a folder as a personal folder

In this exercise, you create a new folder in Outlook for your exported SBS Practice Inbox messages and then export them to your laptop so you can work on the quarterly report at home.

①   In the Folder List, right-click the Outlook Today – [Personal Folders] folder, and then on the shortcut menu, click New Folder.

The Create New Folder dialog box appears.

②   In the Create New Folder dialog box, in the Name box, type **Old Inbox**

③   Be sure that Mail Items is displayed in the Folder Contains box, and click OK.

The Create New Folder dialog box closes and the Add Shortcut To Outlook Bar dialog box appears.

④   In the Add Shortcut To Outlook Bar dialog box, click No.

The Add Shortcut To Outlook Bar dialog box closes and the Old Inbox folder appears in the Folder List.

10

Managing Your Files

5 In the Folder List, select the Old Inbox folder.

6 On the File menu, click Import And Export.

The Import And Export Wizard dialog box appears.

7 In the Import And Export Wizard dialog box, in the Choose An Action To Perform list, select Export To A File, and then click the Next button.

The Export To A File dialog box appears.

8 In the Create A File Of Type list, select Personal Folder File (.pst), and then click the Next button.

The Export Personal Folders dialog box appears.

9 In the Export Personal Folders dialog box, in the Select The Folder To Export From box, be sure that Old Inbox is selected, and then click the Next button.

10 In the Export Personal Folders dialog box, click the Finish button.

11 The Old Inbox folder is copied as Export.pst to the My Documents folder on your hard disk.

important

To complete the next exercise, you must have Microsoft Word installed.

Export a folder to another program

To assist you as you draft your report, in this exercise, you export your Notes folder to Microsoft Word.

1 On the Outlook Bar, click the Notes shortcut.

The contents of the Notes folder are displayed in the Information viewer.

2 On the File menu, click Import And Export.

The Import And Export Wizard dialog box appears.

3 In the Choose An Action To Perform list, select Export To A File, and then click the Next button.

The Export To A File dialog box appears.

4 In the Create A File Of Type list, select Tab Separated Values (Windows), and then click the Next button.

The next page of the Export To A File dialog box appears.

5 In the Select Folder To Export From box, be sure that the Notes folder is selected, and then click the Next button.

The next page of the Export To A File dialog box appears.

6 In the Save Exported File As box, type **Notes** and then browse to select a folder on your hard disk. Click Next.

The next Export To A File dialog box appears.

7 In the Export To A File dialog box, click the Finish button.

The Notes folder is copied to the Notes.txt file in the location you chose.

8 On the Windows taskbar, click the Start button, point to Programs, and then click Microsoft Word.

Microsoft Word opens.

9 On the Insert menu, click File.

The Insert File dialog box appears.

10 In the Insert File dialog box, in the Look In drop-down list, double-click the folder in which you saved Notes.txt, and then in the Files Of Type lists, select All Files.

Your screen should look similar to the following illustration.

11 In the Insert File Information viewer, click Notes, and then click the Insert button.

The Notes file contents are inserted into the Word document.

12 On the File menu, click Exit, and when prompted to save your file, click No.

Archiving Files Manually or Automatically

Archiving is a method of saving old Outlook information that you might need later but will not use often, enabling you to avoid the clutter of these older items as you work with more current ones. Unlike exporting, however, when you archive, you actually remove the folder contents from Outlook and store them elsewhere in an archive file.

You can archive items in any Outlook folder except Contacts. When you archive items, the items are stored on your hard disk in the same folder and, if applicable, organized in the same subfolders they were in Outlook so that they are readily identifiable should you need to retrieve them later. The folder and subfolders also remain in Outlook, along with the non-archived contents; but the archived contents are removed. If you need to work with or refer to archived items, the folders are easily retrieved from the archive by importing them back into Outlook, where you can work with the folders as you would any other Outlook folder.

Outlook folders can be archived either manually or automatically. Manual archiving enables you to archive old items as the need arises, while AutoArchiving enables you to establish a systematic method of archiving your files automatically.

To assist you in automating the archiving process, several of the main Outlook folders have *default aging periods* that are automatically turned on at setup. For example, your Calendar folder has a default aging period of six months. This means that unless you change the default setting, any items in your Calendar folder and subfolders that are older than six months will be automatically archived if you activate AutoArchive when you open Outlook each day. This table shows the default periods for the Outlook folders.

AutoArchive is	for this folder	with a default aging period of
Turned on at setup	Calendar	Six months
	Deleted Items	Two months
	Journal	Six months
	Sent Items	Two months
	Tasks	Six months
	Inbox	Six months
Turned off at setup	Drafts	Three months
	Junk E-mail	Three months
	Notes	Three months
	Outbox	Three months
Not available	Contacts	Not applicable

Archiving in Outlook can be customized to fit your particular work requirements. You can set:

- The frequency with which Outlook prompts you to AutoArchive your folders. For example, you may want to AutoArchive on a daily, weekly, or monthly basis—or at another time interval—depending on the rate at which your items accumulate or become outdated.

- The aging period and other parameters by which individual folder items are archived. For example, you may find that the six-month default aging period for your Inbox folder may be too long, resulting in a mass of old messages that get in the way of your easily finding the newer ones. If this is the case, you may want to change the default aging period to two or three months.

- Exceptions for individual folder items. For example, you may want to prevent items on a certain subject or from a certain contact from being archived at all.

In this lesson, you decide that you have too many e-mail messages in your Inbox, so you manually archive the ones that are older than two months. Next you change the Outlook AutoArchive setting to search for old e-mail messages daily, and then you change the AutoArchive default setting for the Inbox folder so that all items older than one month are archived. Finally, you retrieve your archived messages in order to prepare a quarterly report.

Archive folders manually

In this exercise, you archive all messages in your Inbox and its subfolders that are more than two months old.

1 On the Outlook Bar, click the SBS Practice Inbox shortcut.

The contents of the SBS Practice Inbox are displayed in the Information viewer.

If you do not see Archive in the menu, click the double arrows at the bottom of the menu to view more menu commands.

2 On the File menu, click Archive.

The Archive dialog box opens with the SBS Practice Inbox selected and the path to the default archive file displayed in the Archive File box. Your screen should look similar to the following illustration.

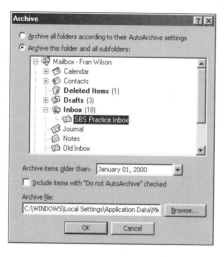

important

Normally, you would select a date from the past as your Archive Items Older Than date. To complete the archiving steps in this lesson, though, you use dates that accommodate the dates given to the practice messages.

❸   In the Archive dialog box, be sure that the Archive This Folder And All Subfolders option is selected, and in the Archive Items Older Than box, click the drop-down arrow.

A monthly calendar appears.

❹   Scroll through the calendar, and then select the date January 1, 2000.

❺   Be sure that the Include Items With "Do Not AutoArchive" Checked box is cleared.

❻   Position the insertion point in the Archive File box, and press the Right arrow key until the word *archive* is displayed.

❼   Select *archive*, type **testarchive** and click OK.

The Archive dialog box closes and the SBS Practice Inbox messages older than January 1, 2000, are now archived using the filename Testarchive.pst.

❽   In the Options dialog box, click OK.

Set AutoArchive properties for Outlook

In this exercise, you set AutoArchive to prompt you daily to archive old contents in your Outlook folders.

For a demonstration of how to use AutoArchive, in the Multimedia folder on the Microsoft Outlook 2000 Step by Step CD-ROM, double-click the Archive icon.

1 On the Tools menu, click Options.

The Options dialog box appears.

2 In the Options dialog box, click the Other tab, and then in the AutoArchive area, click the AutoArchive button.

The AutoArchive dialog box appears. Your screen should look similar to the following illustration.

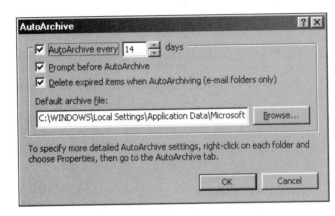

3 In the AutoArchive dialog box, be sure that the AutoArchive Every check box is selected, and then in the AutoArchive Every box, select 1 as the number of days.

Old e-mail messages will automatically be archived the first time that you start Outlook each day.

4 Be sure that the Prompt Before AutoArchive check box is selected.

Before AutoArchiving begins each time, you are prompted to approve the procedures.

5 Be sure that the Delete Expired Items When AutoArchiving (E-mail Folders Only) check box is selected.

AutoArchive will automatically delete rather than archive any expired e-mail messages.

tip
If you set an expiration date for an e-mail message, you make the message unavailable after a specific date. To set the expiration date for an e-mail message, on the Message form Standard toolbar, click the Options button. In the Delivery Options area, select the Expires After check box, and then in the Expires After box, click the drop-down arrow and select the date you want.

Managing Your Files

10

⑥ Position the insertion point in the Default Archive File box, and press the right arrow key until the word *archive* is displayed.

⑦ Select *archive*, type **testarchive** and click OK.

Outlook will automatically prompt you shortly after you start Outlook each day and ask if you want it to search your Outlook folders. If you select Yes, Outlook will then archive any items that meet the AutoArchive requirements specified for each folder.

⑧ Close the Options dialog box, and click OK.

Set AutoArchive properties for a specific Outlook folder

In this exercise, you change the default aging period for your SBS Practice Inbox folder.

➊ On the Outlook Bar, right-click the SBS Practice Inbox shortcut, and then on the shortcut menu, click Properties.

The SBS Practice Inbox Properties dialog box appears.

➋. In the SBS Practice Inbox Properties dialog box, click the AutoArchive tab.

The AutoArchive default settings for the SBS Practice Inbox folder are displayed. Your screen should look similar to the following illustration.

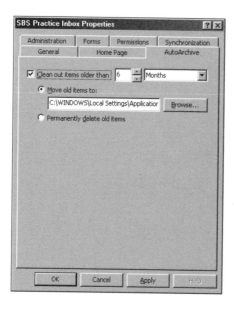

To specify the frequency in days or weeks, in the second Clean Out Items Older Than box, click the drop-down arrow and select from the list.

3 Select the Clean Out Items Older Than check box, and then in the first Clean Out Items Older Than box, type **1** and then in the next box, be sure that Months is selected.

Now all SBS Practice Inbox messages older than one month will be archived automatically.

4 Be sure that the Move Old Items To option is selected, and then position the insertion point in the Move Old Items To box, and press the right arrow key until the word *archive* is displayed.

5 Select the word *archive*, type **test1archive** and click OK.

Messages in your SBS Practice Inbox older than one month will now be automatically archived in a subfolder in your Windows folder with the filename Test1archive.pst.

To automatically delete old items rather than archive them, select Permanently Delete Old Items.

6 Quit Outlook 2000, and then on the Windows taskbar, click the Start button, click Shut Down, and then select the Restart option.

Outlook 2000 closes, and your computer shuts down and then restarts. The AutoArchive dialog box appears, asking if you want to AutoArchive now.

7 In the AutoArchive dialog box, click Yes. The messages in your SBS Practice Inbox older than one month are now archived in a subfolder in your Windows folder with the filename Test1archive.pst.

tip

If you have an item in your folder that you do not want to be archived automatically, open the item, and then on the File menu, click Properties. In the Properties dialog box, select the Do Not AutoArchive This Item check box, and click OK.

Retrieve an archived folder

In this exercise, you retrieve your archived SBS Practice Inbox messages from storage and place them in a folder.

To display the Folder List, on the View menu, click Folder List.

1 In the Folder List, select the Old Inbox folder.

Your screen should look similar to the following illustration.

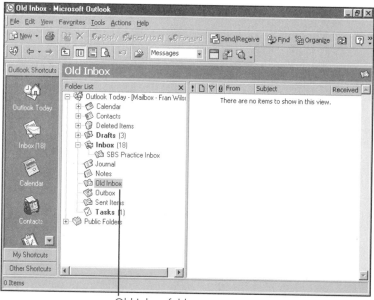

Old Inbox folder

2 On the File menu, click Import And Export.

The Import And Export Wizard dialog box appears.

3 In the Import And Export Wizard dialog box, in the Choose An Action To Perform list, select Import From Another Program Or File, and then click the Next button.

The Import A File dialog box appears. Your screen should look similar to the following illustration.

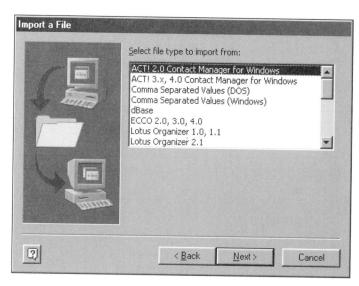

❹ In the Import A File dialog box, in the Select File Type To Import From list, scroll to and select Personal Folder File (.pst), and then click the Next button.

The Import Personal Folders dialog box appears.

❺ In the File To Import area, click the Browse button.

The Open Personal Folders dialog box appears, with the Outlook folders displayed in the Look In drop-down list.

important

If you have not yet been prompted by the AutoArchive dialog box to activate the AutoArchive feature today, use the manually archived file Testarchive.pst to complete step 10.

To locate your archived file, open the Windows folder and then the Local Settings folder, the Application Data folder, the Microsoft folder, and the Outlook folder.

❻ In the Open Personal Folders dialog box, in the Look In drop-down list, select Test1archive.pst, and then click the Open button. (To see the full path of the file, position the insertion point in the File To Import box, and then press the Right arrow key until *Test1archive.pst* is displayed.)

The Open Personal Folders dialog box closes and the Import Personal Folders dialog box reappears. The Test1archive.pst filename is displayed in the File To Import box.

❼ In the Options area, be sure that the Replace Duplicates With Items Imported option is selected, and then click Next.

The next Import Personal Folders dialog box appears.

❽ In the Select The Folder To Import From box, click the plus sign (+) next to Inbox, and then select SBS Practice Inbox.

❾ In the Import Personal Folders dialog box, select the Import Items Into The Current Folder option, and then click the Finish button.

The archived messages are moved from storage and placed in the Old Inbox folder.

Sending Secure E-mail Messages

Sending an e-mail message on the Internet can result in illegal interception by hackers and others intent on viewing your message. To reduce the risk of this occurring, Outlook 2000 offers two primary ways to enhance the security of your e-mail communications. The first method is to attach a *security certificate*, sometimes called a *digital signature* or *digital ID*, to your e-mail messages. Issued by a certified company, the digital ID enables you to prove your identity on the Internet, similar to a driver's license in everyday life. Using a digital ID ensures the intended recipient that the message came from you, and it could be particularly important, for example, in banking and credit card transactions.

The second method is to encrypt the message and attachments. Encrypting a message converts it into mathematical code while it is in transit to ensure that the contents are readable only by the intended recipient. When the recipient receives the encrypted message, it is unencrypted automatically. To send an encrypted message, both you and the intended recipient must have your digital IDs on file.

In the next exercises, you send your company credit information to a bank, attaching your digital signature. Then you send an encrypted message on your company's upcoming merger discussions to a coworker in another office.

Attach your digital signature

In this exercise, you send confidential credit information to a bank and attach your digital signature.

> ### important
>
> You must first obtain a security certificate from a certified company to attach your digital signature to a message and complete this exercise. On the Tools menu, click Options, and then click the Security tab. On the Security tab, click the Get A Digital ID button.

1 On the Outlook Bar, click the SBS Practice Inbox shortcut.

The contents of the SBS Practice Inbox are displayed in the Information viewer.

New Mail Message

2 On the Standard toolbar, click the New Mail Message button.

A blank Message form appears.

3 On the Message form, in the To box, type **someone@microsoft.com** and in the Subject box type **Credit Information**

4 In the message area, type **The company account number is 123456789**.

5 On the Message form Standard toolbar, click the Options button.

The Message Options dialog box appears.

Close

6 In the Message Options dialog box, click the Add Digital Signature To Outgoing Message check box, and then click the Close button.

The Message Options dialog box closes.

7 On the Message form Standard toolbar, click the Send button. If you are not already connected to the Internet, click the Send/Receive button.

The message is sent with your digital signature.

Encrypt the message

In this exercise, you send an encrypted message about merger discussions to your coworker in another office.

> # important
> Before you can complete this exercise and send an encrypted message, you must first have a copy of the recipient's digital ID, received in an e-mail message.

1 Be sure that the SBS Practice Inbox appears in the Information viewer.

2 Click the New Mail Message button.

A blank Message form appears.

3 On the Message form, in the To box, type **someone@microsoft.com** and then in Subject box, type **Status Update**

4 In the message area, type:

The company is in merger negotiations with a major international company.

5 On the Message form Standard toolbar, click the Options button.

The Message Options dialog box appears.

6 In the Message Options dialog box, select the Encrypt Message Contents And Attachments check box, and then click the Close button.

The Message Options dialog box closes.

7 On the Message form Standard toolbar, click the Send button. If you are not already connected to the Internet, click the Send/Receive button.

The encrypted message is sent.

One Step Further ## Using Journal to Log Your Business Activities

With Outlook's Journal, you can track your e-mail, phone, fax, and other communications with your contacts. Journal creates a timeline of the activities that you decide to track during the workday for easy reference.

The following table shows which Outlook-related activities can be tracked both automatically and manually, and which can be tracked manually only in your Contacts folder.

Journal can record	These activities
Manually or automatically	E-mail messages
	Meeting requests
	Meeting responses and cancellations
	Task requests and responses
	Uses of other Microsoft Office applications, such as Access, Excel, Word, and PowerPoint; and Office Binder
Manually	Conversations
	Notes
	NetMeetings
	Phone calls
	Postal letters

When you track an Outlook item in Journal, a record is made each time you create and use that file or item. Because this can use a lot of space on your hard disk, be careful when you select those activities that you want to track. This is particularly important if you track e-mail messages, because all attachments are also saved in Journal.

important

To complete the following exercises in Journal, you need to track your correspondence with a colleague you choose from your own Contact list.

Automatically track activities in Journal

In this exercise, you track your e-mail messages to a colleague.

1 On the Outlook Bar, click the My Shortcuts button, and then click the Journal shortcut.

If you have used Journal before, the current week is displayed in the Information viewer, with today's date selected. If this is the first time you have used Journal, a dialog box will appear prompting you to turn on Journal.

2 If you have used Journal before, skip to step 4.

3 If you need to start Journal, click Yes, and then skip to step 6.

The Journal Options dialog box appears.

4 On the Tools menu, click Options.

The Options dialog box appears, with the Preferences tab active.

⑤ In the Options dialog box, in the Contacts area, click the Journal Options button.

The Journal Options dialog box appears. Your screen should look similar to the following illustration.

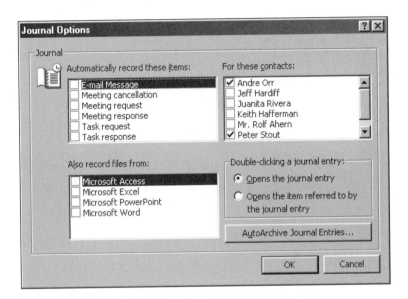

⑥ In the Journal Options dialog box, in the Automatically Record These Items box, select the E-mail Message box and the Meeting Request check box.

⑦ In the Also Record Files From list, clear any items that are selected.

⑧ In the For These Contacts list, select a colleague, and click OK.

The Journal Options dialog box closes, and the Options dialog box reappears.

⑨ In the Options dialog box, click OK.

The Options dialog box closes, and all e-mail messages that you send from now on to your colleague will be recorded in Journal.

Manually track activities in Journal

After completing a call with your colleague, in this exercise, you begin tracking each telephone call with your colleague in Journal.

① On the Outlook Bar, click the Contacts shortcut.

The Contacts list is displayed in the Information viewer.

② Double-click a colleague's name.

The Contact form for your colleague is displayed.

To select another type of entry to record in your Journal, click the Entry Type box drop-down arrow, and then scroll to select the desired activity.

❸ On the Contact form, click the Activities tab.

The Activities tab becomes active.

❹ On the Actions menu, click New Journal Entry For Contact.

The Journal Entry form for your colleague appears with Phone Call displayed in the Entry Type box. Your screen should look similar to the following illustration.

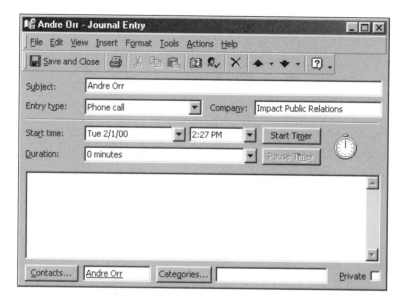

❺ Be sure today's date is shown in the Start Time box. In the time box, click the drop-down arrow, and then scroll to select 8:30 A.M.

❻ In the Duration box, click the drop-down arrow and then click 10 minutes.

❼ On the Journal Entry form Standard toolbar, click the Save And Close button.

The Journal Entry form for your colleague closes, and the Contact form reappears.

❽ On the Contact form, in the Show box, click the drop-down arrow and select Journal.

An entry for the phone call appears in the view area of the Activities tab for your colleague.

tip

To view records that have been tracked in your Journal, on the Outlook Bar, click the Journal shortcut. In the Information viewer, click the plus button (+) for the type of entry that you want to view. Each item tracked appears in the Information viewer.

Close

9 On the Contact form, click the Close button.

important

Tracking contact activities in Journal uses up valuable hard disk memory. Unless you want to continue tracking contact activity with the colleague selected for this exercise, turn off the Journal tracker. On the Tools menu, click Options. In the Contacts area, click the Journal Options button, and then in the For These Contacts box, clear the check box next to your colleague's name. Then click OK. To delete old items in Journal but continue tracking items in the future, right-click the plus button (+) or minus button (-), whichever is displayed, and on the shortcut menu, click Delete.

Finish the lesson

Delete

1 To continue to the next lesson, on the File menu, click Close All Items.

2 To delete the practice Notes files, click the Notes shortcut. In the Information viewer, select the first practice Notes file from the list, and then while holding down the Shift key, select the remaining practice Notes files. On the Standard toolbar, click the Delete button.

3 To reset your system clock, on the taskbar, right-click the status bar time area, and then on the shortcut menu, click Adjust Date/Time. In the Date/Time Properties dialog box, on the Date & Time tab, click the year box down arrow, and then select the current year. Click OK.

4 If you have finished using Outlook for now and are working in a Workgroup environment, click File, and then click Exit And Log Off. If you are working in an Internet only environment, click File, and then click Exit.

Lesson 10 Quick Reference

To	Do this
Export a folder as a personal folder	In the Folder List, click the folder to be exported, and then on the File menu, click Import And Export. In the Import And Export Wizard dialog box, select Export To A File, and then click the Next button. In the Export To A File dialog box, select Personal Folder File (.pst), and then click the Next button. In the Save Exported File As box, type the filename, and then click the Finish button.

Managing Your Files

10

Lesson 10 Quick Reference

To	Do this
Export a folder to another program	In the Folder List, click the folder to be exported, and then on the File menu, click Import And Export. In the Import And Export Wizard dialog box, select Export To A File, and then click the Next button. In the Export A File dialog box, click Tab Separated Values (Windows), and then click the Next button. In the Select The Folder To Export From dialog box, be sure that the folder you want is selected, and then click the Next button. In the Save Exported File As box, be sure that the correct path is specified, click the Finish button, and click OK. Then open the application to which you want to export the file. On the Insert menu of the application, click File. In the Insert File dialog box, in the Look In drop-down list, locate and click the file to be imported. Click the Insert button.
Archive folders manually	In the Folder List, click the folder that you want to archive. On the File menu, click Archive. In the AutoArchive dialog box, select options and frequency. In the Archive Items Older Than drop-down list, select the date before which files are to be archived. Select or type the name of the archive folder, and click OK.
Set AutoArchive properties for Outlook	On the Tools menu, click Options, click the Other tab, and then in the AutoArchive area, click the AutoArchive button. In the AutoArchive dialog box, select the frequency and other options that you want. In the Default Archive File box, type the name of the archive file, and click OK.

Lesson 10 Quick Reference

To	Do this
Set AutoArchive properties for a specific Outlook folder	On the Outlook Bar, right-click the shortcut that you want. On the shortcut menu, click Properties, and then click the AutoArchive tab. In the Clean Out Items Older Than box, select the time period that you want. Be sure that the Move Old Items To option is selected and, if desired, position the insertion point in the box and scroll to the end of the box, select the word *archive* and replace it with the desired folder name. Then click OK. Quit Outlook 2000, and then on the Windows taskbar, click the Start button, click Shut Down, and then click the Restart option. If you want to AutoArchive immediately, in the message box, click Yes.
Retrieve an archived folder	In the Folder List, right-click the Outlook Today—[Personal Folders] folder, and on the shortcut menu, click New Folder. In the Create New Folder dialog box, type the new name for the folder, and click OK. In the Folder List, select the new folder, and then on the File menu, click Import And Export. In the Import And Export Wizard dialog box, select Import From Another Program Or File, and then click the Next button. In the Import A File dialog box, scroll to and select Personal Folder File (.pst), and then click the Next button. In the File To Import area, click Browse, click the archive file that you want, and then click the Open button. Click Next, and then click Finish.
Attach your digital signature	After you have written an e-mail message, on the Message form Standard toolbar, click the Options button. In the dialog box, click the Add Digital Signature To Outgoing Message check box, and then click the Close button. To obtain a digital signature, on the Tools menu, click Options, and then click the Security tab. Click the Get A Digital ID button and follow the instructions for how to obtain a digital ID.

Managing Your Files

10

Lesson 10 Quick Reference

To	Do this
Encrypt an e-mail message	On the Outlook Bar, click the Inbox shortcut, and then on the Standard toolbar, click the New Mail Message button. Enter the information you want for the message. On the Message form Standard toolbar, click the Options button. In the dialog box, click the Encrypt Message Contents And Attachments check box, and then click the Close button. On the Message form Standard toolbar, click the Send button.
Automatically track activities in Journal	On the Outlook Bar, click the Journal shortcut. On the Tools menu, click Options. In the Contacts area, click the Journal Options button. In the Automatically Record These Items list, select the items to be tracked, and then in the For These Contacts list, select the contacts to be tracked. Click OK twice to close the dialog boxes.
Manually track Contact activities in Journal	On the Outlook Bar, click the Contacts shortcut. Double-click the name of the contact you want to track. On the Contact form, click the Activities tab. On the Actions menu, click New Journal Entry For Contact. On the Journal Entry form, enter the information in the Start Time boxes and in the Duration box. Click the Save And Close button. On the Contact form, in the Show box, click the drop-down arrow and select Journal. Click the Close button.

LESSON 11

Using Outlook with Other Connections

ESTIMATED
TIME
40 min.

In this lesson you will learn how to:

✔ *Grant coworkers access to your Outlook folders to act on your behalf.*

✔ *Share Outlook folders with workgroup members.*

✔ *Use Net Folders to share Outlook folders with other Internet users.*

✔ *Share your Calendar as a Web page.*

In this lesson, you learn how to share information in your Microsoft Outlook folders with others. By sharing folders with another person, you give the person direct access to the folder information that you select. This can enable you to communicate more efficiently on project work and can even enable another person to act on your behalf while you are away or busy—by responding to e-mail messages and meeting requests, for example. When you decide to share an Outlook folder with another person, you can grant access levels ranging from allowing the person only to read your folder items to allowing the person to also edit information in the folder and even create new entries for you.

There are three ways to share folder information:

■ By granting a delegate from your workgroup the permission to access your folders and act on your behalf—for example, to answer your e-mail messages or to schedule your meetings while you are away. All e-mail messages sent by the delegate are marked with your name plus "on behalf of" the delegate's name.

■ By simply sharing your folder information with your coworkers—for example, to share project information among members of your project team.

■ By using Net Folders to share folder information with other Outlook users on the Internet—for example, to review work with a colleague with whom you are collaborating.

If you work in a workgroup environment, you can utilize all three ways of sharing information. If you work in an Internet-only environment, you can employ only the third method, using Net Folders. Skip the first two exercises since they do not apply to you.

Getting Ready for the Lesson

In this exercise, you start Outlook 2000 and prepare the practice files and folders that you need.

Start Outlook and copy the practice files

*Microsoft
Outlook*

❶ On the desktop, double-click the Microsoft Outlook 2000 icon.

Outlook 2000 opens.

❷ If necessary, maximize the Outlook window.

Maximize

important

Before proceeding to the next step, you must have installed this book's practice folder on your hard disk and created a practice Contacts folder and shortcut. If you have not yet created a practice folder and practice shortcut for your work, see Lesson 5, "Organizing Your Contacts."

*SBS Practice
Contacts*

*For a detailed
example of
how to copy
practice files
to a practice
folder, see the
exercise "Set
Up Practice
E-mail" in
Lesson 1.*

❸ Click the SBS Practice Contacts shortcut.

❹ Drag the practice Contacts files, indicated by address card icons, from the Lesson11 folder in the Outlook 2000 SBS Practice folder to your SBS Practice Contacts folder in the Folder List.

Granting Permission to Workgroup Delegates to Act on Your Behalf

Workgroup

If you work in a workgroup environment, you can grant access to your Outlook folders to coworkers serving as your *delegate*, that is, someone who will act on your behalf. For example, you can permit:

- Your assistant to access your Calendar folder to set appointments and to your Contacts folder to return phone calls and address letters.

- A coworker to access your Inbox folder to handle project-related e-mail messages while you are out of town.

- Your manager to access your Journal folder to track progress on your projects.

- Your project team members to access your Notes folder to keep abreast of project information.

When you assign permission to a coworker to serve as your delegate, you indicate both the folders the coworker can access and the level of access you want the coworker to have. In any folder, you can assign a delegate to one of three permission levels, ranging from a *Reviewer* at the lowest level to an *Editor* at the highest level. You can change or revoke permissions at any time. If you are given delegate permissions to an Outlook folder by another coworker, you can perform the functions granted to you in that folder on your coworker's behalf.

With this permission level	A delegate can perform these actions on your behalf
Reviewer	Read any folder items.
Author	Read and create items, and modify and delete only the items he or she created themselves.
Editor	Read, create, and modify any items.

For a delegate to act on your behalf, the coworker must be given Editor-level permissions in the desired folder or folders. In addition, the coworker must also be given at least Reviewer-level access to your Inbox, since the communications your coworker makes on your behalf take place through the Inbox. With this access level, the specific activities that a delegate can perform on your behalf depend on the folder.

In this folder	An Editor can act on your behalf to
Calendar	Schedule appointments.
Tasks	Accept and reject task requests.
Inbox	Send and reply to e-mail messages.

In the next exercises, you grant delegate permission to your coworker to act on your behalf while you are on vacation. When you return, you reciprocate the favor while your coworker is away and then cancel your coworker's delegate permissions in your folders.

important

To complete the exercises in this section, you need to recruit the help of a co-worker in your workgroup who is willing to serve as your delegate and also grant you delegate permissions in his or her Inbox and Notes folders.

Grant permissions to a delegate

As you prepare to leave on vacation, in this exercise, you grant permission to your coworker to act on your behalf in your Inbox, Calendar, and Tasks folders.

❶ On the Tools menu, click Options.

The Options dialog box opens.

❷ Click the Delegates tab.

The Delegates tab becomes active.

❸ Click the Add button.

The Add Users dialog box appears.

❹ In the Add Users dialog box, in the Show Names From The box, be sure Global Address List is selected. Select your coworker's name from the global address list, click Add, and click OK.

The Delegate Permissions dialog box opens with your coworker's name displayed on the title bar.

Your screen should look similar to the following illustration.

⑤ In the Delegate Permissions dialog box, your coworker is automatically as-signed Editor permissions in the Calendar and Tasks boxes. In the Calendar area, be sure that the Delegate Receives Copies Of Meeting-Related Mes-sages Sent To Me check box is selected.

⑥ Click the Inbox drop-down arrow, and then select Editor.

⑦ Select the Automatically Send A Message To Delegate Summarizing These Permissions check box, and then click OK.

⑧ On the Delegates tab, be sure the Send Meeting Requests And Responses Only To My Delegates, Not To Me check box is selected, and click OK.

The Options dialog box closes. Your coworker has been granted delegate permissions and will automatically receive a subscription invitation in his or her Inbox. The recipient must click the Accept button to subscribe. The Net Folder then appears in the subscriber's Outlook Folder list, but is accessible only to subscribers. Recipients not using Outlook receive a notification mes-sage instead of a subscription invitation.

Other Connections

11

Your coworker's message should look similar to the following illustration.

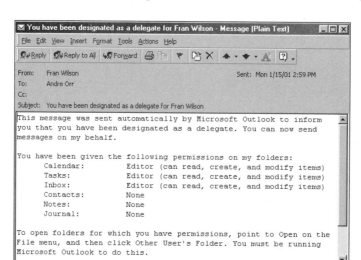

Hide personal items from a delegate

In this exercise, before granting your coworker delegate permissions in your Contacts folder, you hide your personal contacts by creating a new Outlook folder and moving your personal contacts to the new folder.

1 On the Outlook Bar, click the SBS Practice Contacts shortcut.

The contents of the SBS Practice Contacts folder are displayed in the Information viewer.

2 On the View menu, be sure Folder List is selected.

3 Right-click the Outlook Today folder, and then on the shortcut menu, click New Folder.

The Create New Folder dialog box appears.

4 In the Create New Folder dialog box, in the Folder Contains drop-down list, select Contact Items.

5 In the Create New Folder dialog box, in the Name box, type **Personal Contacts** and click OK. In the Add Shortcut To Outlook Bar message box, click No.

The Personal Contacts folder is added to the Folder List.

6 In the Contacts list, select the Contacts cards for Mario Rodas and Lester Tilton, and drag them into the Personal Contacts folder.

The items in the SBS Practice Contacts folder are moved to the Personal Contacts folder, and when your coworker is granted permissions to your Contacts list, these contacts will not be present.

tip

If you have a few items in a folder that you wish to hide from your delegate, you can conceal them individually by opening the item and then selecting the Private check box in the lower-right corner of the form. This process applies to items in all Outlook folders except the Inbox. To conceal an Inbox item, open the message. On the View menu, click Options, and then in the Sensitivity list, select Private.

Read folder items as a delegate

In this exercise, you have been granted delegate permissions as Reviewer in your coworker's Notes folder, and you read an item in the folder.

important

To complete this exercise, you need to recruit a coworker in your workgroup to grant you delegate permissions as Editor in his or her Inbox folder and as Reviewer in his or her Notes folder.

1 On the Outlook Bar, click the Notes shortcut.

The contents of your Notes folder are displayed in the Information viewer.

2 On the File menu, point to Open, and then click Other User's Folder.

The Open Other User's Folder dialog box appears.

3 In the Open Other User's Folder dialog box, click the Name button.

The Select Name dialog box opens.

4 In the Select Name dialog box, in the Show Names From The box, be sure Global Address List is selected. Select your coworker's name in the global address list, and click OK.

The Open Other User's Folder dialog box appears with your coworker's name displayed in the Name box.

5 In the Folder box, be sure that Notes is selected, and click OK.

Your coworker's Notes folder appears as a window on your screen.

Your screen should look similar to the following illustration.

Your Notes folder   Coworker's Notes folder

⑥ Maximize your coworker's Notes folder, and then in the Information viewer, double-click the first item.

The contents of the item are displayed in the Information viewer.

⑦ In the Note, click the Close button.

The Note closes.

⑧ In the window containing your coworker's Notes folder, click the Close button.

Close

Send a message as a delegate

In this exercise, you have been granted delegate permissions as Editor in your coworker's Inbox folder, and you send an e-mail message on your co-worker's behalf.

important

If you have not already done so for the preceding exercise, you need to recruit a coworker in your workgroup to grant you delegate permissions as Editor in his or her Inbox folder. You might want to also enlist the help of an additional co-worker so that you can respond to a message sent to your coworker.

1   On the Outlook Bar, click the Inbox shortcut.

The contents of the Inbox are displayed in the Information viewer.

2   On the File menu, point to Open, and then click Other User's Folder.

The Open Other User's Folder dialog box opens.

3   In the Open Other User's Folder dialog box, click the Name button.

The Select Name dialog box opens.

4   In the Select Name dialog box, click the name of your coworker, and click OK.

The coworker's name is displayed in the Name box.

5   In the Folder box, be sure that Inbox is selected, and click OK.

Your coworker's Inbox appears as a window on your screen, and any mail is displayed in the window. Your screen should look similar to the following illustration.

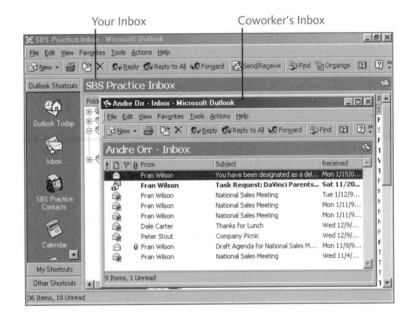

Your Inbox   Coworker's Inbox

6   In your coworker's Inbox, maximize the window, and then in the Information viewer, double-click a message.

The message opens.

7   On the Message form Standard toolbar, click the Reply button.

A blank Message form appears, with the original sender's name in the To box.

8   Type a reply to the message. and then click the Send button.

Your message is sent. The message the recipient receives should look similar to the following illustration.

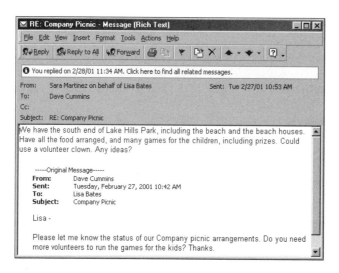

9   Click the close button in both the Message form and your coworker's inbox.

Workgroup

tip

If you have been delegated Editor permissions in your coworker's Calendar and Tasks folders, you can accept or reject requests that appear in your coworker's Inbox by opening the request and selecting the appropriate response. First review the contents of your coworker's Calendar or Tasks folder before making the response. On the File menu, point to Open, and then click Other User's Folder. Select your coworker's name, and then select the folder you want to view.

Sharing Folders with Workgroup Members

If you do not need a coworker to act on your behalf to respond to e-mail messages, meeting requests, and task requests, you can still grant access to your Outlook folders by simply *sharing* a folder with coworkers. For example, when you share your Contacts folder with the marketing team members, they can access the information group-wide. You decide the level of access you want your coworker(s) to have, selecting from several default permission levels. The level you select for a coworker can vary from folder to folder.

With this permission level	A coworker can perform these actions in your folder
Contributor	Create his or her own items.
Reviewer	Read any folder items.
Nonediting Author	Create and read any folder items.
Author	Read any items, and create or modify his or her own items.
Publishing Author	Read any items, and create or modify his or her own items or subfolders.
Editor	Read, create, or modify any items.
Publishing Editor	Read, create, or modify any items or subfolders.
Owner	Read, create, or modify any items or subfolders, and change others' access permissions.

If you are a member of a project team, you might want to share your Calendar, Tasks, and Notes folders with your team. You can grant Author-level access to your fellow team members and Publishing Editor-level access to the same folders to your team manager. In this way, your fellow team members can coordinate their schedules and tasks with yours and will be able to review your project notes. Your team manager will be able to change schedules, tasks, and notes to keep the project on track.

To attach additional mailboxes to your Folder List, you must first share your *Outlook mailbox* with your coworker. The Outlook mailbox is the collection of all of your Outlook folders (Calendar, Tasks, Inbox, Calendar, Notes, Journal, and any others you may have created). To share an Outlook folder, you select the specific folder(s) to which you want to grant access. Assign the permission level, and your coworker will only have access to the folders you allow.

In the next exercises, you share your Outlook mailbox with your project team, and then give the team access to your Notes folder. You have been granted similar access to the Notes folder of another team member, and you review an item in that person's folder. Then you remove your Notes folder from the shared files list to revoke shared file permissions.

important

To complete the exercises in this section, you need to recruit at least one coworker in your workgroup to grant you permission to share his or her Notes folder.

11

Other Connections

Grant mailbox permission

In this exercise, you grant Author permission to a coworker.

important

In a Workgroup environment, your personal folders are named Mailbox—*Your Name* or Outlook Today—[Mailbox—*Your Name*]. Your user name is substituted for the phrase *Your Name*.

① On the View menu, be sure the Folder List is selected.

② In the Folder List, right-click the Mailbox folder. On the shortcut menu, click Properties For Mailbox.

The Mailbox Properties dialog box opens.

③ In the Mailbox Properties dialog box, click the Permissions tab.

Your screen should look similar to the following illustration.

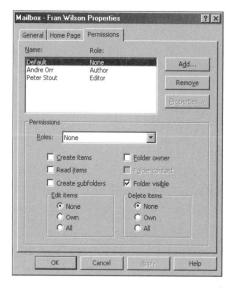

To add more than one co-worker, select the name and then click the Add button for each coworker to be added. Then click OK.

④ On the Permissions tab, click the Add button.

The Add Users dialog box opens.

⑤ In the Add Users dialog box, in the Type Name Or Select From List area, select the name of the coworker to whom you wish to grant access, click the Add button, and click OK.

The Mailbox Properties dialog box displays the name of the person you selected in the Name box and a default entry in the Role box displayed as None.

6 Be sure your coworker's name is selected in the Mailbox Properties dialog box, and in the Roles drop-down list, select Author.

The permissions associated with the Author role are automatically displayed below the Roles box.

7 Click OK.

The Mailbox Properties dialog box closes.

Share a folder with coworkers

In this exercise, you share a folder with a coworker.

1 In the Folder List, right-click the Notes folder, and on the shortcut menu, click Properties.

The Notes Properties dialog box opens.

2 In the Notes Properties dialog box, click the Permissions tab.

3 On the Permissions tab, click the Add button.

The Add Users dialog box appears.

4 In the Add Users dialog box, select the name of the coworker to whom you wish to grant access, click the Add button, and click OK.

The Notes Properties dialog box appears.

5 In the Notes Properties dialog box, in the Name Role list, select the name of the coworker.

6 In the Roles drop-down list, select Author, and click OK.

The Notes Properties dialog box closes and the coworker has Author privileges in your Notes folder.

tip

To share another folder with the same coworker, repeat steps 1 through 6. Each time, right-click the folder you want to share.

Revoke folder-sharing permissions for a coworker

In this exercise, you remove permission for your coworker to share your folder.

11

Other Connections

1 On the View menu, be sure the Folder List is selected.

2 In the Folder List, right-click the Notes folder, and then on the shortcut menu, click Properties.

The Notes Properties dialog box opens.

When you remove folder-sharing permission for a coworker, your mailbox still remains available for others with permission to access it.

3 In the Notes Properties dialog box, click the Permissions tab.

4 On the Permissions tab, select your coworker's name from the list, click the Remove button, and click OK.

Your coworker is no longer able to share your folders.

Add a shared mailbox to your Folder List

One of your team members has granted you Author-level access to his or her mailbox. In this exercise, you add your coworker's mailbox to your Folder List and then read items in it.

important

To complete this exercise, you need to recruit at least one coworker in your workgroup to grant you permission to share his or her mailbox. To do this, your coworker will need to complete the steps in the exercise on page 254, "Grant Mailbox Permission."

1 On the Tools menu, click Services.

The Services dialog box opens.

2 On the Services tab, select Microsoft Exchange Server, and then click the Properties button.

The Microsoft Exchange Server dialog box opens.

3 In the Microsoft Exchange Server dialog box, click the Advanced tab.

4 On the Advanced tab, in the Mailboxes area, click the Add button.

The Add Mailbox dialog box opens.

5 In the Add Mailbox dialog box, type the coworker's mailbox name to which you have been granted access, and click OK.

The Add Mailbox dialog box closes and the Microsoft Exchange Server dialog box reappears.

6 On the Microsoft Exchange Server dialog box, click OK, and then in the Services dialog box, click OK.

The two dialog boxes close and the name of the coworker's mailbox appears in your Folder List.

❼ In the Folder List, click the plus sign (+) next to the coworker's mailbox.

Your coworker's shared Notes folder appears in the Folder List. Your screen should look similar to the following illustration.

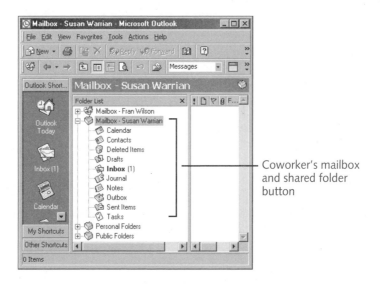

Coworker's mailbox and shared folder button

❽ Click your coworker's Notes folder.

The contents of your coworker's Notes folder are displayed in the Information viewer.

❾ Double-click an item to read it, and then close the item.

Remove a shared mailbox

In this exercise, you remove your coworker's shared mailbox from your Folder List.

❶ On the Tools menu, click Services.

The Services dialog box appears.

❷ On the Services tab, select Microsoft Exchange Server, and then click the Properties button.

The Microsoft Exchange Server dialog box opens.

❸ In the Microsoft Exchange Server dialog box, click the Advanced tab.

❹ On the Advanced tab, in the Mailboxes area, click the mailbox name you want to remove, and then click the Remove button.

A message box appears, prompting you to confirm the deletion of the mailbox.

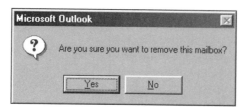

The shared folder is only removed from view. You can access the folder until your coworker revokes permission.

5 In the message box, click Yes, and click OK.

The Microsoft Exchange Server dialog box closes.

6 In the Services dialog box, click OK.

The Services dialog box closes and your coworker's mailbox is removed from your Folder List.

Sharing Folders with Internet Users

Workgroup

Internet only

Although you need to be in a Workgroup environment to either grant delegate permissions or share folders with Workgroup members, you can share folders with other Internet users that use Outlook regardless of whether you work in a Workgroup or Internet only environment. However, if you are in a Workgroup environment, to share folders on the Internet you must first establish a *personal Internet account*, as described later in this lesson. Using your company's *corporate Internet account* will not enable you to access Outlook's folder sharing features on the Internet. You can share any file in a PST format, but you will not be able to share files stored on the network's Exchange server.

Sharing folders on the Internet enables you to:

* Share your Calendar folder with your health care providers to facilitate scheduling appointments.

* Share items in your Notes folder with a colleague to facilitate work on a collaborative effort.

* Share items in your Journal folder with a client to document time charges on a project.

* Share your Contact list with your corporate marketing department in another state.

To share folders on the Internet, you first create a Net Folder, and then you place a copy of the items you want to share into the folder. If you make changes to any items in the folder, the shared Net Folder is updated automatically.

You grant other Internet users access to the Net Folder by first selecting their names and then assigning each person one of four default access levels. These levels range from the Reviewer, who can only read items in the Net Folder, to the Editor, who can read and modify any item in the folder and create new items.

With this permission level	A subscriber can perform these actions in a Net Folder
Reviewer	Read any folder items.
Contributor	Read any items, and create his or her own items.
Author	Read any items, and create or modify his or her own items.
Editor	Read, create, or modify any items.

Recipients not using Outlook receive a notification message instead of a subscription invitation.

After an Internet user has been granted access to a Net Folder, an automatic subscription invitation is sent by e-mail. In the subscription message, the recipient must click the Accept button to subscribe. The Net Folder then appears in the subscriber's Outlook Folder list, but is accessible only to subscribers.

important

Because Net Folders are shared on the Internet, they are not secure from interception. You cannot encrypt Net Folder items.

In the next exercises, you create a Net Folder to share your Notes folder with another Internet user, and then you stop sharing the folder. Next you subscribe to someone else's Net Folder and then unsubscribe.

important

To complete the exercises in this section, you need to recruit the help of another Internet user who uses Outlook 98 or Outlook 2000 and who is willing to share folders with you. If you work in a Workgroup environment, you must first have a *personal Internet account* with an Internet service provider (you will not be able to share files on your network's Exchange server). To obtain a personal Internet account, you need to complete the following exercise. If you work in an Internet only environment, you can skip the first exercise.

11

Other Connections

Add a personal Internet service in a workgroup environment

Workgroup

If you work in a Workgroup environment, you must obtain a personal Internet account from an Internet service provider. In this exercise, you add a personal Internet service account to your user profile.

important

Before you begin this exercise, you must first contact the Internet service provider (ISP) you wish to use and receive from the ISP your personal Internet account information. (You may need to see your system administrator first.) You must also have a dial-up network connection already set up, which is typically established when the Internet account is set up. If your dial-up network connection has not been established, on the desktop, open My Computer, and then open the Dial-up Networking folder. When the folder opens, click the Make New Connection icon and follow the instructions.

Mail

1 On the taskbar, click the Start button, point to Settings, and click Control Panel.

2 In Control Panel, double-click the Mail icon.

The Properties dialog box for the default messaging settings profile opens.

3 In the Properties dialog box, click the Add button.

The Add Service To Profile dialog box opens.

4 In the Add Service To Profile dialog box, in the Available Information Services box, select Internet E-mail, and click OK.

The Mail Account Properties dialog box opens.

5 In the Mail Account Properties dialog box, in the Mail Account area, type **Internet Account**

6 In the User Information area, type your name and organization in the respective boxes.

7 In the User Information area, type your e-mail address in both the E-mail Address and Reply Address boxes. (This information is provided by your Internet service provider.)

If you select the Remember Password check box, you will not be prompted for your password each time you check your e-mail in Outlook.

8 Click the Servers tab.

The Servers tab becomes active.

9 On the Servers tab, in the Server Information area, type the Incoming Mail (POP3) and Outgoing Mail (SMTP) information provided by your ISP.

10 In the Incoming Mail Server area, type your account name and password (provided by your Internet Service Provider).

11   Click the Connection tab.

The Connection tab becomes active.

12   On the Connection tab, in the Connection area, select Connect Using My Phone Line.

13   In the Modem area, in the Use The Following Dial-Up Networking Connection box, click the drop-down arrow, and then select the dial-up networking connection created for your ISP.

14   Click OK.

The Internet Account Properties dialog box closes, and you can now access the Internet using your own account.

tip
If Outlook was open during the previous exercise, you will need to quit Outlook and restart it to activate your new settings.

Share your Net Folder with another Internet user

In this exercise, you create a Net Folder for your SBS Practice Inbox folder and give another Internet user Author-level access to the folder.

1   Be sure Outlook 2000 is open.

2   On the View menu, be sure Folder List is selected.

3   In the Folder List, select the SBS Practice Inbox folder, and drag it to the Personal Folders.

The contents of the SBS Practice Inbox folder move to the Personal Folders.

4   Select the SBS Practice Inbox folder.

5   On the File menu, point to Share, and then click This Folder.

The Net Folder Wizard dialog box appears.

If the name of the Internet user who agreed to help you with this exercise is not listed, add the user's name to your Contacts list before completing step 9.

6   In the Net Folder Wizard dialog box, click the Next button.

7   In the next page of the Net Folder Wizard dialog box, click the Add button.

The Add Entries To Subscriber Database dialog box appears.

8   In the Show Names From The drop-down list, be sure that Contacts is selected.

9   In the Type Name Or Select From List area, select the name of the Internet user who agreed to help you with this exercise, click the To button, and click OK.

11

Other Connections

The name of your Internet colleague is added to the Member List. Your screen should look similar to the following illustration.

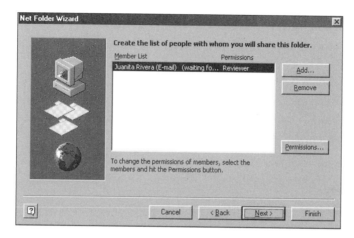

⑩ Be sure the colleague's name is selected, and then click the Permissions button.

The Net Folder Sharing Permissions dialog box opens.

⑪ Select the Author option, and click OK.

Your colleague has been granted Author permission in your SBS Practice Inbox folder.

⑫ Click the Next button, and in the next page of the Net Folder Wizard dialog box, type **Contents of my SBS Practice Inbox folder**, click the Next button, and then click the Finish button.

Your colleague will automatically receive an e-mail message indicating that a Net Folder has been created and inviting him or her to subscribe.

Stop sharing your Net Folder

In this exercise, you have completed the project with your Internet colleague so you stop sharing your SBS Practice Inbox folder.

❶ On the View menu, be sure the Folder List is selected.

❷ In the Folder List, select the SBS Practice Inbox folder that you shared as a Net Folder.

The contents of the SBS Practice Inbox folder are displayed in the Information viewer.

❸ On the File menu, point to Share, and then click This Folder.

The Net Folder Wizard dialog box opens.

④ In the Net Folder Wizard dialog box, click the Stop Sharing This Folder button.

A message confirming that the folder will no longer be shared appears.

⑤ In the message box, click Yes.

The SBS Practice Inbox folder is no longer shared with your colleague.

tip
If you shared your folder with more than one person and want to stop sharing the folder with some but not all of them, in the Net Folder Wizard, instead of clicking the Stop Sharing This Folder button, click the Next button. In the Member List drop-down list, select one of the people you wish to remove, and then click the Remove button. Repeat this process for each member you wish to remove and then click the Finish button.

One Step Further | # Sharing Your Calendar As a Web Page

If you need to schedule appointments with people outside your workgroup, such as clients, colleagues with other companies, and medical providers, you can publish your Calendar to the Web for easy access by those who need to view your schedule. You can decide the time intervals and level of detail you wish to make available.

tip
If you work in a Workgroup environment, to access this feature, you must first have a personal Internet account, in addition to the corporate Internet account. To find out how to establish a personal Internet account, see the "Add a Personal Internet Service in a Workgroup Environment" on page 260.

Share your Calendar as a Web page

In this exercise, you publish a portion of your Calendar to the Web.

① On the View menu, be sure the Folder List is selected.

② In the Folder List, select the SBS Practice Calendar folder.

If you do not want to share detailed information about your appointments, in the Options area, clear the Include Appointment Details check box.

③ On the File menu, click Save As Web Page.

The Save As Web Page dialog box appears.

④ In the Save As Web Page dialog box, in the Duration area, select the start and end dates that you would like to publish.

⑤ In the Save As area, in the Calendar Title box, type your name and then type **Appointment Calendar**

⑥ In the Save As area, in the File Name box, type **My Calendar**

⑦ Click the Save button. If you receive a message asking if you would like to install the Save As Web Page feature, click Yes.

Now your Calendar is formatted and ready to be published.

For more information on publishing, see "Saving and Opening Forms That You Create" in Lesson 12.

Finish the lesson

① To continue to the next lesson, on the File menu, click the Close button.

② If you have finished using Outlook for now and are working in a Workgroup environment, click File, and then click Exit And Log Off. If you are working in an Internet only environment, click File, and then click Exit.

Lesson 11 Quick Reference

To	Do this
Grant permissions to a delegate	On the Tools menu, click Options, and then click the Delegates tab. Click the Add button, select the name you want from the global address list, click the Add button, and click OK. In the Delegate Permissions dialog box, select the permission level you want for each folder.
Hide personal items from a delegate	Before granting permissions to a folder, right-click Outlook Today in the Folder List and then on the shortcut menu, click New Folder. Enter a name for the new folder that will contain the personal items you want to hide. Drag the personal items from the folder to which you will delegate permissions to the new folder.

Lesson 11 Quick Reference

To	Do this
Read folder items as a delegate	On the Outlook Bar, click the shortcut for the type of folder you want to access. On the File menu, point to Open, click Other User's Folder, and then click Name. In the Show Names From The box, be sure Global Address List is selected, click the name of the person whose folder you want to access, and click OK. In the Open Other User's Folder dialog box, be sure that the folder you want to access is displayed in the Folder box. In your coworker's folder, maximize the window, and in the Information viewer, double-click the item you want to read.
Send a message as a delegate	On the Outlook Bar, click the Inbox shortcut. On the File menu, point to Open, click Other User's Folder, and then click Name. In the Select Name dialog box, click the name of the person you want to send the message on behalf of, and click OK. In your coworker's Inbox, maximize the window, and in the Information viewer, double-click the item for which you want to send a reply.
Grant mailbox permission	In the Folder List, right-click the Mailbox folder. On the shortcut menu, click Properties For Mailbox, click the Permissions tab, and then click the Add button. Select the name you want, click the Add button, and click OK. In the Mailbox dialog box, in the Roles drop-down list, select the role you want to assign, and click OK.
Share a folder with coworkers	In the Folder List, right-click the folder you want to share. On the shortcut menu, click Properties, and then click the Permissions tab. Click the Add button, select the name of the coworker you want, select the role, and click OK.
Revoke folder-sharing permissions for a coworker	In the Folder List, right-click the Personal Folders folder. On the shortcut menu, click Properties For Personal Folders, and then click the Permissions tab. Select the co-worker name you want, and then click the Remove button.

Other Connections

11

Lesson 11 Quick Reference

To	Do this
Add a shared mailbox to your Folder List	On the Tools menu, click Services. On the Services tab, select Microsoft Exchange Server, and then click the Properties button. On the Advanced tab, in the Mailboxes area, click the Add button. Type the mailbox name to which you have been granted access, and click OK twice to close the two open dialog boxes.
Remove a shared folder	On the Tools menu, click Services. On the Services tab, select Microsoft Exchange Server, and then click the Properties button. Click the Advanced tab, and in the Mailboxes area, click the mailbox name you want to remove. Click the Remove button, and click OK twice to close all open dialog boxes.
Add a personal Internet service in a Workgroup environment	First contact the desired Internet service provider (ISP) and obtain your account information. On the taskbar, click Start, point to Settings, and then click Control Panel. Double-click the Mail icon, and then click Add. In the Add Service To Profile dialog box, in the Available Information Services box, select Internet E-mail, and click OK. In the Mail Account Properties dialog box, complete the requested user information, and then click the Servers tab. Complete the information provided by your ISP, and then click the Connection tab. In the Connection area, select Using My Phone Line. In the Modem drop-down list, select the connection created for your ISP, and click OK.
Share your Net Folder with another Internet user	On the Outlook Bar, click the shortcut to the folder you want to share. On the File menu, point to Share, and then click This Folder. In the Net Folder Wizard, click the Next button, and then click the Add button. Select the user name you want, click the To button, and click OK. Click the Permissions button, and then select the permission level. Click the Next button. Type a brief message in the next screen, click the Next button, and then click the Finish button.

Lesson 11 Quick Reference

To	Do this
Stop sharing your Net Folder	In the Folder List, select the folder you shared as a Net Folder. On the File menu, point to Share, and then click This Folder. In the Net Folder Wizard dialog box, click the Stop Sharing This Folder button, and in the message box confirming that the folder will no longer be shared, click Yes.
Share your Calendar as a Web page	In the Folder List, select the Calendar folder, and then on the File menu, click Save As Web Page. In the Save As Web Page dialog box, select the start and end dates that you wish to publish. Type your name, the calendar's title, and a filename. Click the Save button. If you receive a message asking if you would like to install the Save As Web Page feature, click Yes.

LESSON 12

Creating Business Forms

**ESTIMATED
TIME
30 min.**

Using forms in business communications is an easy way to ensure that all required information is gathered and stored in an easily retrievable location. Forms can be a very effective means of simplifying and expediting many communications, especially those that include routine, repetitive components. In the preceding lessons, you learned how to use the various standard Microsoft Outlook forms—the Message form, Contact form, Appointment form, Task form, and Journal Entry form. Each of these standard forms can be modified as needed to meet other specialized business needs.

As an account manager at Impact Public Relations, you are responsible for monitoring customer satisfaction among your client groups. To handle this recurring need, you modify the Message form so that it can be sent to customers upon completion of each project for customers to record their satisfaction level. You plan to use this form yourself and make it available to other coworkers to use on their projects.

Start Outlook

Microsoft Outlook

1 On the desktop, double-click the Microsoft Outlook icon.

Outlook 2000 opens.

2 Maximize the Outlook window.

Redesigning an Existing Form

You can create new, customized forms by redesigning existing Outlook forms. To do this, you first select the type of form—the Message form, Contact form, Appointment form, Task form, or Journal Entry form—that most closely meets your business needs. Then you open the form in Design mode, which enables you to change, remove, and add fields, those areas on the form in which you enter data. You can add many types of fields, including drop-down lists to facilitate and standardize user response and text boxes to record individual comments or feedback. You can also format a field to be sure that the data entered is displayed in a standard way (such as in whole dollars), create or delete field labels, and format the final appearance of the form.

In the next exercises, you redesign the Message form to create a customer satisfaction survey for your client base. Using the Message form enables your clients to use the form to respond via e-mail, because all of the features and information needed to send an e-mail message are retained in the form.

> **tip**
> Custom forms created in Outlook 2000 are compatible with older versions of Outlook.

Open a form in Design Mode

To customize the Message form, you open the Message form and switch to Design mode.

New Mail Message

1 On the Outlook Bar, click the Inbox shortcut, and then on the Standard toolbar, click the New Mail Message button.

A blank Message form appears.

2 On the Message form, on the Tools menu, point to Forms, and then click Design This Form.

The blank Message form appears in Design mode, with the Form Design toolbar displayed under the Message toolbar and the Field Chooser dialog

To modify another type of Outlook form, for example, the Task form, click the Tasks folder shortcut and click the New Task button.

box displayed on the right side of the screen. A grid to help you position new fields is displayed on the gray areas of the Message form. Your screen should look similar to the following illustration.

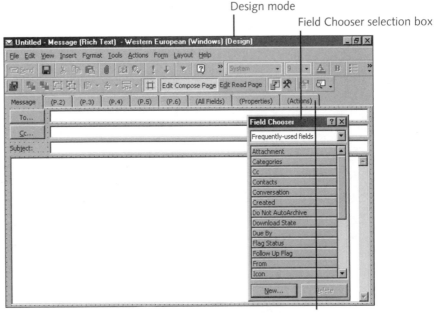

Parentheses indicate that the tab will not be visible in the published form.

❸ On the Form menu, click Separate Read Layout to deselect it.

An Outlook warning message appears, prompting you to continue.

❹ In the message box, click Yes.

The Separate Read Layout is turned off, and the message recipient will view the form as you have designed it rather than in the default Message form.

Rename a field

In this exercise, you rename the Subject field label on the Message form.

❶ On the left side of the Message form, click the word *Subject*.

Sizing handles appear in a box around the word *Subject*.

❷ Click within the box, and then double-click to select *Subject*. Type **Project**

❸ Click anywhere on the form to enter the selection.

The Subject field has been renamed Project.

Delete a field

You delete the message area on the Message form.

❶ On the Message form, select the message area by clicking in it once.

Sizing handles appear in a box around the Message area.

❷ Press the Delete key.

The Message area field is deleted.

Add a field

To readily identify responses that require follow-up, you add the Flag Status field to the Message form.

❶ In the Field Chooser dialog box, scroll to and select the Flag Status field.

❷ Drag the Flag Status field to the Message form grid area below the Project field.

The Flag Status field is automatically aligned with the Project field. Sizing handles appear in a box around the field label and the field text box. Your screen should look similar to the following illustration.

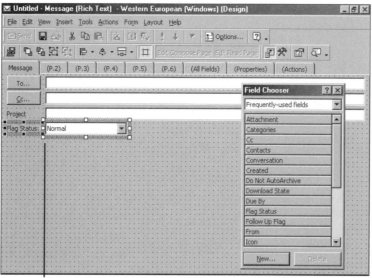

Drag the sizing handles to
change the size or shape of the field.

❸   Click anywhere on the form to enter the selection.

The Flag Status field is added to the Message form.

tip

When you add a new field and drag it below an existing field, Outlook automatically aligns the new field with the existing field. To manually align the new field, be sure that the new field is selected, and then on the Layout menu, click to deselect AutoLayout. Then on the Layout menu, point to Align, and click the appropriate alignment format.

Create a new field

In this exercise, you create the Project Cost field in the Message form.

❶   In the Field Chooser dialog box, click the New button.

The New Field dialog box appears, with Text appearing by default in the Type box and the Format box.

❷   In the New Field dialog box, in the Name box, type **Project Cost**

❸   In the Type box, click the drop-down arrow, and then select Currency.

The default information in the Format box changes.

❹   In the Format box drop-down list, select $12,346 ($12,346).

❺   Click OK.

The Field Chooser dialog box now displays User-Defined Fields In Inbox in the box under the title bar. The newly created Project Cost field is listed on the form.

❻   In the Field Chooser dialog box, click the Project Cost field, and drag the field to the Message form grid area under the Flag Status field.

The Project Cost field is automatically aligned with the Flag Status field. Sizing handles appear in a box around the field label and the field text box.

Your screen should look similar to the following illustration.

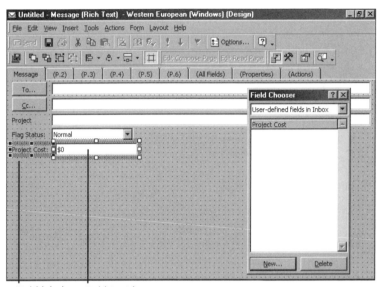

Field label   Field text box

7 Click anywhere on the form to enter the selection.

The Project Cost field is added to the Message form.

For a demon-stration of how to open a form in Design mode and create a custom field, in the Multimedia folder on the Microsoft Outlook 2000 Step by Step CD-ROM, double-click the Design icon.

tip

To add a text box for comments, in the Field Chooser dialog box, click the New button, and then in the Name box, type the label that you want to use for the field. Be sure that Text appears in the Type and Format boxes, and click OK. Drag the field to the appropriate location, and then drag the sizing handles on the field text box to size and shape the response box.

Create a new drop-down field

In this exercise, you create a drop-down list for the customer to select an overall project performance rating.

1 Be sure the Field Chooser dialog box is not blocking your view of the Form Design toolbar.

Control Toolbox

ComboBox

Properties

② On the Message form, on the Form Design toolbar, click the Control Toolbox button.

The Toolbox is displayed.

③ In the Toolbox, click the ComboBox button, and then on the Message form, click the area immediately below the Project Cost box.

A blank field text box with a drop-down arrow is positioned below the words *Project Cost*. Sizing handles appear in a box around the field text box.

④ On the Message form, on the Form Design toolbar, click the Properties button.

The Properties dialog box appears with the Value tab active.

⑤ In the Field And Format Of Control area, click the New button.

The New Field dialog box appears.

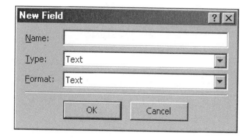

⑥ In the New Field dialog box, in the Name box, type **Performance Rating**

⑦ Be sure that Text is displayed in both the Type box and the Format box, and click OK.

The Properties dialog box appears with Performance Rating shown in the Field And Format Of Control area next to the Choose Field box.

⑧ In the Properties dialog box, be sure that Dropdown appears in the List Type box.

⑨ In the Possible Values box, type **Excellent, Good, Fair, Poor** and click OK.

The field text box drop-down list now has four entries—Excellent, Good, Fair, and Poor—which are displayed when the drop-down arrow is clicked. The name of the drop-down list, *Performance Rating*, does not appear on the form.

Creating Business Forms

12

When you click the drop-down arrow, your screen should look similar to the following illustration.

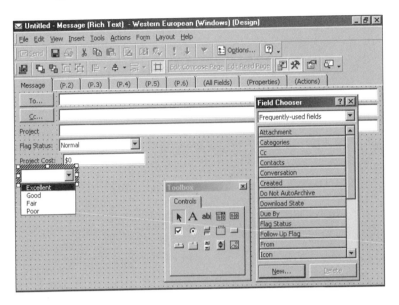

10 In the field text box, click the text area, and then type **Performance Rating**

11 Position the mouse pointer over the middle-right sizing handle on the drop-down list until you see a horizontal double arrow. Click the sizing handle and drag the box to the appropriate size so that *Performance Rating* is fully visible in the box. Then click anywhere on the form to enter the selection.

The Performance Rating field is added to the Message form.

tip
If you need to add another tab to your form, just format the new tab using the Field Chooser dialog box in the same way as you did the Message tab. To remove a tab, click the tab, and then on the Form menu, click to clear Display This Page.

Align the new fields

In this exercise, you finish the form by aligning the fields you added.

1 In the Toolbox, click the Close button.

The Toolbox closes.

Close

2   Holding down the Ctrl key, on the Message form, select the Performance Rating, Flag Status, and the Project Cost field boxes.

3   On the Message form, on the Layout menu, point to Align, and then click Right.

The three boxes are aligned on the right margins.

4   Click anywhere on the form to enter the selection, and then in the Field Chooser dialog box, click the Close button.

The form is complete. Your screen should look similar to the following illustration.

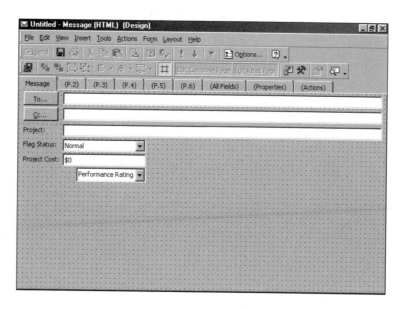

tip

To view how the form will appear to users once it is published, on the Form menu, click Run This Form. To return to Design mode, on the sample form, click the Close button. If you are prompted to save changes, click No.

Saving and Opening Forms that You Create

Once you have completed a new form, you first protect it so that others cannot modify your form without your permission. You then save, or *publish,* the form by filing it in an Outlook folder for easy access. Depending on the folder you select, you can publish it in one of two *Forms Libraries,* which make the form available to others. If you publish to the *Personal Forms Library*, the form will be available for your personal use and to share via the Internet. In a Workgroup environment, you can publish it to the *Organization Forms Library* for your coworkers to access, just as they would any of the standard Outlook forms. In the next exercises, you protect your customer satisfaction message form and then publish it to the Personal Forms Library. After it is published, you then retrieve the form and test it by completing the form and sending it back to yourself.

Protect the form from revision by others

Now that you have completed your form, you protect it with a password so that others cannot change it without your permission.

1 On the Message form, click the (Properties) tab.

2 On the lower-right side of the tab, select the Protect Form Design check box.

The Password dialog box appears.

3 In the Password dialog box, in the Password box, type **test** and press the Tab key.

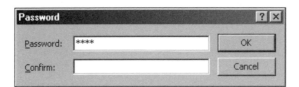

4 In the Confirm box, type **test** and click OK.

The Password dialog box closes and the form you that created is protected from alteration by others by the password.

Publish a form to the Personal Forms Library

In this exercise, you name the form and publish it to the Personal Forms Library so that it is available for you to access at any time.

Publish Form

1 On the Message form, on the Form Design toolbar, click the Publish Form button.

The Publish Form As dialog box appears.

2 In the Publish Form As dialog box, be sure that Personal Forms Library appears in the Look In box.

3 In the Display Name box, type **Customer Satisfaction**

The name is also automatically displayed in the Form Name box.

4 Click the Publish button.

A Microsoft Outlook warning box appears. Review the warning box information and then click Yes.

The warning box closes and the Message form reappears.

5 On the File menu, click Close.

A dialog box appears, prompting you to save the changes.

6 In the dialog box, click Yes.

The Message form closes, and the Inbox is displayed in the Information viewer.

tip
If you work in a Workgroup environment, you can publish the form to a network folder for your coworkers to access when needed. To publish to a network folder, in the Publish Form As dialog box, click Browse, locate the network folder you want, and then click Publish.

Open the form that you published

Workgroup

1 Be sure that the Inbox Information viewer is open, and then on the Tools menu, point to Forms, and click Choose Form.

The Choose Form dialog box appears.

2 In The Choose Form dialog box, in the Look In box, click the drop-down arrow, and then select Personal Forms Library.

The Customer Satisfaction form appears in the list.

3 Select Customer Satisfaction, and then click the Open button.

An untitled Customer Satisfaction Message form appears.

Test the form that you published

1 On the Customer Satisfaction Message form, in the To box, type your e-mail address.

2 In the Project box, type **test**

3 Be sure that the Flag Status box displays the Normal default setting.

4 In the Project Cost box, type **$10,000**

5 In the Performance Rating box, click the drop-down arrow, and then select Excellent.

12

Creating Business Forms

⑥ On the Message form Standard toolbar, click the Send button, and then if you are not already connected to the Internet, click the Send/Receive button.

The Customer Satisfaction Message form closes. The form will soon arrive in your Inbox.

⑦ In the Inbox Information viewer, double-click the Test message, read the form, and then close the form.

⑧ On the Standard toolbar, click the Delete button.

Delete

One Step Further Removing a Form from the Forms Library

Workgroup

Over time, business needs change, and with them the need for business forms can also change. Some of the forms in the forms libraries might become outdated and need to be removed in order to avoid confusion and clutter.

Now that you have created a form and published it to the Personal Forms Library, you practice removing it.

Remove a form from the Personal Forms Library

In this exercise, you remove the Customer Satisfaction form that you created from the Personal Forms Library.

① On the Tools menu, click Options.

The Options dialog box appears.

② In the Options dialog box, click the Other tab, and then click the Advanced Options button.

The Advanced Options dialog box appears.

③ Click the Custom Forms button.

A second Options dialog box appears.

④ Click the Manage Forms button.

The Forms Manager dialog box appears, with the Customer Satisfaction form listed under Personal Forms.

⑤ In the Forms Manager dialog box, select the Customer Satisfaction form, and then click the Delete button. In the message box prompting you to confirm the deletion, click Yes.

The Customer Satisfaction form no longer appears listed under Personal Forms.

Close

6 In the Forms Manager dialog box, click the Close button.

The Forms Manager dialog box closes.

7 In the active Options dialog box, click OK, and then in the Advanced Options dialog box, click OK. In the next Options dialog box, click OK.

Finish the lesson

1 To continue to the last Review & Practice, on the File menu, click Close All Items.

2 If you have finished using Outlook for now and are working in a Workgroup environment, click File, and then click Exit And Log Off. If you are working in an Internet only environment, click File, and then click Exit.

Lesson 12 Quick Reference

To	Do this
Open a form in Design mode	Open the Outlook form that you want to redesign. On the form, on the Tools menu, point to Forms, and then click Design This Form.
Rename a field	Open a form in Design mode. On the form, click the field label, double-click to select the label's text, and then type the new label text. Click anywhere on the form to enter the selection.
Delete a field	Open a form in Design mode. On the form, select the field you want to remove, and then press the Delete key.
Add a field	Open a form in Design mode. In the Field Chooser dialog box, scroll and select the field you want to add, and then drag the field to the gray grid area of the form. Click anywhere on the form to enter the selection.

12

Creating Business Forms

Lesson 12 Quick Reference

To	Do this	Button
Create a new field	Open a form in Design mode. In the Field Chooser dialog box, click the New button. In the New Field dialog box, in the Name box, type the new field name, select the type and format for the data the field is to display, and click OK. In the Field Chooser dialog box, select the field and drag it to the gray grid area on the form. Click anywhere on the form to enter the selection.	
Create a new drop-down list	Open a form in Design mode. On the Design toolbar, click the Control Toolbox button, and then in the Toolbox, click the ComboBox button. In the gray grid, click the location where you want to place the new field, and then on the Form Design toolbar, click the Properties button. On the Value tab, click the New button, and then in the Name box, type the name of the drop-down field. Click OK. In the Properties dialog box, be sure that Dropdown appears in the List Type box. In the Possible Values box, type the list choices you want, separating each by a comma. Click OK. To label the drop-down box, click in the title box and type the label. If necessary, drag the sizing hand to resize the title box.	

Lesson 12 Quick Reference

To	Do this	Button
Align the new fields	In the Toolbox, click the Close button. Hold down the Ctrl key and select the fields that you want to align. On the Layout menu, point to Align, and then click the alignment you want. Click anywhere on the form to enter the selection.	
Protect a form from revision by others	Open a form in Design mode. On the form, click the (Properties) tab, and then select the Protect Form Design check box. Type a password in the Password box, press the Tab key, and then in the Confirm box, type the same password again. Click OK. On the Form Design toolbar, click the Save button.	
Publish a form	Open a form in Design mode. On the Form Design toolbar, click the Publish Form button. In the Publish Form As Dialog Box drop-down list, select the appropriate folder location for the new form. In the Display Name box, type the name for the new form, and then click the Publish button. In the warning dialog box that appears, click Yes, and then on the File menu, click Close.	
Open the form that you published	On the Tools menu, click Forms, and then click Choose Form. In the Look In drop-down list, select the folder containing the form. From the list, select the form, and then click the Open button.	

Creating Business Forms

12

Lesson 12 Quick Reference

To	Do this	Button
Test a form that you published	Open the published form, enter data in each field, and then address the form to your e-mail address. Click the Send button, and then if you are not already connected to the Internet, click the Send/Receive button. When the form arrives in your Inbox, double-click to open the message, read it, and then click the Close button. On the Standard toolbar, click the Delete button.	
Remove a form from the Personal Forms Library	On the Tools menu, click Options, click the Other tab, and then click the Advanced Options button. Click the Custom Forms button, and then click the Manage Forms button. In the Forms Manager dialog box, select the form to be removed, and then click the Delete button. In the message prompting you to confirm the deletion, click Yes. In the Forms Manager dialog box, click the Close button, and click OK three times to close all the dialog boxes.	

Review & Practice

You will review and practice how to:

✔ *Archive an Outlook folder.*
✔ *Share an Outlook folder with a coworker.*
✔ *Create a custom form.*

ESTIMATED TIME
20 min.

Now that you have completed Part 4, you can practice the skills you learned by working through this Review & Practice section. You archive old items in your Inbox, delegate a coworker to act on your behalf in your Inbox, and then create a new form for internal use.

Scenario

As an account manager for Impact Public Relations, you decide to clean out your Inbox, archiving old items for future reference. Then you grant permissions to a coworker to act on your behalf in your Inbox while you are away on vacation. Finally, you create a new form for internal use to record information from coworkers on their contacts.

Step 1:   Archive an Outlook Folder

In this exercise, you archive messages in your Inbox that are older than two months.

① Open the SBS Practice Inbox shortcut.

② Set AutoArchive to review your Outlook folders daily for items that meet the AutoArchive requirements.

③ Set the AutoArchive specifications in your SBS Practice Inbox to archive items that are older than two months.

For more information about	See
Setting AutoArchive properties	Lesson 10
Retrieving archived folders	Lesson 10

Step 2:   Share an Outlook Folder with a Coworker

Before you leave to go out of town, you grant Editor-level delegate permissions in your Inbox to a coworker to handle communications while you are away.

important

If you do not work in a Workgroup environment, you will be unable to complete this exercise. Proceed to step 3.

① Grant your coworker Editor-level permissions as a delegate in your Inbox.

② Hide your personal correspondence from your delegate by creating a new Outlook folder and transferring the personal items into the new folder.

③ Revoke the delegate permissions.

For more information about	See
Granting delegate permissions	Lesson 11
Hiding personal items	Lesson 11
Revoking delegate permissions	Lesson 11

Step 3:   Create a Custom Form

By modifying a standard Outlook message form, you create a new form for internal use.

① Open a blank Message form and create a new form by replacing the Subject field with the Customer field, and replacing the message area with a Comments field and a Flag Status field.

② Protect the form with a password, and then title it Customer Report. If you work in a Workgroup environment, publish it to a network folder.

For more information about	See
Creating a new form	Lesson 12
Protecting and publishing a form	Lesson 12

Finish the Review & Practice

Follow these steps to delete the practice files that you created in this Review & Practice, and then quit Outlook 2000.

① Delete the Customer Report form in your network folder.

② If you are finished using Outlook and are working in a Workgroup environment, on the File menu, click Exit And Log Off. If you are working in an Internet only environment, on the File menu, click Exit.

Index

Catapult, Inc. & Microsoft Press

Microsoft Outlook 2000 Step by Step has been created by the professional trainers and writers at Catapult, Inc., to the exacting standards you've come to expect from Microsoft Press. Together, we are pleased to present this self-paced training guide, which you can use individually or as part of a class.

Catapult, Inc., is a software training company with years of experience. Catapult's exclusive Performance-Based Training system is available in Catapult training centers across North America and at customer sites. Based on the principles of adult learning, Performance-Based Training ensures that students leave the classroom with confidence and the ability to apply skills to real-world scenarios. *Microsoft Outlook 2000 Step by Step* incorporates Catapult's training expertise to ensure that you'll receive the maximum return on your training time. You'll focus on the skills that can increase your productivity the most while working at your own pace and convenience.

Microsoft Press is the book publishing division of Microsoft Corporation. The leading publisher of information about Microsoft products and services, Microsoft Press is dedicated to providing the highest quality computer books and multimedia training and reference tools that make using Microsoft software easier, more enjoyable, and more productive.

Stay in the *running* for maximum productivity.

These are *the* answer books for business users of Microsoft® Office 2000. They are packed with everything from quick, clear instructions for new users to comprehensive answers for power users— the authoritative reference to keep by your computer and use every day. THE RUNNING SERIES—learning solutions made by Microsoft.

- RUNNING MICROSOFT EXCEL 2000
- RUNNING MICROSOFT OFFICE 2000 PREMIUM
- RUNNING MICROSOFT OFFICE 2000 PROFESSIONAL
- RUNNING MICROSOFT OFFICE 2000 SMALL BUSINESS
- RUNNING MICROSOFT WORD 2000
- RUNNING MICROSOFT POWERPOINT® 2000
- RUNNING MICROSOFT ACCESS 2000
- RUNNING MICROSOFT INTERNET EXPLORER 5
- RUNNING MICROSOFT FRONTPAGE® 2000
- RUNNING MICROSOFT OUTLOOK® 2000

Microsoft Press offers *comprehensive* learning solutions to help new users, power users, and professionals get the most from *Microsoft technology.*

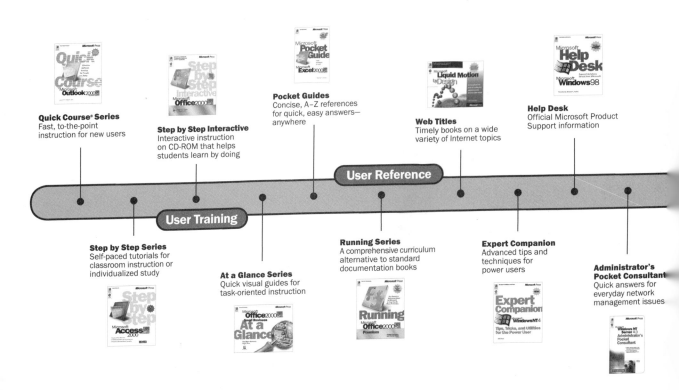

Quick Course® Series
Fast, to-the-point
instruction for new users

Step by Step Interactive
Interactive instruction
on CD-ROM that helps
students learn by doing

Pocket Guides
Concise, A–Z references
for quick, easy answers—
anywhere

Web Titles
Timely books on a wide
variety of Internet topics

Help Desk
Official Microsoft Product
Support information

User Reference

User Training

Step by Step Series
Self-paced tutorials for
classroom instruction or
individualized study

At a Glance Series
Quick visual guides for
task-oriented instruction

Running Series
A comprehensive curriculum
alternative to standard
documentation books

Expert Companion
Advanced tips and
techniques for
power users

**Administrator's
Pocket Consultant**
Quick answers for
everyday network
management issues

With **over 200** *print,*
multimedia, and online resources—
whatever your information
need or learning style,
we've got a solution to help
you *start faster and go farther.*

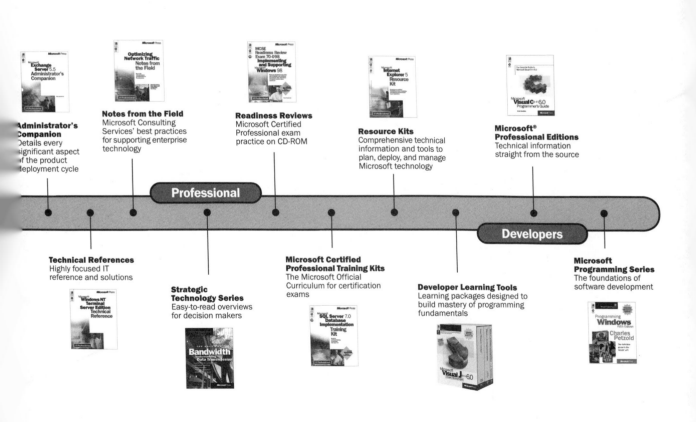

Administrator's Companion
Details every significant aspect of the product deployment cycle

Notes from the Field
Microsoft Consulting Services' best practices for supporting enterprise technology

Readiness Reviews
Microsoft Certified Professional exam practice on CD-ROM

Resource Kits
Comprehensive technical information and tools to plan, deploy, and manage Microsoft technology

Microsoft® Professional Editions
Technical information straight from the source

Professional

Developers

Technical References
Highly focused IT reference and solutions

Strategic Technology Series
Easy-to-read overviews for decision makers

Microsoft Certified Professional Training Kits
The Microsoft Official Curriculum for certification exams

Developer Learning Tools
Learning packages designed to build mastery of programming fundamentals

Microsoft Programming Series
The foundations of software development

Look for them at your bookstore
or computer store today!

mspress.microsoft.com

Get a **Free**
e-mail newsletter, updates,
special offers, links to related books,
and more when you
register on line!

Register your Microsoft Press® title on our Web site and you'll get a FREE subscription to our e-mail newsletter, *Microsoft Press Book Connections.* You'll find out about newly released and upcoming books and learning tools, online events, software downloads, special offers and coupons for Microsoft Press customers, and information about major Microsoft® product releases. You can also read useful additional information about all the titles we publish, such as detailed book descriptions, tables of contents and indexes, sample chapters, links to related books and book series, author biographies, and reviews by other customers.

Registration is easy. Just visit this Web page and fill in your information:

http://www.microsoft.com/mspress/register

Microsoft®

- -

MICROSOFT LICENSE AGREEMENT

Book Companion CD

SOFTWARE PRODUCT LICENSE

The SOFTWARE PRODUCT is protected by United States copyright laws and international copyright treaties, as well as other intellectual property laws and treaties. The SOFTWARE PRODUCT is licensed, not sold.

1. **GRANT OF LICENSE.** This EULA grants you the following rights:

    a. **Software Product.** You may install and use one copy of the SOFTWARE PRODUCT on a single computer. The primary user of the computer on which the SOFTWARE PRODUCT is installed may make a second copy for his or her exclusive use on a portable computer.

    b. **Storage/Network Use.** You may also store or install a copy of the SOFTWARE PRODUCT on a storage device, such as a network server, used only to install or run the SOFTWARE PRODUCT on your other computers over an internal network; however, you must acquire and dedicate a license for each separate computer on which the SOFTWARE PRODUCT is installed or run from the storage device. A license for the SOFTWARE PRODUCT may not be shared or used concurrently on different computers.

    c. **License Pak.** If you have acquired this EULA in a Microsoft License Pak, you may make the number of additional copies of the computer software portion of the SOFTWARE PRODUCT authorized on the printed copy of this EULA, and you may use each copy in the manner specified above. You are also entitled to make a corresponding number of secondary copies for portable computer use as specified above.

    d. **Sample Code.** Solely with respect to portions, if any, of the SOFTWARE PRODUCT that are identified within the SOFTWARE PRODUCT as sample code (the "SAMPLE CODE"):

        i. **Use and Modification.** Microsoft grants you the right to use and modify the source code version of the SAMPLE CODE, *provided* you comply with subsection (d)(iii) below. You may not distribute the SAMPLE CODE, or any modified version of the SAMPLE CODE, in source code form.

        ii. **Redistributable Files.** Provided you comply with subsection (d)(iii) below, Microsoft grants you a nonexclusive, royalty-free right to reproduce and distribute the object code version of the SAMPLE CODE and of any modified SAMPLE CODE, other than SAMPLE CODE, or any modified version thereof, designated as not redistributable in the Readme file that forms a part of the SOFTWARE PRODUCT (the "Non-Redistributable Sample Code"). All SAMPLE CODE other than the Non-Redistributable Sample Code is collectively referred to as the "REDISTRIBUTABLES."

        iii. **Redistribution Requirements.** If you redistribute the REDISTRIBUTABLES, you agree to: (i) distribute the REDISTRIBUTABLES in object code form only in conjunction with and as a part of your software application product; (ii) not use Microsoft's name, logo, or trademarks to market your software application product; (iii) include a valid copyright notice on your software application product; (iv) indemnify, hold harmless, and defend Microsoft from and against any claims or lawsuits, including attorney's fees, that arise or result from the use or distribution of your software application product; and (v) not permit further distribution of the REDISTRIBUTABLES by your end user. Contact Microsoft for the applicable royalties due and other licensing terms for all other uses and/or distribution of the REDISTRIBUTABLES.

2. **DESCRIPTION OF OTHER RIGHTS AND LIMITATIONS.**

    - **Limitations on Reverse Engineering, Decompilation, and Disassembly.** You may not reverse engineer, decompile, or disassemble the SOFTWARE PRODUCT, except and only to the extent that such activity is expressly permitted by applicable law notwithstanding this limitation.

    - **Separation of Components.** The SOFTWARE PRODUCT is licensed as a single product. Its component parts may not be separated for use on more than one computer.

    - **Rental.** You may not rent, lease, or lend the SOFTWARE PRODUCT.

    - **Support Services.** Microsoft may, but is not obligated to, provide you with support services related to the SOFTWARE PRODUCT ("Support Services"). Use of Support Services is governed by the Microsoft policies and programs described in the user manual, in "online" documentation, and/or other Microsoft-provided materials. Any supplemental software code provided to you as part of the Support Services shall be considered part of the SOFTWARE PRODUCT and subject to the terms and conditions of this EULA. With respect to technical information you provide to Microsoft as part of the Support Services, Microsoft may use such information for its business purposes, including for product support and development. Microsoft will not utilize such technical information in a form that personally identifies you.

- **Software Transfer.** You may permanently transfer all of your rights under this EULA, provided you retain no copies, you transfer all of the SOFTWARE PRODUCT (including all component parts, the media and printed materials, any upgrades, this EULA, and, if applicable, the Certificate of Authenticity), **and** the recipient agrees to the terms of this EULA.

- **Termination.** Without prejudice to any other rights, Microsoft may terminate this EULA if you fail to comply with the terms and conditions of this EULA. In such event, you must destroy all copies of the SOFTWARE PRODUCT and all of its component parts.

3. **COPYRIGHT.** All title and copyrights in and to the SOFTWARE PRODUCT (including but not limited to any images, photographs, animations, video, audio, music, text, SAMPLE CODE, REDISTRIBUTABLES, and "applets" incorporated into the SOFTWARE PRODUCT) and any copies of the SOFTWARE PRODUCT are owned by Microsoft or its suppliers. The SOFTWARE PRODUCT is protected by copyright laws and international treaty provisions. Therefore, you must treat the SOFTWARE PRODUCT like any other copyrighted material **except** that you may install the SOFTWARE PRODUCT on a single computer provided you keep the original solely for backup or archival purposes. You may not copy the printed materials accompanying the SOFTWARE PRODUCT.

4. **U.S. GOVERNMENT RESTRICTED RIGHTS.** The SOFTWARE PRODUCT and documentation are provided with RESTRICTED RIGHTS. Use, duplication, or disclosure by the Government is subject to restrictions as set forth in subparagraph (c)(1)(ii) of the Rights in Technical Data and Computer Software clause at DFARS 252.227-7013 or subparagraphs (c)(1) and (2) of the Commercial Computer Software—Restricted Rights at 48 CFR 52.227-19, as applicable. Manufacturer is Microsoft Corporation/One Microsoft Way/Redmond, WA 98052-6399.

5. **EXPORT RESTRICTIONS.** You agree that you will not export or re-export the SOFTWARE PRODUCT, any part thereof, or any process or service that is the direct product of the SOFTWARE PRODUCT (the foregoing collectively referred to as the "Restricted Components"), to any country, person, entity, or end user subject to U.S. export restrictions. You specifically agree not to export or re-export any of the Restricted Components (i) to any country to which the U.S. has embargoed or restricted the export of goods or services, which currently include, but are not necessarily limited to, Cuba, Iran, Iraq, Libya, North Korea, Sudan, and Syria, or to any national of any such country, wherever located, who intends to transmit or transport the Restricted Components back to such country; (ii) to any end user who you know or have reason to know will utilize the Restricted Components in the design, development, or production of nuclear, chemical, or biological weapons; or (iii) to any end user who has been prohibited from participating in U.S. export transactions by any federal agency of the U.S. government. You warrant and represent that neither the BXA nor any other U.S. federal agency has suspended, revoked, or denied your export privileges.

DISCLAIMER OF WARRANTY

NO WARRANTIES OR CONDITIONS. MICROSOFT EXPRESSLY DISCLAIMS ANY WARRANTY OR CONDITION FOR THE SOFTWARE PRODUCT. THE SOFTWARE PRODUCT AND ANY RELATED DOCUMENTATION IS PROVIDED "AS IS" WITHOUT WARRANTY OR CONDITION OF ANY KIND, EITHER EXPRESS OR IMPLIED, INCLUDING, WITHOUT LIMITATION, THE IMPLIED WARRANTIES OF MERCHANTABILITY, FITNESS FOR A PARTICULAR PURPOSE, OR NONINFRINGEMENT. THE ENTIRE RISK ARISING OUT OF USE OR PERFORMANCE OF THE SOFTWARE PRODUCT REMAINS WITH YOU.

LIMITATION OF LIABILITY. TO THE MAXIMUM EXTENT PERMITTED BY APPLICABLE LAW, IN NO EVENT SHALL MICROSOFT OR ITS SUPPLIERS BE LIABLE FOR ANY SPECIAL, INCIDENTAL, INDIRECT, OR CONSEQUENTIAL DAMAGES WHATSOEVER (INCLUDING, WITHOUT LIMITATION, DAMAGES FOR LOSS OF BUSINESS PROFITS, BUSINESS INTERRUPTION, LOSS OF BUSINESS INFORMATION, OR ANY OTHER PECUNIARY LOSS) ARISING OUT OF THE USE OF OR INABILITY TO USE THE SOFTWARE PRODUCT OR THE PROVISION OF OR FAILURE TO PROVIDE SUPPORT SERVICES, EVEN IF MICROSOFT HAS BEEN ADVISED OF THE POSSIBILITY OF SUCH DAMAGES. IN ANY CASE, MICROSOFT'S ENTIRE LIABILITY UNDER ANY PROVISION OF THIS EULA SHALL BE LIMITED TO THE GREATER OF THE AMOUNT ACTUALLY PAID BY YOU FOR THE SOFTWARE PRODUCT OR US$5.00; PROVIDED, HOWEVER, IF YOU HAVE ENTERED INTO A MICROSOFT SUPPORT SERVICES AGREEMENT, MICROSOFT'S ENTIRE LIABILITY REGARDING SUPPORT SERVICES SHALL BE GOVERNED BY THE TERMS OF THAT AGREEMENT. BECAUSE SOME STATES AND JURISDICTIONS DO NOT ALLOW THE EXCLUSION OR LIMITATION OF LIABILITY, THE ABOVE LIMITATION MAY NOT APPLY TO YOU.

MISCELLANEOUS

This EULA is governed by the laws of the State of Washington USA, except and only to the extent that applicable law mandates governing law of a different jurisdiction.

Should you have any questions concerning this EULA, or if you desire to contact Microsoft for any reason, please contact the Microsoft subsidiary serving your country, or write: Microsoft Sales Information Center/One Microsoft Way/Redmond, WA 98052-6399.

PN 097-0002296